Fundamentals of Fire Protection for the Safety Professional

LON H. FERGUSON, CSP
and
CHRISTOPHER A. JANICAK, CSP, ARM

D1521300

Government Institutes
An imprint of
THE SCARECROW PRESS, INC.
Lanham, Maryland • Toronto • Oxford
2005

Ĝ Government Institutes

Published in the United States of America
by Government Institutes, an imprint of The Scarecrow Press, Inc.
A wholly owned subsidiary of
The Rowman & Littlefield Publishing Group, Inc.
4501 Forbes Boulevard, Suite 200
Lanham, Maryland 20706
http://govinst.scarecrowpress.com

PO Box 317
Oxford
OX2 9RU, UK

British Library Cataloguing in Publication Information Available

Library of Congress Cataloging-in-Publication Data

Ferguson, Lon H., 1958–
   Fundamentals of fire protection for the safety professional / Lon H. Ferguson and Christopher A. Janicak.
      p.   cm.
   Includes bibliographical references and index.
   ISBN 0-86587-988-5 (pbk. : alk. paper)
   1. Fire protection engineering.   I. Janicak, Christopher A.   II. Title.
   TH9146.F47   2005
   628.9′2—dc22   2005006977

∞ ™ The paper used in this publication meets the minimum requirements of American National Standard for Information Sciences—Permanence of Paper for Printed Library Materials, ANSI/NISO Z39.48-1992.
Manufactured in the United States of America.

Contents

Figures and Tables

FIGURES

1

Introduction to Industrial Fire Protection

Safety science is a twenty-first-century term for everything that goes into the prevention of accidents, illnesses, fires, explosions, and other events that harm people, property, or the environment (ASSE and BCSP 2000, 3). Of these events, fire losses can be one of the greatest threats to an industrial organization in terms of financial losses, loss of life, loss of property, and property damage. Therefore, industrial fire protection and prevention are crucial components of any safety professional's job, be it serving as a loss-control consultant or a safety manager.

Fires can strike any type of workplace at any time, resulting in property damage, injuries, and deaths. The adverse financial effects can be felt by an organization long after the fire is extinguished. Fire is a hazard that can potentially strike any workplace. The problem of "fire" in the United States today can be summarized as follows (U.S. Fire Administration [USFA] 1987, 22):

- The United States has one of the highest fire-death rates per capita in the industrialized world.
- Each year, fires kill more Americans than all other natural emergencies combined, including floods, hurricanes, tornadoes and earthquakes.

Fire experience in the United States indicates that fires are a major problem. The United States, along with Canada, still has the worst fire-death rate for all the industrialized countries for which we have comparable data. U.S. fire deaths, based on one million per population, are almost twice the average fire-death rates for other industrialized countries (USFA 1987, 50).

As the federal government agency responsible for setting the national standards for worker safety and health, the Occupational Safety and Health Administration (OSHA) has established standards addressing each of the three key elements of fire safety (OSHA 2004, www.osha.gov):

1. Fire prevention
2. Safe evacuation of the workplace in the event of fire
3. Protection of workers who fight fires or who work around fire-suppression equipment

Industrial fire protection and prevention involves recognizing those situations that may result in an unwanted fire, evaluating the potential for an unwanted event, and developing control measures that can be used to eliminate or reduce those fire risks to an acceptable level. As is the case with any safety control measure, these controls can range from engineering strategies to administrative strategies or a combination of the two. Included in fire protection and prevention is emergency response. Emergency response involves organizing, training, and coordinating skilled employees with regard to emergencies such as fires, accidents, or other disasters (ASSE and BCSP 2000, 6).

FIRE PREVENTION VERSUS FIRE PROTECTION

It is important to make the distinction between *fire prevention* and *fire protection*. Each term is unique, and the responsibilities of the safety professional for each aspect differ. Fire prevention is the elimination of the possibility of a fire being started. In order to start, every hostile fire requires an initial heat source, an initial fuel source, and something to bring them together (NFPA 1997, 1–9).

Prevention can occur through successful action on the heat source, the fuel source, or the behavior that brings them together (NFPA 1997, 1–9). Examples of programs that can be instituted in the workplace to prevent fires include housekeeping programs and inspection programs. Housekeeping can eliminate unwanted fuel sources and ignition sources. Inspection programs can effectively identify fire-ignition and fuel hazards, then take appropriate steps to eliminate them.

Effective fire prevention requires vigilance, action, and cooperation (OSHA 2004, www.osha.gov). Vigilance involves regular inspection of the workplace to identify fire hazards. Action is necessary to correct hazardous situations by cleaning up debris, installing effective storage and ventilation systems for hazardous materials that could ignite or fuel a fire, establishing and enforcing work rules and maintenance policies that prevent hazardous situations from arising, shielding or ventilating heat sources, and repairing or replacing faulty equipment or electrical systems. Cooperation between employers and employees is necessary to ensure understanding of their common interests in fire prevention and to ensure maximum effort by all concerned to see and correct fire hazards (OSHA 2004, www.osha.gov).

Fire-protection engineers use the basic tools of engineering and science to help protect people, property, and operations from fire and explosions (ASSE and BCSP 2000, 23). Aspects of fire-engineering-safety jobs include evaluating buildings to determine fire risks, designing fire-detection-and-suppression systems, and researching materials and consumer products.

Safety professionals also recognize that prevention will never be 100 percent successful. Therefore, it is necessary to plan and design to mitigate damages when fire occurs (NFPA 1997, 1–11). This process is referred to as fire protection. Fire-protection strategies are those activities designed to minimize the extent of the fire. Fire protection includes reducing fire hazards by inspection, layout of facilities and processes, and design of fire-detection-and-suppression systems (ASSE and BCSP 2000, 23).

It is important, therefore, to include in workplace fire-safety planning considerations for fire suppression or extinguishment and for evacuation of persons in the event of a fire emergency (www.osha.gov). Fire-extinguishment systems include sprinkler systems, rated fire doors and walls, portable fire extinguishers, and standpipe hose systems. Evacuation of persons includes means of egress, detection-and-notification systems, and emergency planning and preparedness.

Fire protection requires the development of an integrated system of balanced protection that uses many different design features and systems to reinforce one another and to cover for one another in case of the failure of any one (NFPA 1997, 1–12). The National Fire Protection Association (NFPA) describes fire protection as a series of six opportunities to inter-

vene against a hostile fire, arrayed along a time line of potential growth in
fire severity (NFPA 1997, 1–3).

1. Prevent the fire entirely.
2. Slow the initial growth of the fire.
3. Detect fire early, permitting effective intervention before the fire
   becomes too severe.
4. Provide ability for automatic or manual suppression.
5. Provide ability to confine the fire in a space.
6. Move the occupants to a safe location.

Fire protection includes the use of active systems such as automatic detection systems and passive fire-protection systems that stop fire and smoke
(NFPA 1997, 1–12). As one can see, the activities designed to prevent fires
are different from those activities geared toward minimizing the extent of
the fire once it has occurred. Thus, an effective fire-safety program
requires both prevention and protection aspects. Throughout this book,
fire-prevention and fire-protection strategies will be presented for a variety of common fire hazards found in the workplace.

IMPORTANCE OF FIRE SAFETY

Protecting the workplace from fires is a major job responsibility for safety
managers. Not only do they have to ensure that the property is adequately
protected to prevent catastrophic financial losses to the organization, but
there is also the moral obligation to protect the workers and members of
the community from the devastating effects that a fire can have upon the
entire community. Over the years, there are numerous examples of the
effects that industrial fires have had upon both the workers involved and
the communities in which they occurred. Some examples of the largest
and most devastating industrial fires in the United States include the Triangle Shirtwaist Company fire, the Imperial Foods processing plant fire,
the Phillips Petroleum chemical plant explosion and fire, and the Crescent
City, Illinois, fire.

HISTORICAL MAJOR FIRE LOSSES IN THE
UNITED STATES

Throughout U.S. history, a number of major industrial fires have resulted
in significant loss of life and property damage. Table 1.1 summaries these
events (Emergency and Disaster Management, 2003):

Table 1.1   Summary of Major Fire Losses in the United States

1911, March 25	New York, NY: The Triangle Shirtwaist Factory fire killed 145 young workers
1927, November 14	Pittsburgh, PA: A tank filled with 5 million cubic feet of natural gas exploded when a maintenance worker controlled it with an open-flame lamp; 28 people died, hundreds were injured.
1947, February 20	Los Angeles, CA: South of Downtown Pico Blvd. and Stanford Ave., a blast at the O'Connor Electroplating Company destroyed/damaged more than 55 structures in a 300-foot radius; 150 people were injured, and 15 people perished. The incident resulted in the city's first ordinance stipulating regulations for the storage, transportation, production, processing, and use of hazardous chemicals and led to one of the first Haz-Mat Dictionaries in the United States.
1947, April 16	Texas City/Port, TX: The explosion of the S.S. *Grandcamp* loaded with ammonium nitrate killed 561 people, including all 27 members of the Texas City Volunteer Fire Department.
1947, June 22	Los Angeles, CA: On Wilmington Mormon Island, the S.S. *Markey,* loaded with more than 3 million gallons of butane and other petroleum products, exploded.
1991, September 3	NC: At the Hamlet Imperial Food Products chicken-processing plant, 25 worker died in a fire. The building was without fire alarms or sprinkler systems; many exit doors were locked to prevent employees from stealing.
2003, January 29	Kinson, NC: An explosion in the West Pharmaceutical Services plant killed 3 people and injured more than 20.

TRENDS IN FIRES IN THE UNITED STATES

Overall, fire deaths in the United States have fallen nearly two-thirds since their peak levels around World War I (NFPA 1997, 1–4). When examining the fire impact of industrial occupancies, the NFPA is the foremost authority on keeping track of reported fires, fire injuries, and property losses. The NFPA defines an industrial occupancy as all industrial, manufacturing, defense, and utility properties and all storage facilities excluding dwelling garages (NFPA 1997, 1–6). The U.S. Department of Labor, Bureau of Labor Statistics (BLS) Census of Fatal Occupational Injuries is the foremost authority on occupational fatalities in the United States.

ECONOMIC IMPACT OF INDUSTRIAL FIRES IN THE UNITED STATES

The challenge in any assessment of the total cost of fire is twofold: deciding what impacts of fire should be counted as costs and finding good bases for including the elements selected. Some elements are fairly straightforward, such as the direct cost of career fire departments. Some are clearly costs involved in fire prevention or mitigation but are hard to estimate with available data, such as the portion of annual construction expenditures spent only to comply with fire-protection rules (Hall 2002, 1). Analysis of costs associated with fire losses used the following estimating rules (Hall 2002, 3):

- Each year, 2 percent of reported nonresidential structure fires, excluding fires in storage facilities and special structures (e.g., vacant properties, properties under construction, structures that are not buildings) result in business closings. For the purposes of this analysis, a closing was estimated to imply indirect losses equal to four times the reported average direct loss in those types of fires.
- Indirect losses (principally business interruption costs) also add 65 percent in losses for manufacturing and industrial properties to direct loss, reported or unreported.

The economic impact of fires in industry can be felt as losses in business sales and production. Employment can be impacted as workers who once worked in a facility involved in a fire may lose time at work waiting for operations to get back up and running. In some cases, they may never return to work since the business is forced to close following the fire. Thus, individuals involved and their family members suffer the loss of income. The municipality suffers losses in taxes since workers are now not bringing in an income. Loss of income means decreased spending in local businesses and, as a result, lower sales-tax revenues to the local government as well. Because unemployment can increase from the loss of work or jobs in the area, increased demands upon social services are experienced. Finally, if the company ceases to exist following a major fire, unemployed workers may have no alternative but to move to another area to seek employment, resulting in population shifts in a region.

DEATHS AND INJURIES DUE TO INDUSTRIAL FIRES

A variety of agencies keep statistics on the fire experience in the United States. These agencies include the NFPA, National Safety Council, and the BLS. The NFPA, for example, found that an average of 16,900 reported structure fires cause 18 civilian deaths, 556 civilian injuries, and $789.6 million in direct property damage per year. One-fifth of these structure

Table 1.2   Structure Fires in Industrial and Manufacturing Facilities, 1994–1998 Annual
Averages

Occupancy	Fires	Direct Civilian Deaths	Direct Civilian Injuries	Direct Property Damage (in $ million)
Industry, Utility, and Defense	**4,200**	**3**	**62**	**136.0**
Energy production facility	200	1	6	22.9
Laboratory	300	0	17	4.8
Communication, defense, or document facility	200	0	4	7.1
Energy distribution property or utility facility	500	1	10	12.2
Agricultural or farm production facility	2,300	2	11	57.0
Forest, fish hatchery, or hunting area	100	0	0	0.8
Mine or quarry	200	0	3	6.5
Nonmetallic mineral or mineral product manufacturing facility	300	0	10	15.1
Unclassified or unknown type of industry, utility, or defense	200	0	3	9.7
Manufacturing	**12,700**	**15**	**494**	**653.6**
Food-product manufacturing	1,200	1	27	77.2
Beverage, tobacco, or related oil product manufacturing	200	0	9	3.7
Textile manufacturing	500	1	21	150.0
Wearing apparel, leather, or rubber product manufacturing	400	0	19	38.3
Wood, furniture, paper, or printing product manufacturing	3,000	0	68	112.8
Chemical, plastic, or petroleum product manufacturing	1,300	6	106	54.6
Metal or metal-product manufacturing	3,700	4	166	140.4
Vehicle assembly or manufacturing	600	1	28	22.5
Other manufacturing	1,000	0	27	30.9
Unclassified or unknown type of manufacturing	800	3	23	23.1
Total	**16,900**	**18**	**556**	**789.6**

Note: These are fires reported to U.S. municipal fire departments and, so, exclude fires reported only to federal or state agencies or industrial fire brigades. Fires are rounded to the nearest hundred, deaths and injuries to the nearest one, and direct property damage to the nearest hundred thousand dollars. Sums may not equal totals due to rounding errors. Damage has not been adjusted for inflation.

Source: National estimates based on NFIRS and NFPA survey (NFPA, June 2001, Ahrens, p. 156).

Table 1.3   Causes of Fires and Direct Property Damage in Industrial and Manufacturing
Structure Fires, 1994–1998 Annual Averages

Cause	Fires (n [%])		Property Damage ($ million, [%])	
Other equipment	6,600	(39.1)	277.4	(35.1)
Working or shaping machine	1,000	(5.6)	21.0	(2.7)
Unclassified or unknown-type processing equipment	900	(5.5)	65.5	(8.3)
Furnace, oven, or kiln	900	(5.4)	26.4	(3.3)
Unclassified or unknown-type special equipment	500	(2.9)	31.3	(4.0)
Heat-treating equipment	300	(1.8)	11.0	(1.4)
Separate motor or generator	300	(1.7)	6.2	(0.8)
Waste-recovery equipment	300	(1.6)	4.4	(0.6)
Casting, molding, or forging equipment	300	(1.5)	14.9	(1.9)
Conveyor	200	(1.1)	13.1	(1.7)
Open flame, ember, or torch	2,300	(13.8)	101.0	(12.8)
Torch	1,400	(8.2)	75.3	(9.5)
Open fire	300	(1.6)	2.4	(0.3)
Rekindling or reignition	200	(1.2)	2.6	(0.3)
Electrical distribution	1,700	(10.3)	86.6	(11.0)
Fixed wiring	500	(2.9)	29.1	(3.7)
Light fixture, lamp holder, ballast, or sign	200	(1.3)	12.0	(1.5)
Power-switch gear or overcurrent protection device	200	(1.2)	11.1	(1.4)
Heating equipment	1,200	(7.1)	32.3	(4.1)
Fixed area heater	300	(1.7)	10.5	(1.3)
Central-heating unit	200	(1.2)	6.8	(0.9)
Natural causes	1,100	(6.6)	40.6	(5.1)
Spontaneous ignition or chemical reaction	700	(4.1)	23.7	(3.0)
Lightning	300	(1.5)	9.0	(1.1)
Incendiary or suspicious	1,000	(6.1)	158.6	(20.1)
Appliance, tool, or air conditioning	800	(4.8)	21.5	(2.7)
Dryer	300	(1.8)	3.9	(0.5)
Other heat source	700	(3.9)	16.2	(2.1)
Cooking equipment	500	(2.9)	24.1	(3.1)
Exposure (to other hostile fire)	500	(2.7)	17.1	(2.2)
Smoking materials	400	(2.1)	13.1	(1.7)
Child playing	100	(0.5)	1.1	(0.1)
Total	**16,900**	**(100.0)**	**789.6**	**(100.0)**

Unknown-cause fires are allocated proportionally.

U.S. Fire Problem Overview Report 161, NFPA Fire Analysis and Research, Quincy, MA.

Note: These are fires reported to U.S. municipal fire departments and, so, exclude fires reported only to federal or state agencies or industrial fire brigades. Fires are expressed to the nearest hundred and property damage is rounded to the nearest hundred thousand dollars. Property damage figures have not been adjusted for inflation. The twelve major cause categories are based on a hierarchy developed by the U.S. Fire Administration. Sums may not equal totals due to rounding errors.

Source: National estimates based on NFIRS and NFPA survey (NFPA, June 2001, Ahrens, p. 161).

Table 1.4 Estimates of 2002 Structure Fires and Property Loss by Property Use

Property Use	Structure Fires Estimate (thousands)	Property Loss[1] Estimate (hundred thousands)
Public assembly	14	342
Educational	7	92
Institutional	6.5	26
Residential (total)	401	6.055
One- and two-family dwellings[2]	300.5	5.005
Apartments	88.5	926
Other residential[3]	12	124
Stores and offices	24	604
Industry, utility, defense[4]	12.5	658
Storage in structures	32	627
Special structures	22	338
Total	519	8,742

Notes:
1. This includes overall direct property loss to contents, structure, vehicles, machinery, vegetation, or anything else involved in a fire. It does not include indirect losses (e.g., business interruption or temporary shelter costs). No adjustment was made for inflation in the year-to-year comparison.
2. This includes manufactured homes.
3. This includes hotels and motels, college dormitories, boarding houses, and so forth.
4. Incidents handled only by private fire brigades or fixed suppression systems are not included in the figures shown here.

The estimates are based on data reported to the NFPA by fire departments that responded to the 2002 National Fire Experience Survey.

fires occur in facilities manufacturing metal or metal products. The average number of structure fires, casualties, and direct property damage per year from 1994 through 1998 in industrial and manufacturing properties are listed in table 1.2 (Ahrens 2001, 157). Summaries of the fire experience in the United States are provided in tables 1.3 and 1.4.

The BLS keeps data on the occupational injuries, illnesses, and fatalities in the United States involving fires. Data from the BLS identified the following occupational injuries and fatalities due to fires and explosions in the U.S. workplace. Fires and explosions accounted for approximately 3,711 occupational injuries in 2001 with the majority occurring in the construction industry. Trend data involving fires and explosions from 1992 to 2000 indicated that fires and explosions account for approximately 3 percent of all nonfatal occupational injuries and illnesses involving days away from work (see tables 1.5 and 1.6). Between 1992 and 2000, fires and explosions accounted for approximately 1,760 deaths in the workplace. From 1994 to 1998, structure fires in manufacturing and industrial properties averaged approximately 16,900 fires annually and $789.6 million in property losses with the greatest percentage of fires start-

Table 1.5 Number of Nonfatal Occupational Injuries and Illnesses Involving Days Away from Work[1] by Event or Exposure Leading to Injury or Illness and Industry Division, 2001

Event	Private Industry[2]	Agriculture[3]	Mining[4]	Construction	Manufacturing	Transportation	Wholesale Trade	Retail Trade	Finance, Insurance, Real Estate	Services
Fires and explosions	3,711	48	35	846	520	418	652	801	—	362
Fires, unintended or uncontrolled	2,472	—	—	586	339	270	484	521	—	220
Fire, unspecified	864	—	—	147	89	—	113	375	—	112
Fire in residence, building, or other structure	864	—	—	147	89	—	113	375	—	112
Forest, brush, or other outdoor fire	18	—	—	—	—	—	—	—	—	—
Ignition of clothing from controlled heat sources	216	—	—	—	73	—	—	—	—	47
Fire, n.e.c	1,044	—	—	349	137	166	231	93	—	36
Explosion	1,225	—	32	261	181	148	167	276	—	132
Explosion, unspecified	222	—	—	121	18	53	—	—	—	—
Explosion of battery	64	—	—	—	—	—	—	—	—	—
Explosion of pressure vessel or piping	581	—	12	80	67	68	165	103	—	81
Explosion, n.e.c	358	—	17	—	94	—	—	123	—	47

Notes:
Dashes indicate data that are not available. Because of rounding, dots may not sum to totals.
n.e.c. = not elsewhere classified.

1. Days-away-from-work cases include those that result in days away from work with or without restricted work activity.
2. This excludes farms with fewer than eleven employees.
3. Data conforming to OSHA definitions for mining operators in coal, metal, and nonmetal mining are provided to BLS by the Mine Safety and Health Administration (MSHA), U.S. Department of Labor. Independent mining contractors are excluded from the coal, metal, and nonmetal mining industries. Data for mining (Division B in the Standard Industrial Classification Manual, 1987 ed.) include establishments not governed by the MSHA rules and reporting, such as those in oil and gas extraction.
4. Data conforming to OSHA definitions for employers in railroad transportation are provided to BLS by the Federal Railroad Administration, U.S. Department of Transportation.

Source: Bureau of Labor Statistics, U.S. Department of Labor, 2002, p. 7.

Table 1.6 Number of Fatal Occupational Injuries by Detailed Event of Exposure, 1992–2000

Event	1992	1993	1994	1995	1996	1997	1998	1999	2000	2000 (%)
Fires and explosions	167	204	202	207	186	196	206	216	177	3.0
Fires, unintended or uncontrolled	59	91	106	97	98	87	117	115	100	1.7
Fires, unspecified	—	9	6	—	5	5	—	—	5	0.1
Fire in residence, building, or other structure	31	53	52	57	64	39	69	74	56	0.9
Forest, brush, or other outdoor fire	5	—	20	9	10	8	14	6	6	0.1
Ignition of clothing from controlled heat source	—	—	—	—	—	7	—	6	—	—
Explosion	105	11	96	107	85	109	89	99	76	1.3
Explosion, unspecified	18	8	5	7	—	5	—	5	—	—
Explosion of pressure vessel or piping	36	39	32	42	46	37	39	38	30	0.5

Note: Totals for major categories may include subcategories not shown separately. Percentages may not add up to totals because of rounding. Dashes indicate no data reported or data that do not meet publication criteria.

Source: U.S. Department of Labor, Bureau of Labor Statistics, Census of Fatal Occupational Injuries, 2002, p. 94.

ing in the process or manufacturing areas of the facilities (see table 1.7). The National Safety Council estimates that from 1992 to 2000, the manufacturing industry accounted for the greatest number of fire- and explosion-related deaths, with 409 (see table 1.8).

OSHA AND FIRE SAFETY

As the federal government agency responsible for setting the national standards for worker safety and health, OSHA has established standards addressing each of the three key elements of fire safety: (1) fire prevention, (2) safe evacuation of the workplace in the event of fire, and (3) protection of workers who fight fires or who work around fire-suppression equipment. These issues are addressed by a variety of detailed OSHA rules applicable to general industry (all businesses except construction, shipbuilding, and longshoring) in 29 C.F.R. § 1910 (www.osha.gov). OSHA has adopted a number of standards dealing with fire protection and prevention in the workplace. The following list summarizes the 29 C.F.R. § 1910 standards for fire protection and prevention (www.osha.gov):

- *General Industry*
  - 1910, Occupational Safety and Health Standards
    - 1910.36, Design and construction requirements for exit routes
    - 1910.37, Maintenance, safeguards, and operational features for exit routes
    - 1910.38, Emergency-action plans
    - 1910.94, Ventilation
    - 1910.103, Hydrogen
    - 1910.104, Oxygen
    - 1910.106, Flammable and combustible liquids
    - 1910.107, Spray finishing using flammable and combustible materials
    - 1910.108, Dip tanks containing flammable or combustible liquids
    - 1910.109, Explosives and blasting agents
    - 1910.110, Storage and handling of liquefied petroleum gases
    - 1910.111, Storage and handling of anhydrous ammonia
    - 1910.119, Process-safety management of highly hazardous chemicals
    - 1910.120, Hazardous-waste operations and emergency response
    - 1910.178, Powered industrial trucks

Table 1.7   Structure Fires in Industrial and Manufacturing Properties, by Area of Origin, 1994–1998 Annual Averages

Area of Origin	Fires [n (%)]		Civilian Deaths [n (%)]		Civilian Injuries [n (%)]		Property Damage [$ millions (%)]	
Process or manufacturing area	3,300	(19.7)	6	(34.6)	198	(35.6)	163.5	(20.7%)
Machinery room or area	1,800	(10.4)	2	(9.5)	76	(13.8)	67.8	(8.6%)
Product storage area, tank, or bin	1,000	(5.7)	2	(12.0)	26	(4.8)	99.9	(12.7%)
Maintenance shop or area	800	(4.9)	1	(7.9)	38	(6.9)	42.8	(5.4%)
Unclassified area of origin	700	(4.3)	0	(1.3)	9	(1.6)	20.5	(2.6%)
Duct	700	(4.1)	0	(1.0)	17	(3.1)	25.1	(3.2%)
Attic or ceiling/roof assembly or concealed space	600	(3.6)	0	(1.0)	9	(1.7)	35.1	(4.4%)
Heating equipment room	500	(3.2)	0	(0.0)	16	(2.9)	52.3	(6.6%)
Exterior wall surface	500	(2.9)	0	(0.0)	3	(0.5)	24.3	(3.1%)
Exterior roof surface	400	(2.6)	0	(0.0)	5	(0.9)	7.0	(0.9%)
Unclassified service or equipment area	400	(2.1)	0	(0.0)	12	(2.2)	10.1	(1.3%)
Trash or rubbish area or container	400	(2.1)	0	(0.0)	6	(1.0)	4.9	(0.6%)
Supply storage room or area	400	(2.1)	0	(1.3)	12	(2.2)	18.4	(2.3%)
Unclassified storage area	300	(2.0)	1	(2.9)	4	(0.7)	19.4	(2.5%)
Unclassified structural area	300	(2.0)	1	(3.2)	5	(0.9)	14.5	(1.8%)
Wall assembly or concealed space	300	(1.7)	0	(0.0)	2	(0.4)	9.7	(1.2%)
Kitchen	300	(1.5)	0	(0.0)	6	(1.1)	4.4	(0.6%)
Switchgear area or transformer vault	300	(1.5)	2	(10.4)	12	(2.2)	13.1	(1.7%)
Shipping, receiving, or loading area	200	(1.4)	1	(5.0)	9	(1.6)	15.5	(2.0%)
Lawn, field, or open area	200	(1.3)	0	(0.0)	0	(0.0)	2.3	(0.3%)
Conveyor	200	(1.3)	0	(0.0)	3	(0.6)	4.8	(0.6%)
Office	200	(1.3)	0	(1.3)	3	(0.6)	13.6	(1.7%)
Electronic equipment room or area	200	(1.3)	0	(0.0)	4	(0.7)	11.7	(1.5%)
Unclassified function area	200	(1.2)	0	(0.0)	8	(1.5)	8.0	(1.0%)
Laboratory	200	(1.2)	0	(0.0)	18	(3.3)	3.2	(0.4%)
Ceiling/floor assembly or concealed space	200	(1.1)	0	(0.0)	1	(0.2)	13.2	(1.7%)
Laundry room or area	200	(1.0)	0	(0.0)	2	(0.3)	2.1	(0.3%)
Other service or equipment area	600	(3.6)	0	(0.0)	9	(1.7)	11.0	(1.4%)
Other known function area	400	(2.3)	1	(2.9)	10	(1.7)	27.2	(3.4%)
Other known assembly area	200	(1.2)	0	(2.2)	4	(0.7)	7.7	(1.0%)
Other known means of egress	200	(1.1)	0	(0.0)	2	(0.4)	7.6	(1.0%)
Other known area	700	(4.2)	1	(3.6)	22	(4.0)	29.2	(3.7%)
Total	**16,900**	**(100.0)**	**18**	**(100.0)**	**556**	**(100.0)**	**789.6**	**(100.0%)**

Unknown-area fires allocated proportionally.

U.S. Fire Problem Overview Report 163, NFPA Fire Analysis and Research, Quincy, MA.

Note: These are fires reported to U.S. municipal fire departments and, so, exclude fires reported only to federal or state agencies or industrial fire brigades. Fires are rounded to the nearest hundred, deaths and injuries to the nearest one, and direct property damage to the nearest hundred thousand dollars. Sums may not equal totals due to rounding errors. Damage has not been adjusted for inflation. *Source:* National estimates based on NFIRS and NFPA survey (NFPA, June 2001, Ahrens, p. 163).

14

Table 1.8   Number of Nonfatal Occupational Injuries and Illnesses Involving Days
Away from Work and Fatal Occupational Injuries Due to Fires and Explosions in the
United States

	Nonfatal Cases, 2000	Fatalities, 1992–2000
Agriculture, forestry, and fishing	192	101
Mining, quarrying, and oil and gas extraction	73	154
Construction	952	270
Manufacturing	795	409
Transportation and public utilities	178	132
Wholesale trade	242	88
Retail trade	778	102
Finance, insurance, and real estate	34	10
Services	495	237
Government	—	248
All industries	3,656	1,760

Source: National Safety Council 2002, Injury Facts, pp. 67–77.

- 1910.252, General requirements
- 1910.253, Oxygen-fuel gas welding and cutting
- 1910.255, Resistance welding
- 1910.261, Pulp, paper, and paperboard mills
- 1910.263, Bakery equipment
- 1910.265, Sawmills
- 1910.266, Logging operations
- 1910.269, Electric power generation, transmission, and distribution
- 1910.272, Grain-handling facilities
- 1910.305, Wiring methods, components, and equipment for general use
- 1910.308, Special systems
- 1910.1200, Hazard communication (HAZCOM)

SOURCES OF INFORMATION

Occupational Safety and Health Administration (OSHA)

OSHA is responsible for the promulgation of federal legislation for safety and health in the workplace. It also has the responsibility for enforcing the standards it develops. Generally speaking, all private employers with one or more employees are required to comply with OSHA standards applicable to their industry. Some states have state plans in which the state is responsible for developing and enforcing its safety and health standards. The following lists the contact information for federal OSHA offices:

NATIONAL OFFICE

U.S. Department of Labor
Occupational Safety and Health Administration
200 Constitution Avenue, N.W.
Washington, DC 20210
Website: www.osha.gov

REGION 1

Regional Office

JFK Federal Building, Room E340
Boston, MA 02203
Phone: (617) 565-9860
Fax: (617) 565-9827

Area Offices

Connecticut, Massachusetts, Maine, New Hampshire, Rhode Island, Vermont

REGION 2

Regional Office

201 Varick Street, Room 670
New York, NY 10014
Phone: (212) 337-2378
Fax: (212) 337-2371

Area Offices

New Jersey, New York, Puerto Rico, Virgin Islands

REGION 3

Regional Office

U.S. Department of Labor/OSHA
The Curtis Center, Suite 740 West
170 S. Independence Mall West
Philadelphia, PA 19106-3309
Phone: (215) 861-4900
Fax: (215) 861-4904

Area Offices

Washington, DC, Delaware, Maryland, Pennsylvania, Virginia, West Virginia

REGION 4

Regional Office

61 Forsyth Street, SW
Atlanta, GA 30303
Phone: (404) 562-2300
Fax: (404) 562-2295

Area Offices

Alabama, Florida, Georgia, Kentucky, Mississippi, North Carolina, South
Carolina, Tennessee

REGION 5

Regional Office

230 S. Dearborn Street, Room 3244
Chicago, IL 60604
Phone: (312) 353-2220
Fax: (312) 353-7774

Area Offices

Illinois, Indiana, Michigan, Minnesota, Ohio, Wisconsin

REGION 6

Regional Office

525 Griffin Street, Room 602
Dallas, TX 75202
Phone: (214) 767-4731
Fax: (214) 767-4693

Area Offices

Arkansas, Louisiana, New Mexico, Oklahoma, Texas

REGION 7

Regional Office

City Center Square
1100 Main Street, Suite 800
Kansas City, MO 64105
Phone: (816) 426-5861
Fax: (816) 426-2750

Area Offices

Iowa, Kansas, Missouri, Nebraska

REGION 8

Regional Office

1999 Broadway, Suite 1690
P.O. Box 46550
Denver, CO 80201-6550
Phone: (303) 844-1600
Fax: (303) 844-1616

Area Offices

Colorado, Montana, North Dakota, South Dakota, Utah, Wyoming

REGION 9

Federal Contact Numbers

71 Stevenson Street, Room 420
San Francisco, California 94105
Phones: (415) 975-4310 (main public: 8:00 AM to 4:30 PM Pacific)
         (800) 475-4019 (for technical assistance)
         (800) 475-4020 (for complaints—accidents/fatalities)
         (800) 475-4022 (for publication requests)
Fax: (415) 975-4319
   For issues involving federal agencies or private companies working for federal agencies in Arizona, California, Guam, Hawaii, and Nevada, call the numbers listed above. For issues involving private or state government employers in these states, refer to the appropriate state office in Arizona, California, Hawaii, or Nevada.

REGION 10

Regional Office

1111 Third Avenue, Suite 715
Seattle, WA 98101-3212
Phone: (206) 553-5930
Fax: (206) 553-6499

Area Offices

Alaska, Idaho, Oregon, Washington

U.S. Department of Transportation (USDOT)

   USDOT is responsible for ensuring that the nation's transportation systems operate in a safe and efficient manner. Transportation safety organizations and programs related to fire protection and prevention include the following:

- National Response Center (NRC). The NRC is the sole federal point of contact for reporting oil and chemical spills.
- Transportation Safety Institute. This organization supports USDOT's vital mission to ensure the safety and security of the nation's transportation system through instruction to both those entrusted with enforcement and those obligated to comply with safety standards.
- Hazardous Materials Safety. The office responsible for coordinating a national safety program for the transportation of hazardous materials by air, rail, highway, and water.

U.S. Department of Transportation
400 7th Street, S.W.
Washington, DC 20590
Phone: (202) 366-4000
Website: www.dot.gov

National Safety Council (NSC)

The NSC is a not-for-profit organization whose mission is to educate and influence society to adopt safety, health, and environmental policies, practices, and procedures that prevent and mitigate human suffering and economic losses arising from preventable causes.

1121 Spring Lake Drive
Itasca, IL 60143-3201
Phone: (630) 285-1121
Fax: (630) 285-1315
Website: www.nsc.org

U.S. Fire Administration (USFA)

The USFA is an entity of the Federal Emergency Management Agency (FEMA) and the Department of Homeland Security. The mission of the USFA is to reduce life and economic losses due to fire and related emergencies, through leadership, advocacy, coordination, and support.

U.S. Fire Administration
16825 S. Seton Avenue

Emmitsburg, MD 21727
Phone: (301) 447-1000
Fax: (301) 447-1052
Website: www.usfa.fema.gov

National Institute for Occupational Safety and Health (NIOSH)

The Occupational Safety and Health Act of 1970 created both NIOSH and OSHA. OSHA is part of the U.S. Department of Labor and is responsible for developing and enforcing workplace safety and health regulations. NIOSH is in the U.S. Department of Health and Human Services and was established to help assure safe and healthful working conditions for working men and women by providing research, information, education, and training in the field of occupational safety and health. NIOSH provides national and world leadership in preventing work-related illness, injury, disability, and death by gathering information, conducting scientific research, and translating the knowledge gained into products and services. NIOSH's mission is critical to the health and safety of every American worker.

National Institute for Occupational Safety and Health
John Howard, M.D., M.P.H., J.D., LL.M.
Director, NIOSH
Hubert H. Humphrey Building
200 Independence Avenue, S.W., Room 715H
Washington, DC 20201
Phone: (202) 401-6997
Website: www.cdc.gov/niosh

Factory Mutual (FM) Global

FM Global is one of the world's largest commercial and industrial property-insurance and risk-management organizations specializing in property protection. FM Global's property-loss-prevention research offers product certification through their independent, third-party testing laboratory, FM Approvals. Manufacturers rely on FM Approvals to test and approve their products and services, certifying their reliability. Products or services that sufficiently meet FM Approvals' rigorous testing standards may bear the FM APPROVED mark.

Factory Mutual Insurance Company
1301 Atwood Avenue
P.O. Box 7500
Johnston, RI 02919
Phone: (401) 275-3000
Fax: (401) 275-3029
Website: www.fmglobal.com

National Fire Sprinkler Association (NFSA)

The mission of NFSA is to create a market for the widespread acceptance of competently installed automatic fire-sprinkler systems in both
new and existing construction, from homes to high-rises.

The National Fire Sprinkler Association
P.O. Box 1000
Patterson, NY 12563
Phone: (845) 878-4200
Website: www.nfsa.org

National Association Fire Equipment Dealers (NAFED)

NAFED was established in 1963 with the mission of continuously
improving the economic environment, business performance, and technical competence of the fire-protection industry.

National Association of Fire Equipment Distributors
104 S. Michigan Avenue, Suite 300
Chicago, IL 60603
Phone: (312) 263-8100
Fax: (312) 263-8111
Website: www.nafed.org

National Fire Academy (NFA)

As a result of the landmark document *America Burning: The Report of
the National Commission on Fire Prevention and Control*, Public Law 93-
498, the Federal Fire Prevention and Control Act of 1974, was signed into
law on October 29, 1974. With the passage of PL93-498, the USFA and its
delivery arm, the NFA, were created. It is estimated that since 1975, over

1.4 million students have received training through a variety of course-delivery methods.

U.S. Fire Administration
16825 S. Seton Avenue
Emmitsburg, MD 21727
Phone:(301) 447-1000
Fax: (301) 447-1052
Website: www.usfa.fema.gov/fire-service/nfa/nfa.shtm

American Petroleum Institute (API)

The mission of the API is to influence public policy in support of the strong, viable, U.S. oil and natural-gas industry essential to meet the energy needs of consumers in an efficient, environmentally responsible manner. API's health and safety programs promote safety and accident prevention through development of effective industry standards and practices on safety and fire prevention.

American Petroleum Institute
1220 L Street, N.W.
Washington, DC 20005-4070
Phone: (202) 682-8000
Website: www.api.org

American Welding Society (AWS)

The AWS was founded in 1919 as a multifaceted, nonprofit organization with the goal of advancing the science, technology, and application of welding and related joining disciplines. Headquartered in Miami, Florida, AWS serves more than 48,500 members in the United States and around the world. AWS provides fact sheets covering aspects of safety and health applicable to welding and cutting, including subjects like fumes and gases, radiation, noise, and electrical hazards. These are produced by the Labeling and Safe Practices Subcommittee of the AWS Safety and Health Committee.

550 N.W. LeJeune Road
Miami, FL 33126
Website: www.aws.org
Phone: (800) 443-9353

Compressed Gas Association (CGA)

Since 1913, the CGA has been dedicated to the development and promotion of safety standards and safe practices in the industrial-gas industry. More than two hundred member companies worldwide work together through the committee system to create technical specifications, safety standards, and training and educational materials; to cooperate with governmental agencies in formulating responsible regulations and standards; and to promote compliance with these regulations and standards in the workplace.

Compressed Gas Association
4221 Walney Road, 5th Floor,
Chantilly, VA 20151-2923
Phone: (703) 788-2700
Fax: (703) 961-1831
Website: www.cganet.com

Society of Fire Protection Engineers (SFPE)

The SFPE was established in 1950 and incorporated as in independent organization in 1971. It is the professional society representing those practicing in the field of fire-protection engineering. The society has approximately thirty-five hundred members in the United States and abroad, and fifty-one regional chapters, ten of which are outside the United States. The purpose of SFPE is to advance the science and practice of fire-protection engineering and its allied fields, to maintain a high ethical standard among its members, and to foster fire-protection engineering education.

Society of Fire Protection Engineers
7315 Wisconsin Avenue, Suite 1225 W.
Bethesda, MD 20814
Phone: (301) 718-2910
Fax: (301) 718-2242
Website: www.sfpe.org

Underwriters Laboratories (UL)

UL is an independent, not-for-profit, product-safety testing and certification organization. UL offers services to consumers, manufacturers, and regulators. Annual lists of manufacturers whose products have proved acceptable under appropriate standards are available.

Underwriters Laboratories
333 Pfingsten Road
Northbrook, IL 60062
Website: www.ul.com

Alliance of American Insurers

The alliance is a property- and casualty-insurance trade association that works with interested safety professionals and stakeholders from the public sector, private industry, labor, and academia. It organizes local coalitions interested in developing new public-policy approaches to protecting employees working in small businesses.

Alliance of American Insurers
Safety and Environment Department
3025 Highland Parkway, Suite 800
Downers Grove, IL 60515-1289
Phone: (630) 724-2100
Website: www.allianceai.org

American Association of Occupational Health Nurses (AAOHN)

This group is an association of registered, professional nurses employed by business and industrial firms, as well as nurse educators, nurse editors, nurse writers, and others interested in occupational-health nursing. AAOHN provides workplace information referrals and related services. In addition, it has several publications of interest to small business and provides a speakers bureau.

American Association of Occupational Health Nurses
2920 Brandywine Road, Suite 100
Atlanta, GA 30341
Phone: (770) 455-7757
Fax: (770) 455-7271
Website: www.aaohn.org

American Conference of Governmental Industrial Hygienists (ACGIH)

ACGIH is a professional society of occupational and environmental safety and health professionals devoted to the development of the administrative and technical aspects of worker-health protection. ACGIH functions mainly as a medium for the exchange of ideas and the promotion of standards and techniques in industrial health.

American Conference of Governmental Industrial Hygienists
1330 Kemper Meadow Drive, Suite 600
Cincinnati, OH 45240
Phone: (513) 742-2020
Fax: (513) 742-3355
Website: www.acgih.org

American Industrial Hygiene Association (AIHA)

AIHA is a professional society of industrial hygienists that promotes the study and control of environmental factors affecting the health and well-being of workers. AIHA sponsors continuing-education courses in industrial hygiene, a government-affairs program, and public relations.

American Industrial Hygiene Association
2700 Prosperity Avenue, Suite 250
Fairfax, VA 22031-4319
Phone: (703) 849-8888
Fax: (703) 207-3561
Website: www.aiha.org

American National Standards Institute (ANSI)

ANSI serves as a clearinghouse for nationally coordinated voluntary standards for fields ranging from information technology to building construction. ANSI gives American National Standards status to standards developed for definitions, terminology, symbols, and abbreviations; materials, performance characteristics, procedures, and methods of rating; methods of testing and analysis; size, weight, volume, and rating; and practice, safety, health, and building construction. ANSI provides information on foreign standards and represents U.S. interests in international standardization work.

American National Standards Institute
25 West 43rd Street, 4th Floor
New York, NY 10036
Phone: (212) 642-4900

Fax: (212) 398-0023
Website: www.ansi.org

American Society of Safety Engineers (ASSE)

ASSE is a professional society of safety engineers, safety professionals, safety directors, and others concerned with accident prevention, environmental protection, and safety and health programs. ASSE develops and publishes ANSI safety-related standards and other technical literature.

American Society of Safety Engineers
1800 East Oakton Street
Des Plaines, IL 60018
Phone: (847) 699-2929
Fax: (847) 768-3434
Website: www.asse.org

American Society for Testing and Materials (ASTM)

ASTM establishes standards for materials, products, systems, and services. ASTM has 131 technical committees (each having 5 to 50 subcommittees). New committees are organized periodically to keep pace with technological advances. ASTM has developed more than ten thousand standard test methods, specifications, classifications, definitions, and recommended practices now in use. Information is available about the prices of ASTM standards with related material.

American Society for Testing and Materials
100 Barr Harbor Drive
P.O. Box C700
West Conshohocken, PA 19428-2959
Phone: (610) 832-9585
Fax: (610) 832-9555
Website: www.astm.org

National Fire Protection Association (NFPA)

NFPA develops, publishes, and disseminates standards (prepared by approximately two hundred fifty technical committees) that are intended to minimize the possibility and effects of fire and explosion. NFPA also conducts fire-safety education programs for the general public. NFPA pro-

vides information on fire protection, prevention, and suppression; com-
piles annual statistics on causes and occupancies of fires, large-loss fires
(over $1 million in damage), fire deaths, and firefighter casualties. NFPA
provides field service by specialists on electricity, flammable liquids and
gases, and marine fire problems. NFPA also sponsors seminars on the Life-
Safety Code, the National Electrical Code, hotel and motel fire safety, ship-
yard fire protection, fire safety in detention and correctional facilities, and
other timely topics.

National Fire Protection Association
1 Batterymarch Park
Quincy, MA 02269-9101
Phone: (617) 770-3000
Toll-free: (800) 344-3555 (publications only)
Website: www.nfpa.org

SUMMARY

A safety professional is a person engaged in the prevention of accidents,
incidents, and events that harm people, property, or the environment
(www.bcsp.org). Fire protection and prevention are just two of the many
responsibilities expected of the safety professional working with industrial
occupancies. The potential for a fire is always present in the workplace.
The risk and the severity of a hazard in terms of losses and injuries in the
workplace can vary greatly from industry to industry. These fire hazards
can be properly controlled with appropriate measures.

The prevention and control of fires can be achieved through a variety
of techniques, including planning a safe workplace through the selection
of appropriate tools and equipment, proper work practices designed to
prevent the contact of fuel sources with heat sources, the control of fires
once they have started with proper fire-protection and identification systems, and, finally, the protection of building occupants and the community through providing proper notification and appropriate means of
egress.

History has shown us that when fire protection is not a primary concern of the organization or when appropriate measures are not taken to
prevent fires and protect the workers, the results can be devastating. While
there has been much improvement in the fire losses experienced in the

U.S. workplace, history has also shown us that major fires and loss of life still occur and are still possible today.

CHAPTER QUESTIONS

1. Compare the fire-death rates in the United States to the fire-death rates in other industrialized countries.
2. Effective fire prevention requires what three components?
3. Describe the opportunities one has to intervene in a fire.
4. Differentiate between fire protection and fire prevention.
5. Describe some of the job activities a fire-protection engineer may engage in.
6. Describe the trends in fire-death experience in the United States since World War I.
7. What impact do fires have upon occupational fatalities and injuries in the United States?
8. What are some major sources of ignition in the workplace based upon reported fires?
9. Describe some aspects of fire safety that OSHA has regulated in the workplace.
10. Describe OSHA's three key elements of fire safety.

REFERENCES

Ahrens, Marty. (2001). *Selections from the U.S. Fire Problem Overview Report: Leading Causes and Other Patterns and Trends: Industrial and Manufacturing Properties, June 2001.* Quincy, MA: NFPA.

American Society of Safety Engineers (ASSE), Foundation and Board of Certified Safety Professionals (BCSP). (2000). *Career Guide to the Safety Profession,* 2nd ed. Des Plaines, IL: ASSE and BCSP.

Emergency and Disaster Management. (2003). Los Angeles, CA, June 6, at www.emergency-management.net (accessed June 22, 2005).

Hall, John R., Jr. (2002). *The Total Cost of Fire in the United States.* Quincy, MA: NFPA, Fire Analysis and Research Division, August 2002.

National Fire Protection Association (NFPA). (1997). *Fire Protection Handbook,* 18th ed. Quincy, MA: NFPA.

National Safety Council. (2002). *Injury Facts, 2002.* Itasca, IL: National Safety Council, 67–77.

Occupational Safety and Health Administration (OSHA). (2004). Available at www.osha.gov (accessed June 22, 2005).

U.S. Bureau of Labor Statistics. (2002). *Table R64: Number of Nonfatal Occupational Injuries and Illnesses Involving Days Away from Work by Event or Exposure Leading to Injury or Illness and Industry Division, 2001*. Washington, DC: Bureau of Labor Statistics.

U.S. Bureau of Labor Statistics. (2002). *Fatal Workplace Injuries in 2000: A Collection of Data and Analysis. Bureau of Labor Statistics, September 2002. Report 961*. Washington, DC: Bureau of Labor Statistics.

U.S. Fire Administration (USFA). (1973). *America Burning: The Report of the National Commission on Fire Prevention and Control*. Washington, DC: National Commission on Fire Prevention and Control.

USFA. (1987). *America Burning Revisited: National Workshop, Tyson's Corner, Virginia, November 30–December 2, 1987*. Washington, DC: Federal Emergency Management Agency, USFA.

Chemistry and Physics of Fire

In order to prevent fires from occurring and to extinguish them successfully after they have started, an understanding of the chemical and physical characteristics of fire is important. The chemistry of fire involves the
ways in which fires can be started and sustained at the molecular level of
the fuel source. The chemical implications of the combustion process, as
well as the potential hazards of combustion by-products to workers, will
also be discussed. The physical aspects of fire involve its thermal properties, methods of heat transfer, and method of extinguishment. Because fire
is a chemical reaction, it is important to understand not only which hazardous materials pose fire hazards in the workplace but also the by-products of the combustion process, which can often be more hazardous than
the hazardous material involved in the fire. Control measures include the
use of established labeling, classification systems, and handling procedures
for hazardous materials. Examples of these systems include the Department of Transportation Hazardous Materials Classification Labeling System, the National Fire Protection Association (NFPA) Labeling System,
and additional references on hazardous materials.

FIRE TETRAHEDRON

For many years, it was believed the fire process could be described by what
was referred to as a *fire triangle*. This concept basically indicated that there
were three elements essential to initiate and sustain fire: oxygen, heat or
some other energy source, and fuel. In more recent years, we have
expanded the fire triangle into what is now referred to as the *fire tetrahedron* (Klinoff 2003, 85). This concept contains the three elements dis-

cussed above; however, it adds a fourth element, which is often referred to as the *chemical chain reaction*. Figure 2.1 depicts the fire tetrahedron.

In terms of oxygen supplies, air is the most common source of oxygen with, on average, 21 percent of air being oxygen. However, it should be noted that sources of oxygen can also include oxidizers. *Oxidizers* are substances that acquire electrons from a fuel in a chemical reaction and release oxygen during combustion. Examples of common oxidizers include elements of fluorine, chlorine, hydrogen peroxide, nitric acid, sulfuric acid, and hydrofluoric acid.

In its simplest form, the source of energy that heats the material to its ignition temperature as part of the fire tetrahedron is the *ignition source* or *energy source*. Some examples of ignition sources for fires in industrial occupancies include excessive electrical current, heating equipment, flames and sparks, and lightning. When discussing heat or energy sources, an important concept to understand is *ignition temperature*, the minimum temperature of a material required to initiate or cause self-sustained combustion of the material (Klinoff 2003, 88). Some examples of ignition temperatures of common building materials include plywood (390°C), gypsum board (565°C), carpet (412°C), and asphalt shingles (378°C) (Quintiere 1998, 241). Ignition temperature can vary. Oxygen in the air is also one influencing factor: the richer the oxygen levels, the lower the ignition temperature. The rate of heat rise, the duration of heating, and the size and shape of material will also influence ignition material. A classic example illustrating how ignition material is influenced by the size and shape of material is wood. Wood shavings ignite at a lower ignition temperature than bulk wood because of the size and shape of the material.

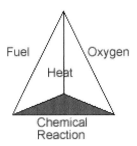

FIGURE 2.1
Fire tetrahedron

It should also be noted that spontaneous ignition can occur when the ignition source is slow oxidation with very limited heat loss that produces a temperature rise above the ignition temperature of the material. An example of spontaneous ignition in industrial occupancies are oil-soaked rags stored in 55-gal. waste drums.

The third element to the fire tetrahedron is fuel. Most fires involve a fuel that contains carbon and hydrogen, such as wood, paper, and flammable and combustible liquids and gases (Klinoff 2003, 87). Another potential fuel is a combustible metal, such as aluminum or magnesium. For fire-extinguishment purposes, the fuels are classified as follows (Klinoff 2003, 102):

- *Class A:* carbon-based products such as wood and paper
- *Class B:* flammable gases and liquids
- *Class C:* combustible materials where electricity may be present
- *Class D:* combustible metals, such as aluminum, magnesium, titanium, and zirconium
- *Class K:* liquid cooking media

Each fuel classification also has a unique symbol. Fire extinguishers are an example of a piece of equipment that uses these fuel-classification symbols. A summary of the fuel classifications and their symbols appears in figure 2.2.

The fourth and final element to the fire tetrahedron is the chemical chain reaction. This chemical chain reaction occurs within the material itself when the fuel is broken down by heat, producing chemically reactive free radicals, which then combine with the oxidizer (Klinoff 2003, 85–86).

COMBUSTION

Combustion can be defined as an exothermic chemical reaction between some substance and oxygen. Combustion consists of chain reactions involving free hydrogen atoms, H_2, hydroxyl free radicals, OH, and free oxygen molecules (NFPA 2000, 2). The combining of the hydrogen H_2 with oxygen O_2 forms water molecules and new hydrogen molecules, which in turn combine with oxygen molecules, forming more water molecules and more hydrogen molecules. This chemical chain reaction continues until all of the fuel is consumed by the fire.

To truly understand combustion, we must also understand *oxidation.*

Symbol	Types of Materials
 A Ordinary Combustibles	Ordinary combustibles wood, paper
 B Flammable Liquids	Flammable and combustible liquids, oils, grease
 C Electrical Equipment	Electrical fires
 D Combustible Metals	Metal fires
	Cooking oils

FIGURE 2.2
Classifications of fuels

Oxidation can be defined as the chemical combination of any substance with an oxidizer (Klinoff 2003, 475). With combustion, the energy that accompanies oxidation is commonly given off as heat and light. The speed at which oxidation occurs varies from that of rusting iron and yellowing paper to that of combustion. The difference between a slow oxidation like rusting and combustion is that combustion occurs so rapidly that the heat is generated faster than it is dissipated, causing a substantial temperature rise in the substance.

The rates of combustion of gases, liquids, and solids vary depending on several factors. For solids, the rate of combustion varies primarily based on the size of the solid particles, with smaller particles having a higher rate of combustion. For flammable liquids, the rate of combustion will vary based on whether the combustion occurs in a still pool, flowing current, or spray or foam. For flammable gases, the rate of combustion varies based on the extent to which the gas mixes with air prior to combustion and on the degree of motion and turbulence of the gases (Klinoff 2003, 475).

There are four major products of combustion: heat, smoke, light, and fire gases (Ladwig 1991, 38). These products of combustion are critical for fire purposes not only in terms of extinguishment but also in terms of life safety and building design. The primary loss of life in a fire is due to the toxic fire gases.

Heat affects the body in several ways, but the two major factors that determine its effect on the body include the length of exposure and the temperature. As a rule of thumb, one should not enter areas exceeding 120°F without proper personal protective equipment. Exposure to excessive heat causes an increased heart rate, dehydration, exhaustion, burns, and possibly a blockage of the upper respiratory tract.

Smoke, the second product of combustion, is the result of airborne solids and liquid particulates and fire gases that result from combustion (Cote and Bugbee 2001, 59). Smoke is a major killer in fires, causing 50 to 75 percent of deaths. Smoke reduces visibility and irritates eyes and lungs, and in many cases, the fire gases carried in smoke are lethal. The amount and kind of fire gases will vary depending on the chemical composition of the material burning, the amount of oxygen, the temperature, and the possibility of the mixture of particles and gases producing synergistic effects (Friedman 1998, 159). The effects of these fire gases on the body is influenced by the concentration of the gases present, the length of exposure time, and the physical condition of the individual exposed. In a fire situation, carbon monoxide is the gas produced in the greatest quantities (as high as 5 to 6 percent by volume), with its toxicity based on carbon monoxides' affinity for carboxyhemoglobin in the blood (Cote and Bugbee 2001, 56). The effects of carbon monoxide are initiated at approximately 1,000 parts per million (ppm), where headaches will be experienced; concentrations of 4,000 ppm or more are fatal in less than an hour (Sax 1984, 470). Another common gas produced during a fire is carbon dioxide. Carbon dioxide is low in toxicity and is not normally considered a significant toxin in smoke. However, carbon dioxide does increase the speed and depth of breathing, thereby increasing carboxyhemoglobin in the blood from carbon monoxide. Combustion of materials containing nitrogen bonds, such as wool and silk, result in the release of hydrogen cyanide (HCN). The amount of HCN released is temperature dependent, with higher levels generated as the temperature increases (Clayton and Clayton 1994, 3686).

The toxicity of HCN is based on the fact that it inhibits cells from using oxygen (a condition called histoxic hypoxia). Levels of HCN of 135 ppm are lethal within thirty minutes (Cote and Bugbee 2001, 57). It should also be noted that during combustion, oxygen is consumed; therefore, oxygen-deficient atmospheres are an important consideration when considering the toxicity of smoke. The usual concentration of oxygen in air is 21 percent, with levels below 17 percent causing diminished muscular control. In addition to the toxicity of smoke, it is also important to consider the effect smoke has on vision. Smoke obscures the passage of light, thereby possibly blocking the visibility of exits and impeding escape from a fire (NFPA 2000, 4–18). The development of smoke in sufficient quantities to obscure exits happens very quickly and is often the first hazard of a fire. In addition, eye irritation, which is primarily based on the concentration of irritants in the smoke, may also impact the vision of the individual trying to escape.

UNIQUE COMBUSTION PHENOMENA
Five unique combustion phenomena that may occur during a fire include explosions, deflagrations, detonations, flashovers, and back drafts. An *explosion* is the rapid release of high-pressure gas into the environment (NFPA 2000, 1–69). The main difference between a fire and an explosion is the rate at which energy is released. In a fire situation, an example of an explosion is a boiling-liquid expanding-vapor explosion (BLEVE). To illustrate a BLEVE, consider a fire contacting the surface of a flammable-liquid storage tank. The flame causes the gases in the tank to expand and open the emergency vents so that the pressure can be relieved. If the vents cannot relieve the pressure fast enough, the tank will fail and the gas will be released. Sources of explosions in industry are most commonly associated with combustion explosions (44 percent) that involve fuels (Ladwig 1991, 225). Many times the explosions are the result of improper lighting

procedures or inadequate safeguards on the fuel appliances, such as low-gas shutoffs. Other sources of explosions in industry include flammable-liquid vapors, combustible dusts, trapped steam, gas leakage, ruptured pressure vessels, nuclear or atomic explosions, and thermal explosions due to unstable materials decomposing.

A *deflagration* is the burning of a gas or aerosol that is characterized by a combustion wave. The combustion wave moves through the gas and oxygen, burning until all the fuel is used. With a deflagration, the rate of travel of the combustion wave is less than the speed of sound, and no shock wave is produced. Most explosions that occur in industry are deflagrations (Ladwig 1991, 226).

A *detonation*, another unique combustion phenomenon, is the burning of a gas or aerosol characterized by a shock wave. With detonation, the shock wave travels at a speed greater than the speed of sound, and the wave is characterized by very high pressure initiated by a very rapid release of energy (Ladwig 1991, 226). The very high pressure created from the shock wave also serves to create a heat source for igniting other combustibles.

Methods for controlling explosions include containment, quenching, dumping, venting, and isolation (NFPA 1997b, 1–80). *Containment* involves designing a container to withstand maximum pressure. *Quenching* is the removal of heat or chemical inhibition to stop a reaction. *Dumping* is the release of the reaction mixture, which does not stop the reaction but rather transfers the reaction to an area that can handle it. *Venting* releases the energy and gases from the explosion in a controlled manner. *Isolation* involves the separation of the process from surrounding areas that may be affected by an explosion. This can be accomplished by physical separation or through the use of blast-resistant structures.

A *flashover* is a fire in an enclosed area that fosters the buildup of heat; when the temperature reaches the ignition temperature of the majority of combustibles in the area, there is spontaneous combustion of the combustibles in the area (Schroll 1992, 52).

The last unique combustion phenomenon is referred to as a *back draft*. A back draft is sometimes referred to as a smoke explosion because it is a fire in an enclosed area that consumes the oxygen supply and generates carbon monoxide and heat. As the oxygen is being used up the fire tends to smoke a lot; then, if outside air is introduced, the carbon monoxide will burn rapidly with explosive force (Schroll 1992, 52).

HEAT VERSUS TEMPERATURE

It is important to make a distinction between temperature and heat. Heat is a flow of energy between two objects due to a temperature difference, while temperature is a quantity that determines when objects are in thermal equilibrium (Giambattista, Richardson, and Richardson 2004, 442). Common units of measure for temperature are

- *Celsius (C):* 0°—water freezes; 100°—water boils
- *Fahrenheit (F):* 32°—water freezes; 212°—water boils
- *Kelvin (K):* 0°K = −273.15°C or −459.67°F (also referred to as absolute zero)
  Common units of heat include the following (Cote and Bugbee 2001, 48)
- *Joule (J):* amount of heat energy provided by 1W flowing for one second
- *Calorie (cal):* amount of heat required to raise the temperature of 1g of water by 1°C
- *British thermal unit (Btu):* amount of heat required to raise 1 lb. of water by 1°F

When a material goes through a chemical oxidation reaction such as combustion it releases thermal energy. On an atomic scale, heat is the motion of atoms and molecules within the material, and as the temperature increases, the vibration of the molecules increases as well. From a fire-extinguishment perspective, another important concept related to heat is *specific heat*. Specific heat can be defined as the heat capacity per unit mass, and in the metric system, specific heat is the amount of heat required to raise 1 kg of a substance by 1°K (Giambattista, Richardson, and Richardson 2004, 478). The units for specific heat are 1 Kcal/Kg.K. For fire-extinguishment purposes, it is desirable to have a material that has a high specific heat so that it will absorb the heat generated from a fire, thereby reducing the temperature to below the ignition temperature needed for combustion to occur. Water has a specific heat of 1 Kcal/Kg.K., which is much higher than many other materials, such as copper, which has a specific heat of 0.0920 Kcal/Kg.K.

Heat of Combustion

The amount of heat released from a fire over a specific time period (rate) is based on a material's *heat of combustion*. The heat of combustion can be defined as the energy released by the fire per unit mass of fuel burned (Quintiere 1998, 252). Obviously, this is important for fire purposes because the amount of heat released influences fire spread, fire extinguishment, and life safety. The units for heat of combustion are KJ/ g. Examples of heat of combustion of common materials include wood at 16–19 KJ/g, flammable liquids, which range from 19.9–44.8 KJ/g, and flammable gases, which range from 10.1–12.1 KJ/g (Friedman 1998, 41).

HEAT TRANSFER

Heat energy flows due to a temperature difference, with the direction of the flow being from hot to cold or from a higher energy state to a lower energy state. The rate of heat transfer is often expressed as Btus per hour or joules per second. There are three major mechanisms of heat transfer: conduction, convection and radiation. An understanding of heat transfer in these three modes allows the design of buildings to limit heat transfer and correspondingly fire spread.

Heat transfer by conduction: Heat transfer by conduction occurs when the heat is transferred in the material by molecules that are vibrating and colliding with other molecules, thereby transferring their kinetic energy through the material (Friedman 1998, 62). An example of heat transfer by conduction is the simple placement of the end of a 3-ft. metal rod into a flame; the heat will transfer from one end of the rod to the other. There are four major factors that influence heat transfer by conduction: *distance, temperature, cross-sectional area*, and *composition of material*. In terms of the cross-sectional area, the larger the area, the higher the rate of heat transfer. As the distance increases, the rate of heat transfer decreases. This concept is commonly referred to as a *temperature gradient* ($\Delta T/d$), which is the rate of temperature change with distance (Giambattista, Richardson, and Richardson 2004, 490). In general, thermal conductivity (k) of metals decreases as temperatures increase, while the opposite is true with gases. As the temperature increases in gases, the thermal conductivity also increases. It is also worth noting that solid materials will have higher k values than gases and liquids simply because the gases have molecules that are farther apart; therefore, there are fewer collisions and less heat transfer.

The fourth factor that influences heat transfer by conduction is the composition of the material. For any given material, there is a constant

called a *coefficient of thermal conductivity* that is directly proportional to
the rate at which energy is transferred through the substance. The coefficient of thermal conductivity (k) has units of watts per meter per degree
K, with higher values of K associated with good conductors of heat and
smaller values with poor conductors or insulators. The insulating property
of an insulator is commonly expressed as an R value, which is based on
thermal resistance. The best commercial insulators have fine particles or
fibers of solid substances with a space between them filled with air, such
as fiberglass. Some examples of k values for various materials include the
following (Giambattista, Richardson, and Richardson 2004, 490):

- Copper 401 W/M °K
- Silver 429 W/M °K
- Aluminum 237 W/M °K
- Iron 72.8 W/M/°K
- Concrete 1.7W/M/°K
- Wood 0.13 W/M/°K
- Air 0.023 W/M/°K

To evaluate heat transfer by conduction, one can use Fourier's Law of
Heat Conduction: $Icd = kA\Delta T/d$. In the above formula, *Icd* represents the
rate of heat flow, A is the cross-section area, d is the thickness of the material, ΔT represents the temperature difference, and k is the thermal conductivity of the material (Giambattista, Richardson, and Richardson 2004,
490).

Heat transfer by convection: Heat transfer by convection occurs because
of the movement of a fluid containing the heat (Giambattista, Richardson,
and Richardson 2004, 492). Convection occurs in fluids that include both
liquids and gases, and heat transfer by convection is critical to the spread
of fire. Convection heating occurs in fires when the fire heats air and gases,
and, in turn, the air and gases are hot enough to ignite other materials.
This natural convection occurs because the heated fluid expands, which
results in a lower density than the surrounding cooler fluid, causing it to
rise. The rate of heat transfer by convection is influenced by the following
(Drysdale 1985, 52):

- Fluid properties such as density, viscosity, and thermal conductivity
- Flow parameters such as the velocity and nature of the flow

- Geometry of the surface such as cross-sectional area
- Temperature difference

Fortunately, only one value addresses many of these factors, the *convection heat transfer coefficient* (h). This is a constant for a given material with the units being watts per square meter per degree C. The rate of convective heat flow can be calculated using the following formula: $Icu = hA\Delta T$ (Giambattista, Richardson, and Richardson 2004, 496).

In the above formula, Icu is the rate of heat transfer by convection, h is the convective heat transfer coefficient, A is the surface area over which the fluid moves, and ΔT is the difference in temperature between the fluid and the surface.

Radiant heat transfer: Heat transfer through electromagnetic waves is the basic process through which heat is transferred by radiant heat transfer. Forms of electromagnetic radiation fall into three wavelengths: infrared, visible, and ultraviolet (Giambattista, Richardson, and Richardson 2004, 498).

The electromagnetic waves associated with a fire are typically in the infrared region, with only a small fraction emitted in the visible light region. It is important to note that thermal radiation is not heat energy but was formed from heat energy and becomes heat again when it strikes an object. All matter emits thermal radiation continuously at temperatures above absolute zero (Quintiere 1998, 55). Heat transfer via electromagnetic waves requires no medium; therefore, this type of heat transfer can travel through a vacuum because it does not need molecules to be in contact with one another like heat transfer by convection and conduction. In general, the ability of an object to emit radiation is proportional to its ability to absorb radiation; in other words, a good emitter is also a good absorber. We measure an object's ability to emit thermal radiation by a constant referred to as *emissivity* (e). Emissivity has no units, and the values for a specific material will range from zero to one. A black body has an emissivity value of one, which is the maximum amount of thermal radiation emitted (Giambattista, Richardson, and Richardson 2004, 498). Common examples of emissivity include the following (Friedman 1998, 66):

- Polished metal < 0.1
- Brick 0.8

- Graphite 0.9
- Oak and marble 0.9

In addition to emissivity, two other factors that influence radiant heat transfer are temperature and distance. Radiant heat transfer increases tremendously with increases in temperature, and distance also plays a major role. Specifically, if the distance between two objects doubles, then the rate of heat transfer is reduced to one-fourth; conversely, if you half the distance between two objects, then the rate of heat transfer is increased by a factor of four.

SOURCES OF HEAT

There are numerous heat sources in the work environment capable of starting a fire or keeping it burning once it is started. The following is a description of heat sources (NFPA 1997b, 1-64-67):

1. *Chemical heat.* Heat of combustion is the heat that is released during a substance's complete oxidation. Calorific values of fuel are expressed in joules per gram of material.
2. *Spontaneous heating.* Spontaneous heating is the process by which a material increases temperature without drawing heat from its surroundings. If allowed to heat to combustion temperatures, spontaneous ignition can take place.
3. *Heat of decomposition.* Heat of decomposition is the heat released by the decomposition of compounds that have been formed. Acetylene is an example of a product that, once it starts to decompose, generates heat.
4. *Heat of solution.* This is heat released when a substance is dissolved in a solution.
5. *Electrical heat.* Also called resistance heating, this is heat generated due to the resistance electricity encounters when traveling through a conductor.
6. *Arcing.* Arcing occurs when electrical energy jumps across a gap in the circuit carrying the electrical energy.
7. *Sparking.* This takes place when a voltage discharge is too high for a low-energy output.
8. *Static electrical charge.* This is an electrical charge that accumulates on

the surfaces of two materials that have been brought together, then separated.

9. *Lightning.* This is the discharge of an electrical charge from a cloud to an opposite charge (i.e., another cloud or the ground).
10. *Mechanical heat.* This is the mechanical energy used to overcome the resistance to motion when two solids are rubbed together; it is also known as frictional heat.
11. *Nuclear heat.* This is heat energy released from the nucleus of an atom.

PHYSICS OF COMBUSTION

In addition to the chemical properties of fire, physics plays an important role in the fire behavior of materials. Fuel in a fire can be present in one of three different states of matter: solid, liquid, or gas. Combustion usually occurs when the fuel is converted to a vapor, or the gaseous state, because the oxidizer occurs as a gas, and it takes both oxidizer and fuel in the gaseous state for the recombination to occur (Klinoff 2003, 88).

- *Solids.* Factors that affect the combustion of solid fuels include the size of the particles, their moisture content, and their continuity (Klinoff 2003, 89). The smaller the solids, the less heat is needed to burn. A prime example of this is a fire involving dust as is the case in a grain elevator fire. Because the dust particles have a greater surface area as compared to their mass, a smaller ignition source is needed to start combustion.
- *Liquids.* Liquids do not burn. Rather, it is the vapor of the liquid at the surface that is actually burning. Some characteristics of liquids that increase the likelihood that they will produce an ignitable vapor include their flash point, their vapor pressure, and their vapor density. Liquids with low flash points will readily produce vapors in a concentration sufficient to support combustion in the normal work environment. The vapor pressure of the liquid provides an indication as to how readily the vapors will be released from the liquid surface. The specific gravity of a liquid provides an indication as to whether the liquid will float in water or sink. For example, liquids with specific gravities greater than 1.0 will sink in water, while liquids with specific gravities less than 1.0 will float on water.
- *Gases.* Gases can be broadly classified as either flammable or nonflammable. While oxygen itself does not burn, it serves as an oxidizer for a

fire and, in some situations, lowers the ignition temperature necessary to ignite a fuel source; other situations, as in cases involving greases and oils, can result in spontaneous combustion.

FIRE HAZARDS OF MATERIALS

Some of the more common materials found in the workplace can pose potential hazards to the occupants should the materials become involved in a fire. The most widely used materials and the most commonly involved in fires include wood products, textiles, and plastics. Each has its own unique characteristics and composition. Each reacts differently when involved in a fire, and each generates its own unique hazards.

Wood

In order for wood to burn, it must be heated to the point at which combustible gases are released from its surface. When wood burns, it releases approximately 8,000 to 12,000 Btus of energy per pound (NFPA 1997b, 4–31). The physical form of wood will influence its ability to ignite and burn. A characteristic that plays a major role in the ability for wood to serve as a fuel in a fire is its ratio of surface area to its mass. This is why paper will flame and burn with a relatively small ignition source while heavier wood logs will require much more heat. The paper has a greater surface area exposed to oxygen source and less mass than the log; as a result, it requires less energy to continue to burn. Another characteristic of wood that influences its use as a fuel in a fire is its thermal conductivity. The thermal conductivity of a material is the measure of the rate at which absorbed heat will flow through the mass material. Wood is therefore a poor conductor of heat and a good insulator (Cote and Bugbee 2001, 65).

Moisture content also plays a significant role in the ignition and rate of combustion of wood. The moisture content of wood consists of free water (water in the cells) above the fiber saturation point (the fiber saturation point is 25 to 30 percent moisture content) (NFPA 1997b, 4–24.). The higher the water content in wood, the greater the heat source required to evaporate the water from the wood.

Once the wood is heated above its autoignition temperature, ignition will occur. At this temperature, combustible gases are formed and released at the surface. If a moderate heat source is applied for long enough, it will raise the temperature of the material to its autoignition temperature. As wood is heated, it reaches a point where an exothermic reaction takes place. Air velocity around the wood can accelerate the ignition and combustion of wood. The average ignition temperature of wood is about 392°C (Quintiere 1998, 241).

Plastics and Polymers

There are thousands of different types of plastics manufactured. There are approximately thirty different classes of plastics, depending upon components and manufacturing processes. Some special fire hazards of plastics include their rate of burning, the smoke produced, and potentially toxic gases released during their combustion. Although plastics tend to have a higher ignition temperature than wood, some are very easily ignitable with a small flame and will burn rapidly. Some plastics, when burning, will produce large amounts of very dense, sooty, black smoke. And, depending upon the formulation of the plastic, toxic gases such as carbon monoxide, HCN, hydrogen chloride, and phosgene can be released (NFPA 1997b, 4–125). Additional hazards of burning plastics include flaming drips, in which the burning plastic material may flame and drip, causing the fire to spread down and away from the source. This causes secondary fires and corrosion of sensitive electronic equipment resulting from gases released from the burning plastics (NFPA 1997b, 4–125).

Textiles

Fabrics are woven from various types of fibers. The ignitability, flame spread, and so forth for textiles depend upon their fiber content and construction. Textiles can be broadly classified into natural fibers and man-made fibers (NFPA 1997b, 4–46). Natural fibers can be classified as cellulosic fiber and protein fibers. Cotton is the most important (90 percent of all natural fiber is cotton) (NFPA 1997b, 4–46). Cotton is combustible, and when ignited, it produces smoke, heat, carbon dioxide, and carbon monoxide. Protein fibers are the second major type of natural fibers. They are derived from animals and include wool and silk. The fire problem is very small when it comes to protein fibers.

Man-made fibers, the second major division of textiles, consist of regenerated fibers such as rayon and synthetic fibers such as acrylics and nylon. Rayon, which is made from dissolved cellulose, has similar burning characteristics to cotton. Acrylics and nylon, on the other hand, can produce HCN when burned. There are man-made textiles made completely from inorganic materials, which can be considered noncombustible, as in the case of glass fabrics.

To reduce the fire potential of textiles, various fire-retardant treatments have been developed, and their use is required by life-safety and building codes. To make a textile fire retardant, chemical treatments are available; however, age, washing, and dry cleaning may reduce the effectiveness of the treatment. Also, the treatment does not make the textile flameproof; it only makes the textile resistant to ignition by small flame. The textile may still burn when exposed to a large flame. There are four methods by which fire-retardant treatments work (NFPA 1997b, 4–36):

1. They produce noncombustible gases that exclude oxygen.
2. Molecules are released that interfere with the chemical chain reaction.
3. A nonvolatile char or liquid is produced, which reduces the oxygen to the material.
4. Finely divided particles are formed that interfere with the chain reaction.

Examples of textiles required to be flame retardant include aircraft textiles, carpeting, blankets, children's sleepwear, clothing, textiles in motor vehicles, tents, air-supported structures, and curtains or draperies.

HAZARDOUS MATERIALS

The U.S. Department of Transportation (USDOT) defines a hazardous material as a substance or material capable of posing an unreasonable risk to health, safety, and property when transported in commerce (USDOT 2003, 22). It should be noted that there is not a consensus on a definition for hazardous materials, and in many cases, there is simply a listing of materials rather than a definition of the term itself, such as with the Pennsylvania Right-to-Know Law. Both the DOT and the *North American Emergency Response Guidebook* place hazardous materials into nine primary classes: explosives, gases, flammable and combustible liquids, flammable solids, oxidizers and organic peroxides, poisonous and infectious substances, radioactive substances, corrosives, and miscellaneous hazardous materials (USDOT 2002, 11). A description of each of these classes follows (49 C.F.R. § 173).

- *Class 1.* Explosives are any chemical compound, mixture, or device, the primary or common purpose of which is to function by explosion, with substantially instantaneous release of gas and heat. There are three classes of explosives and an additional class for blasting agents. Class A explosives are explosives that detonate and present the maximum hazard. Class B explosives function by rapid combustion rather than detonation and include some explosive devices such as special fireworks, flash powders, and propellant explosives. Class C explosives are certain types of manufactured articles containing Class A or Class B explosives in restricted quantities. Examples of Class C explosives are common fireworks, small-arms ammunitions, and ammonium nitrate. Blasting agents are materials designed for blasting that have been tested in accordance with the DOT Standards and found to be so insensitive that there is very little probability of accidental initiation to explosion or to transition from deflagration to detonation.

- *Class 2.* Gases are any compressed gas meeting the requirements for lower flammability, flammable range, flame projection, or flame propagation as specified by the DOT. Examples of flammable gases include liquefied petroleum gas, acetylene, and hydrogen. A nonflammable gas is any compressed gas other than a flammable compressed gas, such as carbon dioxide and argon.

- *Class 3.* Flammable and combustible liquids are any liquids having a flash point above 100°F and below 200°F. Examples of combustible liquids include fuel oils and ethylene glycols. Flammable liquids are any liquid having a flash point below 100°F. Examples of flammable liquids include acetone, gasoline, and methyl alcohol. A pyroforic liquid is any liquid that ignites spontaneously in dry or moist air at or below 130°F. An example of a pyroforic liquid is aluminum alkyl and alkyl borane.

- *Class 4.* Flammable solids include any solid material, other than an explosive, liable to cause fire through friction-contained heat from manufacturing or processing or that can be ignited readily and, when ignited, burns so vigorously and persistently as to create a serious transportation hazard. An example of a flammable solid would be magnesium or aluminum powder.

- *Class 5.* Oxidizers are any substance that yields oxygen readily to stimulate the combustion of organic matter. Examples of oxidizers include ammonium-nitrate fertilizer, hydrogen-peroxide solution, or chlorate. Organic peroxide is a separate division within this class.

- *Class 6.* Poisons and infectious substances break down into four classes: Poison A, Poison B, irritating materials, and etiologic agents. A Poison A is an extremely dangerous poisonous gas or liquid of such a nature that a very small amount of the gas or vapor of the liquid mixed with air is dangerous to life. An example of Poison A would be phosgene or arsine. A Poison B is a less dangerous poison that can be a liquid or solid, other than Class A, or irritating materials known to be so toxic to man as to afford a health hazard during transportation. An example of Poison B is methyl bromide. An irritating material is a liquid or solid substance, which on contact with fire or exposed to air, gives off dangerous or irritating fumes but does not release any poisonous materials included within Class A or Class B. Examples of irritating materials include tear gas and xylyl bromide. An etiologic agent is a viable microorganism or its toxins, which cause or may cause human disease such as tetanus, rabies, and anthrax.

- *Class 7.* Radioactive materials are any material or combination of materials that spontaneously emit ionizing radiation and have a specific activity greater than 0.002 c per gram. Examples of radioactive materials include plutonium, cobalt, and uranium.

- *Class 8.* Corrosive materials are any material or solid that causes visible destruction of human skin tissue or a liquid that has a severe corrosion rate on steel. Examples of corrosive materials include hydrochloric acid, sulfuric acid, and caustic soda.

- *Class 9.* Miscellaneous hazardous materials and other regulated materials (ORMs) include any materials that do not meet the definition of a hazardous material, other than a combustible liquid, in packaging with a capacity of 110 gal. or less and specified by the DOT as an ORM or that poses one or more of the characteristics described in ORM Classes A through D. An ORM Class A is a material that has an anesthetic, irritating, noxious, toxic, or other similar property and that can cause extreme annoyance or discomfort to passengers and crew in the event of leakage during transportation. An example would be carbon tetrachloride. An ORM Class B is a material capable of causing significant damage to a transport vehicle from leakage during transportation.

Examples would include a liquid substance with a corrosion rate exceeding 0.25 in./y on aluminum, such as metallic mercury. An ORM Class C is a material that has other inherent characteristics not described in Class A or Class B but that is unsuitable for shipment unless properly identified and prepared for transportation. An example would be bleaching powder. An ORM Class D is a material such as a consumer commodity that, although otherwise subject to the DOT regulations, presents a limited hazard during transportation due to its form, quantity, and packaging. An ORM Class E is a material that is not included in any other hazard class but is subject to the requirements of the DOT regulations. Most hazardous waste falls into this class.

SOURCES OF INFORMATION ON HAZARDOUS MATERIALS

There is a variety of reference sources a safety professional can use when addressing the handling, storage, and shipping of hazardous materials. The first reference is the *Fire Protection Guide to Hazardous Materials* (1997a), published by the NFPA. This guide is divided into four sections. The first contains hazardous-chemicals data and lists data on the health, fire, and reactivity hazards of approximately 323 chemicals. The second section includes the fire-hazard properties of more than thirteen hundred flammable substances. This section also includes Hazard Index Markings (NFPA 2001) for the substances. The third section is a guide to hazardous chemical reactions with over thirty-six hundred mixtures included. The fourth section addresses NFPA 704, which is an identification system for determining the degree of health, flammability, and reactivity hazard of materials. This labeling system, which is illustrated below, has four separate areas. The blue area is used to identify health hazards; the red identifies fire hazards; the yellow identifies chemical reactivity hazards; and the white section is used for miscellaneous categories, such as water-reactive chemicals, pressurized chemicals, or those needed for specific types of personal protective equipment. The ratings that go within this labeling system range from a score of 0 to indicate no hazard to 4, which indicates a severe hazard (NFPA 2001).

This guide typically identifies the hazardous materials by trade name and chemical name and also identifies chemical and physical characteristics of a material, such as flash point, ignition temperature, flammable limits, specific gravity, uses, and possible manufacturer. This reference is useful to a safety professional because it provides recommendations for shipping, storing, and extinguishing hazardous materials.

Another useful reference source for the safety professional regarding hazardous materials is the USDOT, which has the federally mandated responsibility for developing and enforcing the hazardous-materials regulations included within Title 49 of the Code of Federal Regulations. These federal regulations focus on the transportation of hazardous materials. Within USDOT, the Office of Hazardous Materials Safety was created. This office has five primary functions: regulatory development, enforcement, information systems and training, domestic and international standards, and interagency coordination regarding hazardous materials (see www.dot.gov). Table 2.1 illustrates the variety of information available from the Office of Hazardous Materials Safety website (www.hazmat.dot.-gov). The Hazardous Materials Table (HMT) is the backbone of the Hazardous Materials Regulations (USDOT 2002a, 1). This table is included in 49 C.F.R. § 172.101, and a sample of this table is shown in table 2.1.

USDOT has very specific regulations regarding the identification of hazardous material during transportation through the use of placards and labeling. The specific requirements for all labels and placards are included in 49 C.F.R. §§ 192.407 and 172.519. Specific details for labels and placards for the nine classes of hazardous materials, including size, color, and symbols, are included in §§ 172.521–172.560 and are illustrated in figure 2.3.

In addition to Title 49, USDOT has developed a guidebook referred to as the *North American Emergency Response Guidebook*. This guidebook was created in 1996 in collaboration with Canada and Mexico so that one hazardous-materials emergency-response guidebook would be used for all of North America. The primary purpose of this guidebook was to aid first aid responders in identifying the specific or generic classification of the hazardous materials and to protect themselves and the public during the response phase to the hazardous-materials incident (USDOT, Canada, and Mexico 2002, 8). This guidebook is divided into four sections. The first two sections are a listing of hazardous materials both alphabetically and numerically, using the four-digit DOT identification number. The third section describes potential hazards that materials may display in terms of fire or explosion and health effects upon exposure. This section also outlines suggested public-safety measures and emergency-response

Table 2.1 Excerpt of the Hazardous Materials Table

Symbols	Hazardous Materials Description and Proper Shipping Names	Hazard Class or Division	Identification Numbers	PG	Label Codes	Special Provisions (172.102)	Packaging (173.***)			Quantity limitations		Vessel Stowage	
							Exceptions	NonBulk	Bulk	Passenger Aircraft/ Rail	Cargo Aircraft Only	Location	Other
(1)	(2)	(3)	(4)	(5)	(6)	(7)	(8A)	(8B)	(8C)	(9A)	(9B)	(10A)	(10B)
	Accellerene, see p-Nitrosodimethylaniline												
	Accumulators, electric, see Batteries, wet, etc.												
	Accumulators, pressurized, pneumatic, or hydraulic (containing nonflammable gas), see Articles, pressurized, pneumatic, or hydraulic (containing nonflammable gas)												
	Acetaldehyde	3	UN1089	I	3	A3, B16, T11, TP2, TP7	None	201	243	Forbidden	30 L	E	

Source: 49 CFR § 172.101, Hazardous Material Table (HM-215e). This table can provide the safety professional with a variety of information on hazardous materials, such as description and shipping name, hazard class and division, packing group for the hazardous material, labeling, and quantity limitations.

FIGURE 2.3
DOT placarding
Source: 49 CFR §§ 172.522–172.560.

actions and first aid. The fourth section is an additional reference for isolation and protective-action distances where applicable.

The Chemical Transportation Emergency Center (CHEMTREC) was established in 1971 by the Manufacturer Chemists Association, located in Washington, D.C. (Cote and Bugbee 2001, 104). CHEMTREC provides a clearinghouse of information on hazardous materials for emergency response to such incidents. In order to use CHEMTREC, it is important that the emergency responders provide the organization with either a chemical's four-digit DOT identification number or its name. Once this information is received, CHEMTREC can provide the responders with information regarding the hazards of the material and the precautions needed for extinguishment and cleanup.

CHAPTER QUESTIONS

1. T/F Deflagration is the burning of a gas or aerosol that is characterized by a shock wave.
2. T/F Radioactive materials are those materials that spontaneously emit ionizing radiation.
3. T/F Radiant heat transfer occurs through electromagnetic waves that are in the ultraviolet region and travel at the speed of sound.
4. T/F The four major components of combustion are heat, radiation, smoke, and fire.
5. T/F Sensible heat change is a change in the heat content of a material due to a temperature change only.
6. T/F BLEVE stands for:
   a. Boiling-liquid expanding-vapor event
   b. Boiling-liquid expanding-violent explosion
   c. Boiling-liquid enlarging-vessel explosion
   d. Boiling-liquid expanding-vapor explosion
7. Specific heat is the amount of heat required to raise _____ of a substance by _____.
   a. 1 lb.; 1°C
   b. 1 lb.; 1°F
   c. 1 lb.; 1°K
8. Thermal conductivity of metals
   a. Decreases as the temperature increases
   b. Increases as the temperature increases
   c. Decreases as the temperature decreases
   d. Increases as the temperature decreases
9. In the NFPA labeling system:
   a. Blue indicates health hazards; red indicates fire hazards; yellow indicates chemical reactivity.
   b. Blue indicates fire hazards; red indicates chemical reactivity; yellow indicates health hazards
   c. Blue indicates chemical reactivity; red indicates fire hazards; yellow indicates health hazards
   d. Blue indicates fire hazards; red indicates health hazards; yellow indicates chemical reactivity
10. When assessing the effect of heat on the body, two main factors determine the severity:
   a. Amount of body exposed and length of exposure

b. Length of exposure and temperature

c. Temperature and amount of body exposed

d. None of the above

11. List and then briefly describe the four elements of the fire tetrahedron.

12. What are the five factors that influence heat transfer by convection?

13. What is the significance of the *North American Emergency Response Guidebook?*

14. Smoke is the major killer in fires. Explain why.

15. What is a hazardous material as defined by USDOT?

REFERENCES

Brannigan, Francis L. (1999). *Building Construction for the Fire Service.* Quincy, MA: NFPA.

Clayton, George, and Florence Clayton. (1994). *Patty's Industrial Hygiene and Toxicology.* New York: Wiley Interscience.

Cote, Arthur, and Percy Bugbee. (2001). *Principles of Fire Protection.* Quincy, MA: NFPA.

Cote, Arthur E., and Jim L. Linville. (1990). *Industrial Fire Hazards Handbook.* Quincy, MA: NFPA.

Crowl, Daniel A. (2003). *Understanding Explosions.* New York: Center for Chemical Process Safety.

Diamantes, David. (1998). *Fire Prevention, Inspection and Code Enforcement.* Albany, NY: Delmar Publishers.

Drysdale, Dougal. (1985). *An Introduction to Fire Dynamics.* New York: John Wiley & Sons.

Friedman, Raymond. (1998). *Principles of Fire Protection Chemistry and Physics.* Quincy, MA: NFPA.

Giambattista, Alan, Betty Richardson, and Robert Richardson. (2004). *College Physics.* Boston, MA: McGraw-Hill.

Klinoff, Robert. (2003). *Introduction to Fire Protection,* 2nd ed. Clifton Park, NY: Delmar Learning.

Ladwig, Thomas H. (1991). *Industrial Fire Prevention and Protection.* New York: Van Nostrand Reinhold.

National Fire Protection Association (NFPA). (1994a). *Fire Protection Systems— Inspection, Test and Maintenance Manual,* 2nd ed. Quincy, MA: NFPA.

NFPA. (1994b). *NFPA Inspection Manual,* 7th ed. Quincy, MA: NFPA.

NFPA. (1997a). *Fire Protection Guide to Hazardous Materials,* 12th ed. Quincy, MA: NFPA.

NFPA. (1997b). *Fire Protection Handbook*, 18th ed. Quincy, MA: NFPA.

NFPA. (1997c). *Flammable and Combustible Liquids Code Handbook*. Quincy, MA: NFPA.

NFPA. (1999). *National Fire Alarm Code*. Quincy, MA: NFPA.

NFPA. (2000). *NFPA 101 Life-Safety Code*. Quincy, MA: NFPA.

NFPA. (2001). *NFPA 704 Standard System for the Identification of the Hazards of Materials for Emergency Response*. Quincy, MA: NFPA.

NFPA. (2002). *Automatic Sprinklers System Handbook*. Quincy, MA: NFPA.

Quintiere, James G. (1998). *Principles of Fire Behavior*. Albany, NY: Delmar Publishers.

Sax, Iriving. (1984). *Dangerous Properties of Industrial Materials*. New York: Van Nostrand Reinhold.

Schneid, Thomas D., and Larry Collins. (2001). *Disaster Management and Preparedness*. Boca Raton, FL: Lewis Publishers.

Schram, Peter J., and Mark W. Earley. (1997). *Electrical Installations in Hazardous Locations*. Quincy, MA: NFPA.

Schroll, Craig R. (1992). *Industrial Fire Protection Handbook*, Lancaster, PA: Technomic Publishing Co.

Stringfield, William H. (2000). *Emergency Planning and Management*, 2nd ed. Rockville, MD: Government Institutes.

USDOT. (2002a). *Module 1 Training Module: The Hazardous Materials Table*, http://hazmat.dot.gov/training/training.htm (accessed June 23, 2005).

USDOT. (2002b). *Module 3 Training Module: Marking and Labeling*, http://hazmat.dot.gov/training/training.htm (accessed June 23, 2005).

USDOT. (2002c). *Module 4 Training Module: Placarding*, http://hazmat.dot.gov/training/training.htm (accessed June 23, 2005).

USDOT. (2003). *How to Use the Hazardous Materials Regulations*, at www.hazmat.dot.gov (accessed June 23, 2005).

USDOT. (2004). Title 49 of the Code of Federal Regulations.

USDOT, Transport Canada, and Secretariat of Communications and Transportation of Mexico. (2002). *North American Emergency Response Guidebook*. Washington, DC: U.S. Government Printing Office.

Vulpitta, Richard T. (2002). *On-Site Emergency Response Planning Guide*. Chicago, IL: National Safety Council.

Vunker, Merton W., and Wayne D. Moore. (1999). *National Fire Alarm Code Handbook*. Quincy, MA: NFPA.

Common and Special Hazards

Materials and processes commonly found in the industrial workplace pose unique fire hazards. The presence of electrical sources of ignition, in addition to the use of hazardous materials like flammable and combustible liquids and gases, creates the potential for major fire hazards. The proper installation and maintenance of electrical equipment should be part of every fire-prevention program.

Some of the more common and hazardous materials, from a fire standpoint, used in the workplace include flammable and combustible liquids, liquefied petroleum gases, hydrogen gas, oxygen, and acetylene. To control potential fuel and oxidizer sources, proper handling and storage requirements should be followed. Work procedures involving housekeeping and the control of ignition sources should also be taken into account as an integral part of the fire-protection program.

ELECTRICITY AS AN IGNITION SOURCE

Each year, thirty thousand fires are recorded in the United States, and investigations have found that many of those were initiated from electrical sources (Jones and Jones 2000, 15). The most common causes for fires started as a result of electrical failures include short circuits, ground faults, or other electrical failures. Industrial and manufacturing facility fires have a cause profile that reflects the wide variety of industrial processes used and activities conducted. Of the fires in these structures, 39 percent were caused by the wide variety of equipment and processes listed under "other equipment." Open flames, embers or torches ranked second, and electrical distribution equipment ranked third. Industrial fire prevention must address the specific processes and hazards associated with each activity (Ahrens 2001, 157).

In the workplace, a number of electrical sources can be involved in a fire. Examples of these sources include production equipment, electrical wiring, and heating equipment to name a few. Figure 3.1 depicts typical electrical hazards found at a worksite. All electrical installations in the United States should be made, used, and maintained in accordance with the National Electrical Code (NEC) and other standards that apply in special situations (NFPA 1997, 3–11). Two common electric-safety codes in the United States are the NEC and the National Electrical Safety Code. The NEC provides for the practical safeguarding of persons and property from hazards arising from the use of electricity. The NEC was first issued in 1897 by the National Fire Protection Association (NFPA) and is updated every three years (NFPA 1997, 3–11).

Electrical fires can be the result of a variety of electrical problems in the workplace. Improper use of equipment, improper installation, and improper maintenance of equipment are some of the more common rea-

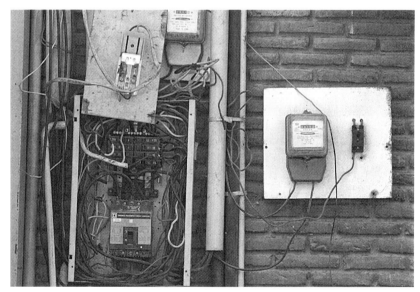

FIGURE 3.1
Electrical hazards present on a job site

sons for electrical fires. Examples of sources of electrical fires in the workplace include the following:

- *Misuse of electric cords.* This includes running the cords under rugs, over nails, or through high traffic areas and the use of extension cords as permanent wiring.
- *Poor maintenance.* This entails a lack of a preventive maintenance program designed to identify and correct potential problems before they occur.
- *Ground failure.* Failure to maintain a continuous path to ground can expose entire electrical systems to damage and can expose the workers using unprotected equipment to electrical hazards.
- *Damaged insulation.* Insulation protecting current-carrying wires can become damaged over time, resulting in exposed wires. If the exposed hot and neutral wires touch, they can create a short circuit and an ignition source for fires.
- *Sparking.* Friction sparking is a form of mechanic heat created when two hard surfaces, at least one of which is metal, impact (NFPA 1997, 1–66).
- *Circuit overload.* A circuit becomes overloaded when there are more appliances on the circuit than it can safely handle. When a circuit is overloaded, the wiring overheats, and the fuse blows or the circuit breaker trips.
- *Short circuit.* A short circuit occurs when a bare hot wire touches a bare neutral wire or a bare grounded wire (or some other ground). The flow of extra current blows a fuse or trips a circuit breaker.
- *Arcing.* This occurs when an electric circuit that is carrying current is interrupted either intentionally or unintentionally (NFPA 1997, 1–66).

HAZARDOUS LOCATIONS AND THE NATIONAL ELECTRICAL CODE

The environment in which the electrical equipment is placed may present a fire hazard. Environments in which concentrations of flammable vapors, ignitable fibers of combustible dusts are present in sufficient concentrations could be ignited by the electrical equipment and installations in the area. To prevent the possibility of electrical equipment and wiring from igniting flammable and combustible vapors, all electrical wiring and equipment used in hazardous locations must meet proper design requirements. The NEC classifies locations according to the potential for the presence of hazardous materials in the atmosphere (NFPA 70 2002). Furthermore, because the electrical equipment may create an ignition source, design specifications have been developed for the equipment to reduce the risk for a fire and explosion hazard.

The NEC classifies hazardous locations into Classes I, II, and III. These major classes are further subdivided into Divisions 1 and 2. The classes differentiate between the type of material that may be present in the air, and the divisions differentiate between the circumstances that may create the presence of hazardous concentrations of the material. Within each class, groupings are assigned. The groupings identify the hazardous material present in the environment. These classes, divisions, and groups are also used by the Occupational Safety and Health Administration (OSHA) for the purposes of classifying hazardous locations and selecting safe electrical equipment for these areas.

Class I Locations

Class I locations are those in which flammable gases or vapors are or may be present in the air in quantities sufficient to produce explosive or ignitable mixtures. Class I, Division 1 locations are locations in which any of the following conditions exist (NFPA 70 2002):

1. Ignitable concentrations of flammable gases or vapors exist under normal operating conditions.
2. Ignitable concentrations of such gases or vapors may exist frequently because of repair or maintenance operations or because of leakage.
3. Breakdown or faulty operation of equipment or processes might release ignitable concentrations of flammable gases or vapors and might also cause simultaneous failure of electric equipment.

Examples of Class I, Division 1 locations include locations where volatile flammable liquids or liquefied flammable gases are transferred from one container to another, the interiors of spray booths, areas containing open tanks of volatile flammable liquids, and all other locations where ignitable concentrations of flammable vapors or gases are likely to occur in the course of normal operations.

Class I, Division 2 locations are locations in which any of the following conditions exist (NFPA 70 2002):

1. Volatile flammable liquids or flammable gases are handled, processed, or used; however, the liquids, vapors, or gases will normally be confined within closed containers or closed systems from which they can escape only in case of accidental rupture or breakdown of such containers or systems or in case of abnormal operation of equipment.
2. Ignitable concentrations of gases or vapors are normally prevented by positive mechanical ventilation and might become hazardous through failure or abnormal operation of the ventilating equipment.
3. The location is adjacent to a Class I, Division 1 location, and ignitable concentrations of gases or vapors might occasionally be communicated to the area unless such communication is prevented by adequate positive pressure ventilation from a source of clean air and effective safeguards against ventilation failure are provided.

This classification usually includes locations where volatile flammable liquids or flammable gases or vapors are used but that would become hazardous only in case of an accident or some unusual operating condition.

Class I locations can also be further subdivided into groups. A group is based upon the specific type of hazardous material in the location. The Class I Hazardous Location Atmospheres Groups include the following (NFPA 2002):

- *Group A Typical:* acetylene
- *Group B Typical:* hydrogen
- *Group C Typical:* ethylene
- *Group D Typical:* propane

Therefore, a Class I, Division I, Group C location is a location in an environment in which ethylene vapors or a closely similar material are present in sufficient concentration to ignite under normal conditions.

Class II Locations

Class II locations are those that are hazardous because of the presence of combustible dust. A Class II, Division 1 location can include any of the following (NFPA 70 2002):

1. Combustible dust is in the air under normal operating conditions in quantities sufficient to produce explosive or ignitable mixtures.
2. Mechanical failure or abnormal operation of machinery or equipment might cause the production of such explosive or ignitable mixtures and might also provide a source of ignition through simultaneous failure of electric equipment, operation of protection devices, or from other causes.
3. Combustible dusts of an electrically conductive nature may be present in hazardous quantities.

Examples of combustible dusts that are electrically nonconductive include dusts produced in the handling and processing of grain and grain products, pulverized sugar and cocoa, oil meal from beans and seeds, and dried hay. Only Group E dusts are considered to be electrically conductive for classification purposes. Dusts containing magnesium or aluminum are particularly hazardous, and the use of extreme caution will be necessary to avoid ignition and explosion.

Class II, Division 2 locations are those where the following conditions exist (NFPA 70 2002):

1. Combustible dust is not normally in the air in quantities sufficient to produce explosive or ignitable mixtures, and dust accumulations are normally insufficient to interfere with the normal operation of electrical equipment or other apparatuses, but combustible dust may be in suspension in the air as a result of infrequent malfunctioning of handling or processing equipment.
2. Combustible dust accumulations on, in, or in the vicinity of the electrical equipment may be sufficient to interfere with the safe dissipation of heat from electrical equipment or may be ignitable by abnormal operation or failure of electrical equipment.

Class II Hazardous Location Atmospheres Groups include the following (NFPA 70 2002):

- *Group E:* atmospheres containing combustible metal dusts, including aluminum, magnesium, and their commercial alloys, or other combustible dusts whose particle size, abrasiveness, and conductivity present similar hazards in the use of electrical equipment

- *Group F:* atmospheres containing combustible carbonaceous dusts that have more than 8 percent total entrapped volatiles or dusts that have been sensitized by other materials so that they present an explosion hazard, including carbon black, charcoal, coal, and coke dusts

- *Group G:* atmospheres containing combustible dusts not included in Group E or F, including flour, grain, wood, plastic, and chemicals

Class III Locations

Class III locations are those that are hazardous because of the presence of easily ignitable fibers or flyings but in which such fibers or flyings are not likely to be in suspension in the air in quantities sufficient to produce ignitable mixtures (NFPA 70 2002). Class III, Division 1 locations are locations in which easily ignitable fibers or materials producing combustible flyings are handled, manufactured, or used. Such locations usually include some parts of rayon, cotton, and other textile mills, combustible-fiber manufacturing and processing plants, clothing manufacturing plants, and woodworking plants. Easily ignitable fibers and flyings include rayon, cotton (including cotton linters and cotton waste), jute, and hemp. Class III, Division 2 locations are locations in which easily ignitable fibers are stored or handled, other than in the process of manufacturing.

DEFINING HAZARDOUS LOCATIONS

In addition to classifying areas when a hazardous environment exists, areas beyond the hazardous location may also be subject to potential environmental fire hazards. Therefore, the NECs and OSHA standards stipulate hazard classifications for areas adjacent to those in which a hazardous environment is present. Under 29 C.F.R. § 1910.307, OSHA stipulates that NFPA 70: National Electrical Code should be followed when determining the type and design of equipment used in hazardous locations (USDOL 2004c, 29 C.F.R. § 1910.307). OSHA standards further stipulate that for dip-tank vapor areas where flammable vapor-air mixtures may exist under normal operations (Class I, Division 1 locations), the Division 1 area shall extend 20 ft. in all directions from all points of vapor liberation (USDOL 2004a, 29 C.F.R. § 1910.108[e]).

Locations where flammable vapor-air mixtures may exist under abnormal conditions for a distance beyond Division 1 locations are classified as Division 2; they include an area within 20 ft. horizontally and 3 ft. vertically beyond a Division 1 area and up to 3 ft. above floor or grade level within 25 ft. if indoors, or 10 ft. if outdoors, from any pump, bleeder, withdrawal fitting, meter, or similar device handling Class I liquids (NFPA 70 2002).

SAFE DESIGN OF ELECTRICAL EQUIPMENT

OSHA established the requirements for electric equipment and wiring in locations that are classified. The type of equipment approved for use in hazardous locations must be selected based upon the properties of the flammable vapors, liquids, or gases or combustible dusts or fibers that may be present therein and the likelihood that a flammable or combustible concentration or quantity is present.

When equipment has been designed specifically for a hazardous environment, it is deemed *intrinsically safe*. Intrinsic safety is a protection concept employed in potentially explosive atmospheres. Intrinsic safety relies on the electrical apparatus being designed so that it is unable to release sufficient energy, by either thermal or electrical means, to cause an ignition of a flammable gas. Equipment, wiring methods, and installations of equipment in hazardous (classified) locations shall be intrinsically safe, approved for the hazardous (classified) location, or safe for the hazardous (classified) location. Requirements for each of these options are as follows (USDOL 2004c, 29 C.F.R. § 1910.307[b]):

1. Equipment and associated wiring approved as intrinsically safe shall be permitted in any hazardous (classified) location for which it is approved.
2. Equipment shall be approved not only for the class of location but also for the ignitable or combustible properties of the specific gas, vapor, dust, or fiber that will be present.
3. Equipment shall be properly marked according to the applicable electrical codes.
4. Equipment that is safe for the location shall be of a type and design that the employer demonstrates will provide protection from the haz-

ards arising from the combustibility and flammability of vapors, liquids, gases, dusts, or fibers.

5. Equipment that has been approved for a Division 1 location may be installed in a Division 2 location of the same class and group.

6. General-purpose equipment or equipment in general-purpose enclosures may be installed in Division 2 locations if the equipment does not constitute a source of ignition under normal operating conditions.

Class I Electrical Equipment Requirements

When examining the requirements for electrical equipment used in hazardous locations involving Class I locations, one term is of importance: *explosionproof*. Equipment that is explosionproof has been designed and constructed to withstand an internal explosion without creating an external explosion or fire. This protection technique is permitted for equipment in Class I, Division 1 or 2 locations (Earley et al. 2003, 624). For Class I, Division 1 equipment, in general, the operating temperature is the maximum temperature of external surfaces of the equipment. For Class I, Division 2 equipment, in general, the operating temperature is the maximum temperature of all parts of the equipment, including internal parts that may be exposed to the flammable material. Equipment must be marked with the operating temperature or operating temperature code if the maximum operating temperature is more than 100°C (212°F). This temperature marking shall not exceed the ignition temperature of the specific gas or vapor to be encountered. Equipment listed or classified for use in Class I locations is not necessarily acceptable for Class II locations as it may not be dust-tight or operate at a safe temperature when blanketed with dust.

Class II Electrical Equipment Requirements

Class II locations entail potential hazards created by the presence of dusts in sufficient concentrations to ignite. Equipment designed for use in Class II locations may be classified as either dust-tight or dustproof. Dust-tight equipment is constructed so that dust will not enter the enclosing case under specified test conditions. Dustproof or dust-ignition-proof equipment is constructed or protected so that dust will not interfere with its successful operation. Dust-ignition-proof equipment for use in Class

II hazardous locations, as defined in the NEC, is tested with respect to acceptability of operation in the presence of combustible dusts in air. Equipment intended for use in a Class II, Division 1 location must be dust-ignition-proof and designated for use in Class II, Division 1 locations. Dust-ignition-proof equipment used in Class II, Division 1 locations is not required to be explosionproof (Earley et al. 2003, 658). Equipment intended for Class II, Division 2 locations must be dust-tight and meet the requirements for a Class II, Division 2 location (Earley et al. 2003, 658).

Class III Electrical Equipment Requirements

Class III areas include textile, clothing, mattress, cotton, batting, rayon, cotton-seed, woodworking industries and those that process similar materials. Easily ignitable fibers and flyings include rayon, cotton, sisal, jute, hemp, cocoa fibers, oakum, Spanish moss, excelsior and similar materials. Electrical equipment used in Class III locations must be approved for such use. Dust-ignition-proof equipment is not required in Class III locations; however, boxes and fittings must be at least dust-tight in both Class III, Division 1 and 2 locations (Earley et al. 2002, 624). Electrical equipment in these areas should be installed to prevent heat buildup or entrance of fibers or flying into enclosures where a spark could ignite them, causing fire. The equipment shall also meet maximum temperature ratings (Earley et al. 2002, 624).

NATIONAL TESTING LABORATORIES

OSHA requires that only approved electrical equipment be used in the workplace. Being approved for a purpose means that the equipment is suitable for a particular application as determined by a recognized testing laboratory, inspection agency, or other organization concerned with product evaluation as part of its labeling or listing program (USDOL DSTM 2004). Nationally recognized testing laboratories (NRTLs) go though a rigorous evaluation procedure before they are recognized by OSHA. NRTLs must have the capability, control programs, complete independence, and reporting and complaint handling procedures to test and certify specific types of products for workplace safety. This means, in part, that an organization must have the necessary capability both as a product-safety-testing laboratory and as a product-certification body to receive

OSHA recognition as an NRTL. Equipment listed or approved by these organizations is acceptable for use in the workplace. The following organizations are currently recognized by OSHA as NRTLs (USDOL DSTM 2004):

- Applied Research Laboratories (ARL)
- Canadian Standards Association (CSA) (also known as CSA International)
- Communication Certification Laboratory (CCL)
- Curtis-Straus LLC (CSL)
- Electro-Test Inc. (ETI)
- Entela (ENT)
- FM Global Technologies LLC (FM) (also known as FM Approvals and formerly Factory Mutual Research Corporation)
- Intertek Testing Services NA (ITSNA) (formerly ETL)
- MET Laboratories (MET)
- NSF International (NSF)
- National Technical Systems (NTS)
- SGS U.S. Testing Company (SGSUS) (formerly UST-CA)
- Southwest Research Institute (SWRI)
- TUV America (TUVAM)
- TUV Product Services GmbH (TUVPSG)
- TUV Rheinland of North America (TUV)
- Underwriters Laboratories (UL)
- Wyle Laboratories (WL)

FLAMMABLE LIQUIDS AND COMBUSTIBLE LIQUIDS

Flammable and combustible liquids pose a unique hazard in the workplace primarily because of the amount of fuel they can provide for a fire and the relatively low heat source necessary to ignite the material. Flammable and combustible liquids are classified as either *flammable* or *combustible* based upon their flash point. The term *flash point* means the minimum temperature at which a liquid gives off vapor within a test vessel in sufficient concentration to form an ignitable mixture with air near the surface of the liquid. When a flammable or combustible liquid is involved in a fire, it is the vapor over the surface of the liquid that burns. The lower the flash point, the more readily a sufficient concentration of vapor is present at a lower temperature.

Flammable Liquids

Flammable liquids are any liquids having a flash point below 100°F, except any mixture having components with flash points of 100°F or higher, the total of which makes up 99 percent or more of the total volume of the mixture. Generally speaking, at normal room temperature, flammable liquids will produce a vapor sufficient to ignite without requiring heating of the liquid to do so. Flammable liquids are known as Class I liquids. Class I liquids are divided into three classes as follows (USDOL 2004b, 29 C.F.R. § 1910.106[a]):

1. *Class IA* shall include liquids having flash points below 73°F and having a boiling point below 100°F.
2. *Class IB* shall include liquids having flash points below 73°F and having a boiling point at or above 100°F.
3. *Class IC* shall include liquids having flash points at or above 73°F and below 100°F.

Combustible Liquids

Combustible liquids typically will require some external heating to produce a sufficient concentration of vapors.

Combustible liquids are any liquid having a flash point at or above 100°F and are divided into two classes. Class II liquids include those liquids with flash points at or above 100°F and below 140°F, except any mixture having components with flash points of 200°F or higher, the total of which makes up 99 percent or more of the total volume of the mixture (USDOL 2004b, 29 C.F.R. § 1910.106[a]).

Class III liquids include those liquids with flash points at or above 140°F. Class III liquids are divided into two subclasses (USDOL 2004b, 29 C.F.R. § 1910.106[a]):

1. *Class IIIA* liquids include those liquids with flash points at or above 140°F and below 200°F, except any mixture having components with flash points of 200°F or higher, the total volume of which makes up 99 percent or more of the total volume of the mixture.

2. *Class IIIB* liquids include those liquids with flash points at or above 200°F. OSHA combustible-liquid requirements do not cover Class IIIB liquids, only Class IIIA liquids.

UPPER AND LOWER EXPLOSIVE LIMITS

As discussed previously, in order for a flammable liquid to burn, it must evolve enough vapors at its surface in a sufficient concentration. At temperatures below the flash point, the liquid cannot evaporate quickly enough to generate enough vapors. The concentration of flammable or combustible vapors in air also determines whether there will be an ignitable concentration or not. If the vapor concentration in air is too low, there will not be enough vapors to ignite. We refer to this concentration as being below the lower flammable limit (LFL) (also referred to as the lower explosive limit [LEL]). People commonly refer to the vapors as being "too lean."

On the other hand, if the vapor concentrations in air are above the upper flammable limit (UFL) (also referred to as the upper explosive limit [UEL]), the vapors will not ignite. This is commonly referred to as the vapors being "too rich." Therefore, flammable and combustible vapors must be present in concentrations in air above the LFL or LEL but below the UFL or UEL in order to burn.

From a safety standpoint, you will see that in many situations, ventilation requirements have been established by OSHA and the NFPA as a means to reduce the potential for accidental ignition of flammable and combustible vapors. The purpose of the ventilation requirements is to keep the concentrations of vapors in the air well below their LFL.

FLAMMABLE- AND COMBUSTIBLE-LIQUID STORAGE

Flammable and combustible liquids can be stored in the workplace in a number of ways. Types of flammable- and combustible-liquid storage include portable-container storage, tank storage, storage cabinets, and storage rooms.

CONTAINERS AND PORTABLE TANKS

It is common in industry to store flammable and combustible liquids in a container. OSHA defines a container as any can, barrel, or drum. A barrel is a container that has a capacity of 42 gal., while a safety can is an

approved container with a maximum capacity of 5 gal. with a spring-closing lid and spout cover. Safety cans are designed to relieve internal pressure when they are subjected to heating. Drums have a capacity of up to
60 gal., and tanks have a capacity of more than 60 gal. Barrels, safety cans,
drums, and tanks used in the workplace must be approved for this type
of use by an NRTL or the U.S. Department of Transportation (USDOT)
(USDOL 2004b, 29 C.F.R. § 1910.106[a]).

Flammable- and combustible-liquid containers may also be made of
glass and plastic, provided that no more than a 1-gal. capacity container
may be used for a Class IA or IB flammable liquid and that storing the
liquid in a metal container is unadvisable (see figure 3.1). The maximum
sizes of containers and portable tanks as allowed by OSHA appear in table
3.1 (USDOL 2004b, 29 C.F.R. § 1910.106[d]).

TRANSFERRING FLAMMABLE AND COMBUSTIBLE LIQUIDS

A common practice in industry is the transferring of flammable and combustible liquids from a one storage container to another. For example, a
worker may need to transfer a flammable liquid from a 55-gal. drum to a
safety can for use on the production line. Several hazards are present during this type of task, including the potential for spilling the liquid, release
of vapors into the work area, and accidental ignition of the vapors. First
of all, flammable liquids must always be kept in approved, covered containers when not in use. Where flammable or combustible liquids are used
or handled, except in closed containers, means shall be provided to dis-

Table 3.1 Maximum Allowable Quantities of Flammable and Combustible Liquids by Container Type

	Flammable Liquids			Combustible Liquids	
Container Type	Class IA	Class IB	Class IC	Class II	Class III
Glass or approved plastic	1 pt.	1 qt.	1 gal.	1 gal.	1 gal.
Metal (other than DOT drums)	1 gal.	5 gal.	5 gal.	5 gal.	5 gal.
Safety cans	2 gal.	5 gal.	5 gal.	5 gal.	5 gal.
Metal drums (DOT specifications)	60 gal.	60 gal.	60 gal.	60 gal.	60 gal.
Approved portable tanks	660 gal.	660 gal.	660 gal.	660 gal.	660 gal.

pose promptly and safely of leakage or spills. To prevent possible ignition of the vapors, Class I liquids may be used only where there are no open flames or other sources of ignition within the possible path of vapor travel.

To prevent both the release of flammable and combustible vapors and the buildup of static electricity, flammable or combustible liquids should be transferred into vessels, containers, or portable tanks within a building only through a closed piping system, from safety cans by means of a device drawing through the top or from a container or portable tank by gravity through an approved self-closing valve. Transferring by means of air pressure on the container or portable tank is prohibited.

Adequate precautions shall be taken to prevent the ignition of flammable vapors. Sources of ignition include but are not limited to open flames; lightning; smoking; cutting and welding; hot surfaces; frictional heat; static, electrical, and mechanical sparks; spontaneous ignition, including heat-producing chemical reactions; and radiant heat. Due to the extreme fire hazards of Class I liquids, they should not be dispensed into containers unless the nozzle and container are electrically interconnected through the use of a bonding wire (see Figure 3.2). An alternative to using a bonding wire is the use of a metallic floor plate while the fill stem is connected to the container (USDOL 2004b, 29 C.F.R. § 1910.106[e]). To prevent the accumulation of flammable vapors in hazardous concentrations, transferring Class I liquids should be done inside buildings unless adequate ventilation is provided. Where mechanical ventilation is required, it should be kept in operation while transferring takes place.

STORAGE CABINETS

Storage cabinets are commonly used to store quantities of flammable and combustible liquids in containers, drums, and barrels. The purpose of the storage cabinet is to protect the liquids inside the cabinet and, if subjected to heat, to limit the internal temperature to not more than 325°F (USDOL 2004b, 29 C.F.R. § 1910.106[d]). The cabinets are constructed to withstand a ten-minute fire test. Additional features of the cabinet include steel construction (wood construction is also acceptable), self-closing doors, venting to the outside where required by code, and raised at least 2 in. above the bottom of the cabinet. Storage cabinets should be approved for use for flammable-liquid storage meeting NFPA standards for the design

FIGURE 3.2
Typical flammable-liquids transferring arrangement

and construction of flammable- and combustible-liquid storage cabinets. The cabinets should also be labeled in conspicuous lettering "Flammable—Keep Fire Away." Figure 3.3 depicts a typical flammable-liquids storage cabinet.

INSIDE STORAGE ROOMS

Storage rooms used in the industry specifically for the storage of flammable and combustible liquids must be properly designed and constructed for that use. The major design aspects of the storage room include fire

FIGURE 3.3
Approved storage cabinet (photo courtesy of Justrite Manufacturing)

protection, spill containment, ventilation, fire resistance, and proper electrical wiring and equipment. To prevent the accidental release of spilled
flammable or combustible liquids from the storage room to other parts of
the facility, openings such as doorways should be protected, and the room
should be liquidtight where the walls join the floor. Common methods for
containing spills at doorways leading into the storage room involve the
use of liquidtight, raised sills at least 4 in. high, ramps, or a floor area in
the storage room that is at least 4 in. below the surrounding floor to hold
spilled liquids within the room. An alternative method of spill control for
the room can be the use of a floor drain that evacuates the spilled liquid
out to a safe location, typically a storage vault located outside the facility,
which can be emptied. Rated self-closing fire doors should be provided to
the room, and if windows are provided in the room, they should be
approved for such use.

Fire protection for a storage room is accomplished by the use of fire
extinguishers. OSHA requires that at least one portable fire extinguisher

having a rating of not less than 12-B units be located outside of, but not more than 10 ft. from, the door opening into any room used for storage. If the storage area contains Class I or Class II liquids, at least one portable fire extinguisher having a rating of not less than 12-B units must be located not less than 10 ft. or more than 25 ft. from any storage area located outside of a storage room but inside a building. Sources of ignition from open flames and smoking are not permitted in flammable- or combustible-liquid storage areas (USDOL 2004b, 29 C.F.R. § 1910.106[d]).

OSHA has also established the maximum quantity of flammable and combustible liquids to be stored in an inside storage room. Factors to take into account when determining maximum quantities include the fire-rating construction of the room and the presence of a sprinkler system (see table 3.2). There shall be one clear aisle at least 3 ft. wide in the storage room to allow for access, and containers over a 30-gal. capacity shall not be stacked one upon the other.

From a hazardous-environment standpoint, flammable- and combustible-liquid storage rooms may be classified as either Class I, Division 1 locations or Class I, Division 2 locations, depending upon the class of liquid stored and whether activities inside the storage room create flammable vapor-air mixtures. If the room is only used for storage of Class I liquids (i.e., no transferring), then the electrical wiring and equipment located in the storage room should meet Class I, Division 2 requirements. If the storage room is used for the storage of Class II and Class III liquids, the electrical equipment should be approved for general use. If flammable vapor-air mixtures may exist under normal operations, then the electrical wiring should meet Class I, Division 1 requirements.

Ventilation is required in storage rooms to keep the flammable and combustible vapors well below their LELs. The ventilation systems should

Table 3.2 Storage in Inside Rooms

Fire Protection Provided	Fire Resistance (hours)	Maximum Floor Area (sq. ft.)	Total Quantities Allowed (gal./sq. ft./floor area)
Yes	2	500	10
No	2	500	5
Yes	1	150	4
No	1	150	2

Source: United States Department of Labor, Occupational Safety and Health Standards for General Industry, 29 C.F.R. § 1910.106(d), 2004.

change over the entire volume of air inside the room at least six times per hour (USDOL 2004b, 29 C.F.R. § 1910.106[d]). Where gravity ventilation is provided, the fresh-air intake, as well as the exhaust outlet from the room, shall be on the exterior of the building in which the room is located.

STORAGE TANKS

Storage tanks are classified according to their operating pressures and are classified as low-pressure tanks, atmospheric tanks, and pressure vessels. Atmospheric tanks are designed to operate at pressures from atmospheric through 0.5 psig; low-pressure tanks are designed to operate at pressures above 0.5 psig but not more than 15 psig; pressure vessels are designed to operate at pressures above 15 psig (USDOL 2004b, 29 C.F.R. § 1910.106[a]).

Tanks used for the storage of flammable and combustible liquids must be built of steel or other approved materials that are compatible with the liquids to be stored, and their design and construction must meet approved standards. Examples of organizations that have standards for the tank construction include FM Global, Underwriters' Laboratories, the American Petroleum Institute (API), and the American Society of Mechanical Engineers (ASME) Boiler and Pressure Vessels Code. The safety requirements for storage tanks for flammable and combustible liquids can be further classified based upon whether they are intended for aboveground or underground use.

OUTSIDE ABOVEGROUND TANKS

Methods for controlling and preventing fires involving outside, aboveground tanks include the separation of storage tanks, diking and drainage, and venting. Separating aboveground storage tanks reduces the spread of fire from one tank to another and provides access to the tanks in the event of a fire. Several factors are examined when determining the minimum separation between two aboveground storage tanks containing flammable and combustible liquids. Figure 3.4 depicts outside, aboveground storage tanks. These factors include the diameters of the tanks, the tank capacities, and the characteristics of liquids being stored. The following are some of the criteria used to determine the minimum spacing between the aboveground storage tanks (USDOL 2004b, 29 C.F.R. § 1910.106[b]):

FIGURE 3.4
Outside aboveground storage tanks

- The minimum distance between any two flammable- or combustible-liquid storage tanks shall not be less than 3 ft.
- The distance between any two adjacent tanks shall not be less than one-sixth the sum of their diameters.
- When the diameter of one tank is less than one-half the diameter of the adjacent tank, the distance between the two tanks shall not be less than one-half the diameter of the smaller tank.
- Where crude petroleum in conjunction with production facilities is located in noncongested areas with capacities not exceeding 126,000 gal. (3,000 barrels), the distance between such tanks shall not be less than 3 ft.
- Where unstable flammable or combustible liquids are stored, the distance between such tanks shall not be less than one-half the sum of their diameters.
- The minimum separation between a liquefied-petroleum-gas container and a flammable- or combustible-liquid storage tank shall be 20 ft., except in the case of flammable- or combustible-liquid tanks operating at pressures exceeding 2.5 psig or equipped with emergency venting that will permit pressures to exceed 2.5 psig.

Venting is used on storage tanks to maintain a constant pressure inside the tank. Pressure inside the tank can change due to temperature changes and the displacement of the liquid inside by either adding or removing liquid. To control pressure changes inside the tank, air movement into and out of it must be allowed. But this can also create additional fire hazards when the flammable or combustible vapors escape through the vent piping and contact a heat source. To alleviate potential fire hazards, when vent-pipe outlets for tanks storing Class I liquids are adjacent to buildings or public ways, they must be located so that the vapors are released at a safe point outside of buildings and not less than 12 ft. above the adjacent ground level. The vent outlets must also be located so that eaves or other obstructions will not trap flammable vapors. The venting equipment must meet applicable standards. Venting also provides protection against over-pressure from any pump discharging into the tank or vessel when the pump-discharge pressure can exceed the design pressure of the tank or vessel.

In addition to venting, emergency relief venting is required on storage tanks to relieve excessive internal pressure caused by fires. This protection may take the form of a floating roof, a lifter roof, a weak roof-to-shell seam, or another approved pressure-relieving construction. Emergency relief venting should meet design capacities to prevent the rupture of the tank. A commercial tank-venting device must have stamped on it the opening pressure, the pressure at which the valve reaches the full open position, and the flow capacity at the latter pressure expressed in cubic feet per hour of air at 60°F and at a pressure of 14.7 psia.

Drainage and diking are means to prevent the accidental discharge of liquid into adjacent properties or waterways or the area around an above-ground tank. OSHA requirements for diking and drainage include the following (USDOL 2004b, 29 C.F.R. § 1910.106[b]):

1. When drainage is used, it must terminate in vacant land or other area or in an impounding basin having a capacity not smaller than that of the largest tank served.
2. When diking is used, the volume of the diked area shall have a volumetric capacity no less than the greatest amount of liquid that can be released from the largest tank within the diked area.
3. If the diked area encloses more than one tank, the capacity should be calculated by deducting the volume of the tanks other than the largest tank below the height of the dike.
4. For a tank or group of tanks with fixed roofs containing crude petroleum with boilover characteristics, the volumetric capacity of the diked area shall be not less than the capacity of the largest tank served by the enclosure, assuming a full tank.
5. The capacity of the diked enclosure shall be calculated by deducting the volume below the height of the dike of all tanks within the enclosure.
6. When constructing the walls for a diked area, the walls may be earth, steel, concrete, or solid masonry designed to be liquidtight and to withstand a full hydrostatic head.
7. Earthen walls 3 ft. or more in height shall have a flat section at the top not less than 2 ft. wide.
8. The maximum height of the walls is an average height of 6 ft. above interior grade.
9. The diked areas shall also be kept free from loose combustible materials.

UNDERGROUND TANKS

Underground storage tanks containing flammable and combustible liquids pose both fire hazards and environmental hazards. Underground storage tanks should be placed in the ground in areas that are free from the potential hazards created by extreme loading generated by buildings and vehicle traffic. The backfill material should be noncorrosive, inert material, such as clean sand, earth, or gravel, well tamped into place, ensuring that the tanks are handled carefully to prevent breaking a weld, puncturing or damaging the tank, or scraping off the protective coating of coated tanks (USDOL 2004b, 29 C.F.R. § 1910.106[b]).

Due to the potential for release of liquid and vapors from an underground tank, the distance from any part of a tank storing Class I liquids to the nearest wall of any basement or pit shall be not less than 1 ft. and to any property line that may be built upon, not less than 3 ft. The distance from any part of a tank storing Class II or Class III liquids to the nearest wall of any basement, pit, or property line shall be not less than 1 ft. (USDOL 2004b, 29 C.F.R. § 1910.106[b]).

To prevent leaking and deterioration of the underground storage tanks due to corrosion, corrosion protection for the tank and its piping shall be provided by one or more of the following methods (USDOL 2004b, 29 C.F.R. § 1910.106[b]):

- Protective coatings or wrappings
- Cathodic protection
- Corrosion-resistant construction materials

Like aboveground storage tanks, underground storage tanks should be equipped with vents to maintain adequate pressure inside the tank during filling and unfilling operations. Design considerations for the vent piping include the following (USDOL 2004b, 29 C.F.R. § 1910.106[b]):

1. The vents must be located in a manner so that the vapors escaping from the tank through the vent cannot be accidentally ignited.
2. Vent pipes from tanks storing Class I liquids must be located so that the discharge point is outside of buildings, higher than the fill-pipe opening, and not less than 12 ft. above the adjacent ground level.
3. If the vent pipe is less than 10 ft. in length or has a nominal inside

diameter greater than 2 in., the outlet shall be provided with a vacuum-and-pressure-relief device, or there shall be an approved flame arrester located in the vent line at the outlet or within the approved distance from the outlet.

4. Vent pipes from tanks storing Class II or Class III flammable liquids shall terminate outside of the building and higher than the fill-pipe opening.

Additional design considerations for underground tanks include tank supports and proper locating of tanks to protect against potential damage to the storage tanks due to floodwaters. All tanks, whether shop built or field erected, must be designed and strength tested in accordance with the applicable codes. The ASME code stamp, API monogram, or the label of the Underwriters' Laboratories on a tank shall be evidence of compliance with this strength test. All piping, valves, and fittings should be approved for use with flammable and combustible liquids. These components should be installed and maintained according to applicable codes and standards.

TANK-VEHICLE AND TANK-CAR LOADING AND UNLOADING

Transferring flammable and combustible liquids from tank vehicles and tank cars poses the same types of hazards one encounters when transferring these liquids from one portable container to another. These hazards include the potential for the presence of flammable and combustible vapors and the potential to create a static-electrical ignition source. To protect adjacent property, loading or unloading facilities involving Class I liquids should not be sited any closer than 25 ft. to the adjacent property or 15 ft. to the loading and unloading facilities for Class II and Class III liquids (USDOL 2004b, 29 C.F.R. § 1910.106[b]). Equipment used in the transfer of liquids from tank cars and rail cars should be approved for use and for the class of liquid being transferred. To prevent accidental spills or overfilling, approved valves should be used that are either self-closing or automatically closing when the vehicle is full or filled to a certain level.

The transfer of liquids to or from the tank car or tank truck can create an electrical-potential difference between the tank car or tank truck and the tank being transferred to. As is the case when transferring between two containers, a means of bonding the tank car or truck to the tank should be provided when Class I liquids are loaded or when Class II or Class III liquids are loaded into vehicles that may contain vapors from previous cargoes of Class I liquids (USDOL 2004b, 29 C.F.R. § 1910.106[b]). Bonding shall be accomplished by connecting a metallic bond wire to the fill stem or to some part of the rack structure to some metallic part in electrical contact with the cargo tank vehicle. The bonding connection is made to the vehicle or tank before dome covers are raised and remains in place until filling is completed and all dome covers have been closed and secured (USDOL 2004b, 29 C.F.R. § 1910.106[b]).

WORKPLACE PRACTICES

To protect employees and property from fire hazards involving flammable and combustible liquids in the workplace, control measures and workplace procedures should be adopted and followed. OSHA, NFPA, and various organizations require procedures to be followed in the storage and handling of flammable and combustible liquids. These regulations also stipulate requirements for housekeeping, fire protection, and the control of ignition sources.

Controlling Sources of Ignition

In locations where flammable vapors may be present, precautions should be taken to prevent ignition by eliminating or controlling sources of ignition. Sources of ignition include open flames, lightning, smoking, cutting and welding, hot surfaces, frictional heat, sparks (static, electrical, and mechanical), spontaneous ignition, chemical and physical-chemical reactions, and radiant heat.

Maintenance and Repairs

When it is necessary to do maintenance work in a flammable- or combustible-liquid processing area, the work shall be authorized by a responsible representative of the employer. Hot work, such as welding or cutting operations, use of spark-producing power tools, and chipping operations, shall be permitted only under supervision of an individual in responsible charge, who shall make an inspection of the area to be sure that it is safe for the work to be done and that safe procedures will be followed for the work specified.

Housekeeping

Maintenance and operating practices shall be in accordance with established procedures, which will tend to control leakage and prevent the accidental escape of flammable or combustible liquids. Spills shall be cleaned up promptly. Adequate aisles shall be maintained for unobstructed movement of personnel and so that fire-protection equipment can adequately reach all areas of the storage room.

Combustible waste material and residues in a building or unit operating area shall be kept to a minimum, stored in covered metal receptacles, and disposed of daily.

Housekeeping can also involve the removal of dust accumulations within the plant. Careful removal of lying dust can eliminate the possibility of secondary dust explosions occurring and also help to prevent some ignition sources. Installing good dust-extraction systems wherever there is a particularly dusty area of the plant should do this. Dust should be removed immediately using either a high-power explosionproof vacuum cleaner or an internal vacuuming system, which removes dust and sends it to a central filtration system.

HYDROGEN

Hydrogen is a nontoxic, colorless gas with no odor. It is flammable and may form mixtures with air that are flammable or explosive. Hydrogen may react violently if combined with oxidizers, such as air, oxygen, and halogens. Hydrogen is an asphyxiant and may displace oxygen in a workplace atmosphere. The concentrations at which flammable or explosive mixtures form are much lower than the concentration at which asphyxiation risk is significant (Voltaix 1996, 1).

Hydrogen can be found in a variety of industries serving a number of useful purposes. It can be stored in containers such as cylinders or it may be part of a tank, piping, and manifold system. Hydrogen can be used in a gaseous form or stored under pressure in a liquefied form. Regardless of the state it is stored in, hydrogen poses an extreme fire hazard; therefore, the safety standards for the storage and handling of hydrogen in the workplace should be closely adhered to.

The containers, whether they are cylinders or tanks, should meet applicable design and construction requirements. For example, OSHA requires hydrogen containers used in the workplace to be designed, constructed, and tested in accordance with appropriate requirements of ASME Boiler and Pressure Vessel Code, Section VIII—Unfired Pressure Vessels, and in accordance with USDOT specifications and regulations. Construction requirements include being equipped with safety relief devices to discharge upward and unobstructed to the open air. Piping and tubing shall conform to "Industrial Gas and Air Piping," Code for Pressure Piping, ANSI B31.1-1967 with addendum B31.1-1969, and shall be suitable for hydrogen service and for the pressures and temperatures involved. Valves, gauges, regulators, and other accessories shall be suitable for hydrogen service. Each portable container and manifolded hydrogen supply unit must be legibly marked with the name "HYDROGEN." The hydrogen storage location shall be permanently placarded as follows: "HYDROGEN—FLAMMABLE GAS—NO SMOKING—NO OPEN FLAMES" or the equivalent.

To prevent the accidental ignition of flammable gas, systems containing hydrogen should be located above ground and away from potential sources of ignition such as electric power lines, flammable-liquid piping, or piping of other flammable gases. The location of a hydrogen system, as determined by the maximum total contained volume of hydrogen, shall be in the order of preference as indicated by Roman numerals in table 3.3 (USDOL 2004d, 29 C.F.R. § 1910.103[b]).

The rooms and facilities used to house hydrogen storage and piping equipment must meet special design considerations. Design features of these facilities include proper venting, fire-resistive building construction, and approved electrical installations. The minimum distance in feet for hydrogen systems to outdoor exposures shall be in accordance with table 3.4 (USDOL 2004d, 29 C.F.R. § 1910.103[b]). Protective structures can be used in lieu of the distances.

Table 3.3   Maximum Capacities of Gaseous Hydrogen Systems

	Size of Hydrogen System		
Nature of Location	Less than 3,000 CF	3,000– 15,000 CF	More than 15,000 CF
Outdoors	I	I	I
In a separate building	II	II	II
In a special room	III	III	Not permitted
Inside buildings, not in a special room, and exposed to other occupancies	IV	Not permitted	Not permitted

Table 3.4   Minimum Safe Distances for Gaseous Hydrogen Systems to Exposures

Type of Outdoor Exposure		Size of Hydrogen System		
		Less than 3,000 CF	3,000 to 15,000 CF	More than 15,000 CF
1. Building or structure	Wood-frame construction	10	25	50
	Heavy timber, noncombustible, or ordinary construction[1]	0	10	252
	Fire-resistive construction[1]	0	0	0
2. Wall openings	Not above any part of a system	10	10	10
	Above any part of a system	25	25	25
3. Flammable liquids above ground	0–1,000 gallons	10	25	25
	In excess of 1,000 gallons	25	50	50
4. Flammable liquids below ground—0 to 1,000 gallons	Tank	10	10	10
	Vent or fill opening of tank	25	25	25
5. Flammable liquids below ground—in excess of 1,000 gallons	Tank	20	20	20
	Vent or fill opening of tank	25	25	25
6. Flammable gas storage, either high pressure or low pressure	0–15,000 CF capacity	10	25	25
	In excess of 15,000 CF capacity	25	50	50
7. Oxygen storage	12,000 CF or less[4]			
	More than 12,000 CF[5]			
8. Fast-burning solids, such as ordinary lumber, excelsior, or paper		50	50	50
9. Slow-burning solids, such as heavy timber or coal		25	25	25
10. Open flames and other sources of ignition		25	25	25
11. Air-compressor intakes or inlets to ventilating or air-conditioning equipment		50	50	50
12. Concentration of people[3]		25	50	50

1. Refer to NFPA No. 220, Standard Types of Building Construction, for definitions of various types of construction (1969 ed.).
2. But not less than one-half the height of adjacent sidewall of the structure.
3. In congested areas such as offices, lunchrooms, locker rooms, and time-clock areas.
4. Refer to NFPA No. 51, Gas Systems for Welding and Cutting (1969).
5. Refer to NFPA No. 566, Bulk Oxygen Systems at Consumer Sites (1969).
Source: United States Department of Labor, Occupational Safety and Health Standards for General Industry, 29 C.F.R. § 1910.103(b), 2004).

LIQUEFIED-HYDROGEN SYSTEMS

To be liquefied, hydrogen has to be compressed and cooled to −250°C. In this state, hydrogen still possesses many of the hazards that it does in a gaseous state. Proper storage and handling of liquid hydrogen is key to preventing fires caused by the material. Therefore, liquefied-hydrogen containers used in the workplace shall be designed, constructed, and tested in accordance with appropriate requirements of the ASME Boiler and Pressure Vessel Code, Section VIII—Unfired Pressure Vessels (1968), or applicable provisions of API Standard 620, *Recommended Rules for Design and Construction of Large, Welded, Low-Pressure Storage Tanks* (2nd ed., June 1963) (USDOL 2004d, 29 C.F.R. § 1910.103[c]). Requirements for proper storage involving liquefied hydrogen in the workplace include the following (USDOL 2004d, 29 C.F.R. § 1910.103[c]):

1. Portable containers shall be designed, constructed, and tested in accordance with USDOT specifications and regulations.
2. Containers shall be legibly marked to indicate "LIQUEFIED HYDRO-GEN—FLAMMABLE GAS."
3. Containers shall be equipped with safety relief devices as required by applicable regulations.
4. Piping, tubing, fittings, and gasket and thread sealants shall be suitable for hydrogen service at the pressures and temperatures involved and shall conform to the applicable standards.
5. Valves, gauges, regulators, and other accessories shall be suitable for liquefied-hydrogen service and for the pressures and temperatures involved.
6. Electrical wiring and equipment located within 3 ft. of a point where connections are regularly made and disconnected must meet requirements for Class I, Group B, Division 1 locations.
7. Electrical wiring and equipment located within 25 ft. of a point where connections are regularly made and disconnected or within 25 ft. of a liquid-hydrogen storage container shall be in accordance with Subpart S of the OSHA standards for Class I, Group B, Division 2 locations.

The location of liquefied-hydrogen storage, as determined by the maximum total quantity of liquefied hydrogen, shall be in the order of preference as indicated by Roman numerals in table 3.5 (USDOL 2004d, 29 C.F.R. § 1910.103[c]):

The minimum distance in feet from liquefied-hydrogen systems of the indicated storage capacity located outdoors, in a separate building, or in a special room, to any specified exposure shall be in accordance with table 3.6 (USDOL 2004d, 29 C.F.R. § 1910.103[c]).

Table 3.5   Maximum Capacities of Liquefied Hydrogen Systems

Nature of Location	Size of Hydrogen Storage (capacity in gallons)			
	39.63 (150 liters) to 50	51 to 300	301 to 600	More than 600
Outdoors	I	I	I	I
In a separate building	II	II	II	Not permitted
In a special room	III	III	Not permitted	Do.
Inside buildings not in a special room and exposed to other occupancies	IV	Not permitted	Do.	Do.

Note: This table does not apply to storage in dewars of the type generally used in laboratories for experimental purposes.

Portable liquefied-hydrogen containers of 50-gal. or less capacity, when housed inside buildings, not located in a special room, and exposed to other occupancies, shall comply with the following minimum requirements (USDOL 2004d, 29 C.F.R. § 1910.103[c]):

1. Be located 20 ft. from flammable liquids and readily combustible materials such as excelsior or paper
2. Be located 25 ft. from ordinary electrical equipment and other sources of ignition including process or analytical equipment
3. Be located 25 ft. from concentrations of people
4. Be located 50 ft. from intakes of ventilation and air-conditioning equipment or intakes of compressors
5. Be located 50 ft. from storage of other flammable gases or storage of oxidizing gases

Containers shall be protected against damage or injury due to falling objects or work activity in the area. They shall be firmly secured and stored in an upright position; welding or cutting operations and smoking shall be prohibited while hydrogen is in the room. As is the case with a hydrogen-gas storage location, liquefied-hydrogen storage must meet requirements for the construction and location of storage buildings, venting, noncombustible construction, electrical wiring, ventilation, and explosion venting.

Table 3.6   Minimum Safe Distances for Liquefied Hydrogen Systems to Exposures[1,2]

Type of Exposure	Liquefied Hydrogen Storage (capacity in gallons)		
	39.63 (150 liters) to 3,500	3,501 to 15,000	15,001 to 30,000
1. Fire-resistive building and fire walls[3]	5	5	5
2. Noncombustible building[3]	25	50	75
3. Other buildings[3]	50	75	100
4. Wall openings, air-compressor intakes, inlets for air conditioning or ventilating equipment	75	75	75
5. Flammable liquids (above ground and vent or fill openings if below ground) (see 513 and 514)	50	75	100
6. Between stationary liquefied-hydrogen containers	5	5	5
7. Flammable gas storage	50	75	100
8. Liquid-oxygen storage and other oxidizers (see 513 and 514)	100	100	100
9. Combustible solids	50	75	100
10. Open flames, smoking, and welding	50	50	50
11. Concentrations of people	75	75	75

1. The distance in Nos. 2, 3, 5, 7, 9, and 12 in table 3.4 may be reduced where protective structures, such as firewalls equal to the height of the top of the container (to safeguard the liquefied-hydrogen storage system), are located between the liquefied-hydrogen storage installation and the exposure.
2. Where protective structures are provided, ventilation and confinement of the product should be considered. The five-foot distance in Nos. 1 and 6 facilitates maintenance and enhances ventilation.
3. Refer to Standard Types of Building Construction, NFPA No. 220-1969, for definitions of various types of construction.

ACETYLENE

Acetylene is most often associated with its use as a fuel in welding and cutting operations. Because acetylene is highly soluble in acetone, large quantities of acetylene can be stored in small cylinders at low pressures (NSC 1992, 589). The gas may be stored in cylinders and tanks, or it may be stored in a manifold system. Acetylene consists of 92.3 percent by weight of carbon and 7.7 percent by weight of hydrogen (NSC 1992, 587). Acetylene is used as a fuel since it produces a much higher flame temperature than other fuels. The gaseous acetylene that comes from cylinders is really evolved from liquid acetone stored in an inert filler material inside the cylinder. As the tank is opened, the acetylene gas is released from the cylinder. Tipping the cylinder on its side can result in the release of liquid acetone from the cylinder.

The in-plant transfer, handling, storage, and use of acetylene in cylinders shall be in accordance with Compressed Gas Association Pamphlet G-1-1966, which is incorporated by reference as specified in 29 C.F.R. § 1910.6 (USDOL 2004e, 29 C.F.R. § 1910.102 [1]). The piped systems for the in-plant transfer and distribution of acetylene shall be designed, installed, maintained, and operated in accordance with Compressed Gas Association Pamphlet G-1.3-1959. Plants for the generation of acetylene and the charging (filling) of acetylene cylinders shall be designed, constructed, and tested in accordance with the standards prescribed in Compressed Gas Association Pamphlet G-1.4-1966 (USDOL 2004d, 29 C.F.R. § 1910.103[c]).

When using acetylene cylinders for oxy-acetylene welding and cutting, the acetylene serves as the fuel, while the oxygen serves as the oxidizer. Hazards with acetylene in welding and cutting include the potential for fires because the fuel and oxidizer are together. Separating the fuel and oxygen cylinders when in storage by 20 ft. will reduce the potential for fires. Figure 3.5 depicts improper storage of oxygen and acetylene cylinders. Because the acetylene is really being formed from the liquid acetone

FIGURE 3.5
Improper storage of oxygen and acetylene cylinders

inside the container, acetylene cylinders should always be stored in the upright position.

OXYGEN

Oxygen is a nonflammable gas, meaning that it does not burn. Oxygen is an oxidizer, serving as an oxygen source for other materials that are consumed as fuel in a fire. Introducing pure oxygen to greases and oils can result in spontaneous combustion. Therefore, equipment making up a bulk oxygen system should be cleaned in order to remove oil, grease, or other readily oxidizable materials before the system is put into service.

Oxygen can be stored in cylinders or in bulk. A bulk oxygen system is an assembly of equipment, comprising oxygen storage containers, pressure regulators, safety devices, vaporizers, manifolds, and interconnecting piping, with a storage capacity of more than 13,000 cu. ft. of oxygen at normal temperature and pressure (NTP) that is connected in service or ready for service or with capacity for more than 25,000 cu. ft. of oxygen (at NTP) including unconnected reserves on hand at the site (USDOL 2004f, 29 C.F.R. § 1910.104[b]).

The bulk oxygen system terminates at the point where oxygen at service pressure first enters the supply line, while oxygen containers may be stationary or movable and the oxygen may be stored as gas or liquid. Bulk oxygen systems shall be designed and installed according to applicable codes. Examples of some provisions pertaining to bulk oxygen systems include the following (USDOL 2004f, 29 C.F.R. § 1910.104[b]):

1. Bulk oxygen storage systems shall be located above ground out of doors or shall be installed in a building of noncombustible construction, adequately vented, and used for that purpose exclusively.
2. The location selected shall be such that containers and associated equipment shall not be exposed by electric power lines, flammable or combustible liquid lines, or flammable gas lines.
3. The minimum safe distance from any bulk oxygen storage container to exposures shall be maintained.
4. Examples of exposures include combustible structures, fire-resistive structures, openings in walls, combustible-liquid storage, and combustible-gas storage.

5. High-pressure gaseous-oxygen containers shall comply with applicable codes, including the ASME Boiler and Pressure Vessel Code, Section VIII—Unfired Pressure Vessels (1968), and USDOT specifications and regulations.

6. Piping, tubing, and fittings shall be suitable for oxygen service and for the pressures and temperatures involved, conforming with "Gas and Air Piping Systems," Code for Pressure Piping, ANSI, B31.1-1967, with addendum, B31.10a-1969.

7. Bulk oxygen storage containers, regardless of design pressure, shall be equipped with safety relief devices as required by the ASME code or USDOT specifications and regulations.

8. Bulk oxygen storage containers designed and constructed in accordance with the ASME Boiler and Pressure Vessel Code, Section VIII—Unfired Pressure Vessel (1968), shall be equipped with safety relief devices meeting the provisions of the Compressed Gas Association Pamphlet *Safety Relief Device Standards for Compressed Gas Storage Containers*, S-1, Part 3.

Valves, gauges, regulators, and other accessories shall be suitable for oxygen service. Any enclosure containing oxygen control or operating equipment shall be adequately vented. The bulk oxygen storage location shall be permanently placarded to indicate "OXYGEN—NO SMOKING—NO OPEN FLAMES" or an equivalent warning.

LIQUEFIED-PETROLEUM GAS

Liquefied-petroleum (LP) gas serves a variety of uses in industry, for example, as a fuel for heating processes or to power equipment such as powered industrial trucks and vehicles and as a propellant in aerosol products. LP gas is extremely flammable. Control measures include using approved equipment to store and transfer LP gas, controlling ignition sources, and using proper handling procedures. Like other gases used in industry, LP gas is commonly stored in portable cylinders, or it may be stored in a manifold system as part of a fixed industrial process.

LP gas stored in USDOT containers should have approved valves, connectors, manifold valve assemblies, and regulators. Containers shall be designed, constructed, and tested following, as appropriate, the Rules for Construction of Unfired Pressure Vessels of the ASME Boiler and Pressure

Vessel Code (USDOL 2004g, 29 C.F.R. § 1910.110[b]). Containers filled on a volumetric basis shall be equipped with a fixed liquid-level gauge to indicate the maximum permitted filling level.

Welding, repairs, and modifications to LP gas containers shall be performed following approved methods to reduce the potential for fires and explosions. LP-gas containers shall be marked with a metal nameplate attached to the container and located in such a manner as to remain visible after the container is installed; information on the nameplate shall include the following (USDOL 2004g, 29 C.F.R. § 1910.110[b]):

1. The name and address of the supplier of the container or the trade name of the container
2. The water capacity of the container in pounds or gallons, U.S. Standard
3. The pressure in psig for which the container is designed
4. The wording "This container shall not contain a product having a vapor pressure in excess of—psig at 100°F."
5. The tare weight in pounds or other identified unit of weight for containers with a water capacity of 300 lb. or less
6. The maximum level to which the container may be filled with liquid at temperatures between 20°F and 130°F (except on containers provided with fixed maximum-level indicators or that are filled by weighing) in increments of not more than 20°F (this marking may be located on the liquid-level gauging device)
7. The outside surface area in square feet

Each individual container shall be located with respect to the nearest important building or group of buildings in accordance with table 3.7 (USDOL 2004g, 29 C.F.R. § 1910.110[b]).

Additional requirements for valves, fittings, piping, and relief valves established by OSHA include the following (USDOL 2004g, 29 C.F.R. § 1910.110[b]):

1. Valves, fittings, and accessories connected directly to the container, including primary shutoff valves, shall have a rated working pressure of at least 250 psig and shall be of material and design suitable for LP-gas service.

Table 3.7   Minimum Distances between Aboveground LP Gas Containers

Water Capacity per Container	Minimum Distances		
	Containers		Between Aboveground Containers
	Underground (ft.)	Aboveground	
Less than 125 gal.[1]	10	None	None
125 to 250 gal.	10	10	None
251 to 500 gal.	10	10	3
501 to 2,000 gal.	25[2]	25[2]	3
2,001 to 30,000 gal.	50	50	5
30,001 to 70,000 gal.	50	75	1/4 of sum of diameters of adjacent containers
70,001 to 90,000 gal.	50	100	1/4 of sum of diameters of adjacent containers

1. If the aggregate water capacity of a multicontainer installation at a consumer site is 501 gal. or greater, the minimum distance shall comply with the appropriate portion of this table, applying the aggregate capacity rather than the capacity per container. If more than one installation is made, each installation shall be separated from another installation by at least 25 ft. Do not apply the minimum distances between aboveground containers to such installations.
2. The above distance requirements may be reduced to not less than 10 ft. for a single container of 1,200 gal. water capacity or less, providing such a container is at least 25 ft. from any other LP-gas container of more than 125 gal. water capacity.

2. Piping, tubing hoses, fittings, and relief valves used for LP-gas systems shall meet applicable requirements.

3. Piping, tubing hoses, fittings, and relief valves shall be installed, tested, and maintained following standards.

4. Relief-valve assemblies shall be of sufficient size to provide the rate of flow required for the container on which they are installed that will discharge the gas to an acceptable location should the valve open.

TANK-CAR AND TRUCK-LOADING OR UNLOADING

Transferring LP gas from tank cars and trucks presents unique fire hazards. To prevent the accidental release of the gas, the following precautions should be taken (USDOL 2004g, 29 C.F.R. § 1910.110[b]):

1. The track of tank car siding shall be relatively level.

2. A "TANK CAR CONNECTED" sign, as covered by USDOT rules, shall be installed at the active end or ends of the siding while the tank car is connected.

3. While cars are on sidetrack for loading or unloading, the wheels at both ends shall be blocked on the rails.

4. The employer shall insure that an employee is in attendance at all times while the tank car, cars, or trucks are being loaded or unloaded.
5. Electrical equipment and wiring shall meet applicable codes for use in an area where LP-gas vapors may be present.
6. Open flames or other sources of ignition shall not be permitted in vaporizer rooms (except those housing direct-fired vaporizers), pump houses, container-charging rooms, or other similar locations.
7. Direct-fired vaporizers shall not be permitted in pump houses or container-charging rooms.
8. Open flames from sources, such as cutting or welding, portable electric tools, and extension lights capable of igniting LP gas, shall not be permitted within specified areas such as storage areas, tank-car-loading and -unloading areas, and LP-gas vehicle recharging areas.

CHAPTER QUESTIONS

1. Describe some of the common electrical hazards that can result in fire ignition sources.
2. Differentiate between the various classes of flammable and combustible liquids.
3. What import do the various classes and groups of flammable and combustible liquids have for the safety manager?
4. Differentiate between the various hazardous-environment classes.
5. What process should be followed when transferring a flammable liquid from a 55-gal. drum to a 5-gal. safety container?
6. What type of fire hazard does oxygen present in the workplace?
7. What fire-prevention and spill-control features would one expect to find on an aboveground storage tank that holds flammable liquids?
8. Describe the safety features found in a flammable-liquid storage room.
9. Describe the safety features of an approved safety container.

REFERENCES

Ahrens, Marty. (2001). *Selections from the U.S. Fire Problem Overview Report: Leading Causes and Other Patterns and Trends: Industrial and Manufacturing Properties, June 2001.* Quincy, MA: NFPA.

Earley, Mark W., et al. (2003). *National Electrical Code 2002 Handbook.* Quincy, MA: NFPA.

Jones, Ray A., and Jane G. Jones. (2000). *Electrical Safety in the Workplace.* Quincy, MA: NFPA.

National Fire Protection Association (NFPA). (1997). *Fire Protection Handbook,* 18th ed. Quincy, MA: NFPA.

NFPA. (2003). *National Fire Codes, Electronic Edition.* Quincy, MA: NFPA.

NFPA. (2002). *NFPA 70: National Electrical Code, 2002 Edition.* Quincy, MA: NFPA.

National Safety Council (NSC). (1992). *Accident Prevention Manual for Business and Industry: Engineering and Technology.* Itasca, IL: NSC.

U.S. Department of Labor (USDOL). (2004a). *Occupational Safety and Health Standards for General Industry, Subpart H: Hazardous Materials: Dip Tanks Containing Flammable or Combustible Liquids, 29 C.F.R. § 1910.108(e).* Washington, DC: USDOL.

USDOL. (2004b). *Occupational Safety and Health Standards for General Industry, Subpart H: Hazardous Materials: Flammable and Combustible Liquids, 29 C.F.R. § 1910.106(a).* Washington, DC: USDOL.

USDOL. (2004c). *Occupational Safety and Health Standards for General Industry, Subpart S: Electrical: Hazardous Locations, 29 C.F.R. § 1910.307(b).* Washington, DC: USDOL.

USDOL. (2004d). *Occupational Safety and Health Standards for General Industry, Subpart H: Hazardous Materials: Hydrogen, 29 C.F.R. § 1910.103(b).* Washington, DC: USDOL.

USDOL. (2004e). *Occupational Safety and Health Standards for General Industry, Subpart H: Hazardous Materials, Acetylene: 29 C.F.R. § 1910.102.* Washington, DC: USDOL.

USDOL. (2004f). *Occupational Safety and Health Standards for General Industry, Subpart H: Hazardous Materials: Oxygen, 29 C.F.R. § 1910.104.* Washington, DC: USDOL.

USDOL. (2004g). *Occupational Safety and Health Standards for General Industry, Subpart H: Hazardous Materials: Storage and Handling of Liquefied Petroleum Gases, 29 C.F.R. § 1910.110.* Washington, DC: USDOL.

USDOL, Directorate of Science, Technology and Medicine (DSTM). (2004). *Nationally Recognized Testing Laboratories.* Washington, DC: USDOL, at www .osha.gov/dts/otpca/nrtl/index.html (accessed June 22, 2005).

Voltaix. (1996). *Material Safety Data Sheet for Hydrogen (H_2).* Branchburg, NJ: Voltaix.

Mechanical and Chemical Explosions

ANATOMY OF AN EXPLOSION

Explosions can result in massive property damage and fires. Explosions can be categorized into either mechanical explosions, as in the failure of a pressure vessel, or chemical explosions, as in the case of ignited dynamite. The term *explosion* is defined as a rapid release of high-pressure gas into the environment (NFPA 1997, 1–69). The high-pressure gas released seeks equilibrium with the pressure of the surrounding environment. The dissipation of the energy from the shockwave into the environment is what can cause damage. The effects of the high-pressure gas upon the environment depends upon the following (NFPA 1997, 1–69):

1. The rate of the release
2. The pressure at release
3. The quantity of the gas released
4. The directional factors governing the release

Explosions can be broadly classified into physical explosions and chemical explosions. In physical explosions, the explosion occurs as the sudden release of pressure due to mechanical means. An example of a physical explosion is the release of energy resulting in the failure of a pressure vessel. In physical explosions, there is no chemical change in the substances involved. In chemical explosions, however, there is some type of chemical reaction taking place in which the composition of the materials involved in the explosion changes form. These chemical changes can occur throughout the entire material, in which case they are referred to as *uniform reactions*. The chemical changes can also take place in such a way that there is a clearer distinction between changed material and unchanged material, in which case they are referred to as *propagating reactions* (NFPA 1997, 1–71). Explosions can be classified as detonations (the flame front speed is greater than the speed of sound in the explosion medium) or deflagrations (the flame front speed is less than the speed of sound). Detonations are much more destructive than deflagrations.

EXPLOSIVES AND BLASTING AGENTS

The U.S. Department of Transportation (USDOT) defines an explosive as any substance or article, including a device, designed to function by explosion (i.e., an extremely rapid release of gas and heat) or that, by a chemical reaction within itself, is able to function in a similar manner even if not designed to function by explosion (USDOT 2003a, 49 C.F.R. § 173.50). Explosives in Class 1 are divided into the following six divisions (USDOT 2003a, 49 C.F.R. § 173.50):

1. Division 1.1 consists of explosives that have a mass-explosion hazard. A *mass explosion* is one that affects almost the entire load instantaneously.
2. Division 1.2 consists of explosives that have a projection hazard but not a mass-explosion hazard.
3. Division 1.3 consists of explosives that have a fire hazard and either a minor blast hazard or a minor projection hazard or both, but not a mass-explosion hazard.
4. Division 1.4 consists of explosives that present a minor explosion hazard. The explosive effects are largely confined to the package and no projection of fragments of appreciable size or range is to be expected. An external fire must not cause virtually instantaneous explosion of almost the entire contents of the package.
5. Division 1.5 consists of very insensitive explosives. This division comprises substances that have a mass-explosion hazard but are so insensitive that there is very little probability of initiation or of transition from burning to detonation under normal conditions of transport.
6. Division 1.6 consists of extremely insensitive articles that do not have a mass-explosion hazard. This division comprises articles that contain

only extremely insensitive detonating substances and that demonstrate a negligible probability of accidental initiation or propagation.

The Occupational Safety and Health Administration (OSHA) defines *explosives* further as including but is not limited to dynamite, black powder, pellet powders, initiating explosives, blasting caps, electric blasting caps, safety fuses, fuse lighters, fuse igniters, squibs, cordeau detonant fuses, instantaneous fuses, igniter cord, igniters, small-arms ammunition, small-arms-ammunition primers, smokeless propellants, cartridges for propellant-actuated power devices, and cartridges for industrial guns (USDOL 2004, 29 C.F.R. § 1910.109). Commercial explosives are those explosives that are intended to be used in commercial or industrial operations.

Materials such as trinitrotoluene (TNT) and dynamite are considered high-explosive materials since they detonate at supersonic speeds greater than 1,100 ft./s. Dynamite is a mixture consisting of an absorbent such as sodium nitrate and diatomaceous earth saturated with nitroglycerin (Schnepp and Gantt 1999, 67). Low explosives, or those that detonate at speeds less than 1,100 ft./s, include materials such as black powder. Black powder is one of the oldest explosives known. It is made up of potassium or sodium nitrate, sulfur, and charcoal.

A blasting agent is defined by OSHA as any material or mixture consisting of a fuel and oxidizer, intended for blasting, not otherwise classified as an explosive, and in which none of the ingredients is classified as an explosive, provided that the finished product, as mixed and packaged for use or shipment, cannot be detonated by means of a No. 8 test blasting cap when unconfined. Blasting agents are those materials used to initiate the higher-order explosives (Schnepp and Gantt 1999, 68). Some explosive materials are not easily detonated until an explosive train is established. The explosive train consists of a smaller precursor explosion used to start the second, higher-order explosion.

LABELS AND PLACARDS
USDOT has established the labeling requirements for hazardous materials, including explosives. Figure 4.1 depicts the proper format for explosives labels and placards for explosives in Divisions 1.1, 1.2, and 1.3 (USDOT 2003b, 49 C.F.R. § 172.522).

The "**" in the figure represents the appropriate division number and

FIGURE 4.1
Labels and placards for explosives divisions 1.1, 1.2, and 1.3 (U.S. Department of
Transportation)

compatibility group letter. The compatibility group letter must be the
same size as the division number and must be shown as a capitalized
Roman letter (USDOT 2003b, 49 C.F.R. § 172.522).

An example label for explosives in Division 1.4 appears in figure 4.2.
The "*" on the label represents the appropriate compatibility group. The
compatibility group letter must be shown as a capitalized Roman letter.

FIGURE 4.2
Labels and placards for explosives division 1.4 (U.S. Department of Transportation)

Labels for explosives in Division 1.5 and 1.6 would have their appropriate division number depicted.

An "EXPLOSIVE" subsidiary label is required for materials identified in USDOT's hazardous materials table. The division number or compatibility group letter may be displayed on the subsidiary hazard label. An example of the "EXPLOSIVE" subsidiary label appears in figure 4.3.

EXPLOSIVES-HANDLING AND -STORAGE PROCEDURES

Magazines used for the storage of explosives are classified as either Class I or Class II magazines. A Class I magazine is required where the quantity of explosives stored is more than 50 lb., while a Class II magazine may be used where the quantity of explosives stored is 50 lb. or less (USDOL 2004, 29 C.F.R. § 1910.109[c]). Magazines used in the workplace must meet design and construction requirements. For example, magazines for the storage of certain types of explosives must be bullet resistant, weather resistant, fire resistant, and ventilated sufficiently to protect the explosive in the specific locality. Safety requirements for heating sources for the magazines and ventilation requirements have also been established. In addition, the property upon which Class I magazines are located and property where Class II magazines are located outside of buildings shall be posted with signs reading "EXPLOSIVES—KEEP OFF" (USDOL 2004,

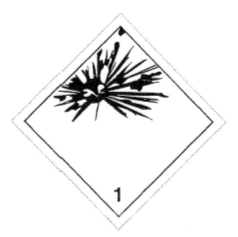

FIGURE 4.3
Explosive subsidiary label (U.S. Department of Transportation)

29 C.F.R. § 1910.109[c]). Magazines must be located a safe distance from other magazines, and locating magazines in certain types of occupancies is prohibited. The storage requirements do not apply to explosives materials such as stocks of small-arms ammunition, propellant-actuated power cartridges, small-arms-ammunition primers in quantities of less than 750,000; smokeless propellants in quantities less than 750 lb.; explosive-actuated power devices in quantities less than 50 lb.; fuse lighters and fuse igniters; and safety fuses other than cordeau detonant fuses (USDOL 2004, 29 C.F.R. § 1910.109[c]). Blasting caps, electric blasting caps, detonating primers, and primed cartridges should not be stored in the same magazine with other explosives.

Sources of ignition such as smoking, matches, open flames, spark-producing devices, and firearms (except firearms carried by guards) are not permitted inside of or within 50 ft. of magazines. The land surrounding a magazine should be kept clear of all combustible materials for a distance of at least 25 ft., and combustible materials should not be stored within 50 ft. of magazines. Magazines should be under the custody of a competent person at all times, and this person should be responsible for enforcing of all safety precautions.

TRANSPORTING EXPLOSIVES

The transportation of explosives shall only be performed by competent employees using approved vehicles and procedures. Employees shall be prohibited from carrying potential sources of ignition while in or near a motor vehicle transporting explosives. No spark-producing metal, spark-producing metal tools, oils, matches, firearms, electric storage batteries, flammable substances, acids, oxidizing materials, or corrosive compounds shall be carried in the body of any motor truck or vehicle transporting explosives, unless the loading of such dangerous articles and the explosives comply with USDOT regulations (USDOL 2004, 29 C.F.R. § 1910.109[d]).

Employees should be required to informing the fire and police departments of when the loading or unloading of explosives will be performed. In the event of breakdown or collision, the local fire and police departments shall be promptly notified to help safeguard such emergencies. Explosives shall be transferred from the disabled vehicle to another only when proper and qualified supervision is provided (USDOL 2004, 29 C.F.R. § 1910.109[e]).

Vehicles used for transporting explosives shall be in good mechanical conditions. Means shall be provided to protect the explosives from sparks and moisture. The vehicles shall be properly placarded according to USDOT regulations. Each motor vehicle used for transporting explosives shall be equipped with a minimum of two extinguishers, each having a rating of at least 10-BC. The fire extinguisher shall be readily accessible to the driver and maintained in proper working condition. OSHA also requires that the motor vehicle used for transporting explosives be given the following inspection to determine that it is in proper condition for the safe transportation of explosives (USDOL 2004, 29 C.F.R. § 1910.109[d]):

1. Fire extinguishers shall be filled and in working order.
2. All electrical wiring shall be completely protected and securely fastened to prevent short-circuiting.
3. Chassis, motor, pan, and underside of body shall be reasonably clean and free of excess oil and grease.
4. Fuel tank and feed line shall be secure and have no leaks.
5. Brakes, lights, horn, windshield wipers, and steering apparatuses shall function properly.
6. Tires shall be checked for proper inflation and defects.
7. The vehicle shall be in proper condition in every other respect and acceptable for handling explosives.

The transportation of the explosives creates hazards for both the driver and the people in the area. A competent driver should be with the vehicle at all times. The driver or other attendant is not to leave the vehicle unattended for any reason. A vehicle is "attended" only when the driver or other attendant is physically on or in the vehicle or has the vehicle within his field of vision and can reach it quickly and without any kind of interference; "attended" also means that the driver or attendant is awake, alert, and not engaged in other duties or activities that may divert his attention from the vehicle, except for necessary communication with public officers, representatives of the carrier shipper, or the consignee or except for necessary absence from the vehicle to obtain food or to provide for his physical comfort (USDOL 2004, 29 C.F.R. § 1910.109[d]). The vehicle should only be parked in designated and secured areas. A designated and secured area is an area that is securely fenced or walled in, with all gates or entrances locked and where parking of the vehicle is otherwise permissible, or at a magazine site established solely for the purpose of storing explosives.

USE OF EXPLOSIVES AND BLASTING AGENTS

The use of explosives and blasting agents is an extremely dangerous activity. OSHA has promulgated standards for the protection of workers engaged in this activity and the people and property that may be in the blasting area. Some of the safety requirements associated with blasting include the following (USDOL 2004, 29 C.F.R. § 1910.109[e]):

1. Blasting should be performed only by qualified individuals.
2. Procedures for loading explosives into blast holes, initiating the explosive charges, and dealing with misfires should adhere to applicable safety standards.
3. Sources of ignition, such as matches, open light, or other fire or flame, should be prohibited at the blasting site to control the potential hazards associated with explosives.
4. Because accidental discharge of electric blasting caps can occur from current induced by radar, radio transmitters, lightning, adjacent power lines, dust storms, or other sources of extraneous electricity, all blasting operations should be suspended and all persons removed from the blasting area during the approach and progress of an electrical storm.
5. Warning signs should be posted against the use of mobile radio transmitters on all roads within 350 ft. of the blasting operations.
6. Precautions should be taken to prevent collateral damage to buildings and structures near the blasting site.
7. Persons authorized to prepare explosive charges or conduct blasting operations shall use every reasonable precaution, including but not limited to warning signals, flags, barricades, or woven wire mats, to insure the safety of the general public and workmen.
8. Whenever blasting is being conducted in the vicinity of gas, electric, water, fire alarm, telephone, telegraph, and steam utilities, the blaster shall notify the appropriate representatives of such utilities at least twenty-four hours in advance of blasting, specifying the location and intended time of such blasting. Verbal notice shall be followed with a written notice.
9. Blasting operations shall be conducted during daylight hours.

OXIDIZING AGENTS

A general definition of an *oxidizing agent* is a chemical substance in which one of the elements has a tendency to gain electrons. NFPA 430: Code for the Storage of Liquid and Solid Oxidizers (1995) has classified oxidizing materials according to their ability to cause spontaneous combustion and how much they can increase the burning rate.

- Class 1 Oxidizers:
  - Slightly increase the burning rate of combustible materials
  - Do not cause spontaneous ignition when they come in contact with them
- Class 2 Oxidizers:
  - Moderately increase the burning rate of combustible materials with which they come into contact
  - May cause spontaneous ignition when in contact with a combustible material
- Class 3 Oxidizers:
  - Severely increase the burning rate of combustible materials with which they come into contact
  - Will cause sustained and vigorous decomposition if contaminated with a combustible material or if exposed to sufficient heat
- Class 4 Oxidizers:
  - Can explode when in contact with certain contaminants
  - Can explode if exposed to slight heat, shock, or friction
  - Will increase the burning rate of combustibles
  - Can cause combustibles to ignite spontaneously

The following common materials are oxidizing agents by this definition:

- *Nitrates:* sodium nitrate ($NaNO_3$)
- *Nitrites:* sodium nitrite ($NaNO_2$)
- *Chlorates:* potassium chlorate ($KClO_3$)
- *Chlorites:* sodium chlorite ($NaClO_2$)
- *Dichromates:* sodium dichromate ($Na_2Cr_2O_7$)
- *Hypochlorites:* sodium hypochlorite ($NaClO$)
- *Perchlorates:* percholoic acid ($HClO_4$)
- *Permaganates:* potassium permanganate ($KMnO_4$)
- *Persulfates:* sodium persulfate ($Na_2O_8S_2$)

Oxidizing agents can make combustible materials ignite at lower temperatures, accelerate combustion, and start fires by causing flames in fuel-
burning appliances to extend beyond their combustion chambers (NFPA
1997, 4-76-77). A primary fire-prevention method for oxidizing agents is
to ensure that they are not stored with flammable and combustible materials. Although the oxidizing agents themselves are not combustible, they
will provide oxygen for the other combustible materials to burn.

AMMONIUM NITRATE

OSHA regulates the handling and storage of ammonium nitrate in the
workplace due to the hazards it poses as an oxidizing agent and an explosion hazard. Ammonium nitrate can be in the form of crystals, flakes,
grains, or prills, including fertilizer grade, dynamite grade, nitrous-oxide
grade, technical grade, and other mixtures containing 60 percent or more
ammonium nitrate (USDOL 2004, 29 C.F.R. § 1910.109[i]). Ammonium
nitrate can be highly reactive with other types of materials. As a precaution, ammonium nitrate should be stored in a separate building or separated by approved-type fire walls of not less than one-hour fire-resistance
rating from organic chemicals, acids, other corrosive materials, materials
that may require blasting during processing or handling, compressed
flammable gases, flammable and combustible materials, or other contami-
nating substances, including but not limited to animal fats, baled cotton,
baled rags, baled scrap paper, bleaching powder, burlap or cotton bags,
caustic soda, coal, coke, charcoal, cork, camphor, excelsior, fibers of any
kind, fish oils, fish meal, foam rubber, hay, lubricating oil, linseed oil (or
other oxidizable or drying oil), naphthalene, oakum, oiled clothing, oiled
paper, oiled textiles, paint, straw, sawdust, wood shavings, or vegetable
oils (USDOL 2004, 29 C.F.R. § 1910.109[i]).

Additional materials for which precautions should be taken to avoid
mixing with ammonium nitrate include the following:

1. Flammable liquids such as gasoline, kerosene, solvents, and light fuel
   oils
2. Sulfur and finely divided metals
3. Explosives and blasting agents

Storage Bins for Ammonium Nitrate

Bins used for the storage of ammonium nitrate should meet applicable
OSHA standards to minimize the potential for fires and explosions due to

situations such as contamination of the ammonium nitrate and the accidental storage of ammonium nitrate with incompatible materials. Guidelines to follow when using bins to store ammonium nitrate include the following (USDOL 2004, 29 C.F.R. § 1910.109[i]):

1. Due to the corrosive and reactive properties of ammonium nitrate and to avoid contamination, galvanized iron, copper, lead, and zinc shall not be used in a bin construction unless suitably protected.
2. Aluminum bins and wooden bins protected against impregnation by ammonium nitrate are permissible.
3. The partitions dividing the ammonium nitrate storage from other products that would contaminate it shall be of tight construction.
4. The ammonium nitrate storage bins or piles shall be clearly identified by signs reading "AMMONIUM NITRATE" with letters at least 2 in. high.
5. Piles or bins shall be so sized and arranged that all material in the pile is moved out periodically in order to minimize possible caking of the stored ammonium nitrate.
6. In no case shall the ammonium nitrate be piled higher at any point than 36 in. below the roof or supporting and spreader beams overhead.

Storage of Ammonium Nitrate

OSHA standards for storing ammonium nitrate apply to facilities storing quantities of 1,000 lb. or more. Buildings used for the storage of ammonium nitrate must meet the following design standards (USDOL 2004, 29 C.F.R. § 1910.109[i]):

1. Provisions shall be made to prevent unauthorized personnel from entering the ammonium nitrate storage area.
2. Storage buildings shall have no basements, unless they are open on at least one side.
3. Storage buildings shall not be over one story in height.
4. Storage buildings shall have adequate ventilation or be of a construction that will be self-ventilating in the event of fire.
5. The wall on the exposed side of a storage building within 50 ft. of a combustible building, forest, pile of combustible materials, or similar exposure hazards shall be of fire-resistive construction. In lieu of the

fire-resistive wall, other suitable means of exposure protection, such as a freestanding wall, may be used.

6. The roof coverings shall meet applicable standards.

7. All flooring in storage and handling areas shall be of noncombustible material or protected against impregnation by ammonium nitrate and shall be without open drains, traps, tunnels, pits, or pockets into which any molten ammonium nitrate could flow and be confined in the event of fire.

8. Buildings and structures shall be dry and free from water seepage through the roof, walls, and floors.

9. Not more than twenty-five hundred tons of bagged ammonium nitrate shall be stored in a building or structure not equipped with an automatic sprinkler system.

Storage of Ammonium Nitrate in Bags, Drums, or Other Containers

To minimize the potential for fires and explosions involving ammonium nitrate materials stored in bags and drums, OSHA has adopted the following safety standards (USDOL 2004, 29 C.F.R. § 1910.109[i]):

1. Bags and containers used for ammonium nitrate must comply with specifications and standards required for use in interstate commerce.

2. Bags of ammonium nitrate shall not be stored within 30 in. of storage-building walls and partitions.

3. The height of piles shall not exceed 20 ft. The width of piles shall not exceed 20 ft., and the length shall not exceed 50 ft.; however, where the building is of noncombustible construction or is protected by automatic sprinklers, the length of piles shall not be limited. In no case shall the ammonium nitrate be stacked closer than 36 in. below the roof or supporting and spreader beams overhead.

4. Aisles shall be provided to separate piles by a clear space not less than 3 ft. in width. At least one service or main aisle in the storage area shall be not less than 4 ft. in width.

BOILING-LIQUID EXPANDING-VAPOR EXPLOSIONS

The phenomenon known as a boiling-liquid expanding-vapor explosion (BLEVE) is the result of a liquid within a container reaching a temperature well above its boiling point at atmospheric temperature, causing the vessel to rupture into two or more pieces (Duval 1998, 3). A BLEVE can occur when fire impinges on the liquefied-petroleum (LP) tank shell at a point or points above the liquid level of the contents of the LP tank (see figure 4.4). This impingement causes the metal to weaken and fail from the internal pressure (Duval 1998, 3). In a typical BLEVE, a tank of liquefied gas is engulfed in a fire. As the fire heats the tank, the fluid inside rises in temperature and pressure. The temperature of the liquid inside is now above its normal boiling point and is superheated with respect to the new pressure outside the tank. As the pressure is released from the tank, either through relief devices or tank failure, the liquid inside begins to boil. This boiling can tear the tank apart, hurling pieces hundreds of yards. If the fluid is flammable, it can ignite, forming a fireball. A vapor explosion results from the rapid and intense heat transfer that may follow contact between a hot liquid and a colder, more volatile one (Berthoud 2000).

Derailment of Toledo, Peoria, and Western Railroad Company's Train No. 20: Crescent City, Illinois

One of the best-known railroad incidents occurred in Crescent City, Illinois, in 1970, when ten tank cars carrying more than 34,000 gal.

FIGURE 4.4
A BLEVE fire

(128,700L) derailed (U.S. Fire Administration [USFA] 1973, 23). Train No. 20, an eastbound freight train of the Toledo, Peoria, and Western Railroad Company, consisting of a four-unit diesel-electric locomotive and 109 cars, derailed the twentieth to the thirty-fourth cars, inclusive, at the west switch of the siding in Crescent City at about 6:30 AM on June 21, 1970 (NTSB 1972, 3). During the derailment, one of the tank cars was punctured, and the leaking propane was immediately ignited, engulfing the other tank cars in the fire.

Included in the fifteen derailed cars were nine tank cars loaded with LP gas. Three BLEVEs resulted, generating enough force to blow people, railroad ballast, ties, and track into the street, destroying most of the business district and several homes (USFA 1973, 23). The National Transportation Safety Board determined that the probable cause of this accident was the breaking of the twentieth car, due to excessive overheating, which permitted the truck side to drop to the track and derail the leading wheels of the car; however, the cause of the overheating could not be determined. The cause of the initial fire was the puncturing of one tank during the derailment, the jumbling of the derailed cars, and the large volume of propane released, which immediately ignited and subjected the other tanks to impingement of fires. Despite the efforts of two hundred fifty firefighters and fifty-eight pieces of apparatus, sixty-four people were injured, twenty-four living quarters were destroyed, and 90 percent of the business district was wiped out.

DUST EXPLOSIONS

A dust explosion occurs when a combustible material is dispersed into the air, forming a cloud, and a flame propagates through it. In order for there to be a dust explosion, the following conditions must be met (Williamson 2002):

- The dust must be combustible.
- The dust must be capable of becoming airborne.
- The dust must have a size distribution capable of flame propagation.
- The dust concentration must be within the explosive range.
- An ignition source must be present.
- The atmosphere must contain sufficient oxygen to support and sustain combustion.

In chapter 3, electrical installations were shown to serve as an ignition source for dust explosions. Preventive measures for dust explosions include meeting the requirements for Class II, Division 1 and Division 2 hazardous locations, preventive maintenance on equipment in dust-prone areas of the facility, engineering controls to eliminate or reduce the development of dust in the workplace, and housekeeping measures to control dust buildup in and around equipment. Locations typically classified as Class II locations include grain elevators and grain-handling facilities (see figure 4.5).

CYLINDER FAILURES

The storage of gases in cylinders may pose two types of hazards: the combustion of the gas inside the cylinder or the combustion of the gas when released from the cylinder. A less frequent, but still significant, hazard of gas stored in containers is the danger of container failure due to overpressure resulting from the combustion of the gas while inside the container (NFPA 1997, 4–75). As a result, a combustion gas explosion occurs when the container is not strong enough to withstand the pressure generated by the combustion of the material. The most common situation resulting in a combustion explosion is the release of the flammable gas from the piping or container.

BOILERS AND UNFIRED PRESSURE VESSELS

A *pressure vessel* is a vessel in which pressure is obtained from an external source or by the application of heat from an indirect or direct source. The vessels may contain gases, vapors, and liquids at various pressures and temperatures. Pressure vessels can be classified as either fired or unfired pressure vessels. Fired pressure vessels use an external heat source to heat their contents, while unfired pressure vessels have no external heat source. Hazards associated with fired pressure vessels include fire hazards involving the fuel source, rupture or failure of the vessel, and explosion hazards. Hazards associated with unfired pressure vessels include the rupture or failure of the vessel and explosion hazards. Boilers can be further classified according to their heat source and operating temperatures. The following are the major classifications of boilers used in industry:

- *Electric boilers:* a power boiler, heating boiler, or high- or low-temperature water boiler in which the source of heat is electricity

FIGURE 4.5
Grain elevator

- *High-temperature water boiler:* a water boiler intended for operations at pressures in excess of 160 psig or temperatures in excess of 250°F
- *Hot-water heating boiler:* a boiler in which no steam is generated, from which hot water is circulated for heating purposes and then returned to the boiler and which operates at a pressure not exceeding 160 psig or a temperature of 250°F at the boiler outlet
- *Process steam generator:* a vessel or system of vessels comprising one or more drums and one or more heat-exchange surfaces as used in waste-heat- or heat-recovery-type steam boilers.
- *Unfired steam boiler:* a vessel or system of vessels intended for operation at a pressure in excess of 15 psig for the purpose of producing and controlling an output of thermal energy
- *Water-heater supply boiler:* a closed vessel in which water is heated by combustion of fuels, electricity, or any other source and withdrawn for use external to the system at a pressure not exceeding 160 psig and which should include all controls and devices necessary to prevent water temperatures from exceeding 210°F

Proper construction, maintenance, and testing of the pressure vessels are ways to prevent some of the accidents associated with these types of equipment. Currently, there is no one specific standard for pressure vessels; however, some OSHA standards require that a pressure vessel be built in accordance with the industry codes and standards. Sections of the ASME Boiler and Pressure Vessel Code include material specifications, specifications for heating boilers, nondestructive testing of boilers, and recommended rules for care and operation and for inspection procedures after installation and repairs. The National Board of Boiler and Pressure Vessel Inspectors comprises the chief inspectors of jurisdictions. This board has developed its national inspection code, the *National Board Inspection Code* (2004), commonly referred to as the "NB code."

To ensure adequate operation of the boiler and to reduce the likelihood of fires and explosions, building owners should follow a prescribed boiler-inspection program. The inspections should be conducted by a qualified person on a regular basis and should include both internal and external inspections. The external inspection should involve as complete an examination as can be reasonably made of the external surfaces and safety devices while the boiler or pressure vessel is in operation. The internal inspection should involve as complete an examination as can be reasonably made of the internal surfaces of the boiler or pressure vessel while it is shut down and while manhole plates and handhole plates are removed as required by the inspector.

Safety appliances found on a boiler include but are not be limited to the following (NSC 1992, 97–98):

1. *Rupture disk device:* a nonreclosing pressure-relief device actuated by inlet static pressure and designed to function by the bursting of a pressure-containing disk
2. *Safety relief valve:* an automatic pressure-relieving device actuated by a static pressure upstream of the valve, which opens further with the increase in pressure over the opening pressure
3. *Temperature limit control:* a control that ensures boiler is operating within acceptable temperature ranges
4. *Low-water cutoffs:* an indicator of when water levels in the boiler have gotten to a low level that shuts down heat source to the boiler
5. *Flame supervisory unit (igniter):* a control that checks to ensure the gas is burning and prevents the accumulation of gas in a room
6. *High- and low-gas-pressure switches:* switches that monitor gas pressure going into boiler
7. *Trial for ignition limiting timer (fifteen seconds):* a timer that checks to ensure that the gas has been ignited and prevents the accumulation of gas in a room

BOILER MAINTENANCE

Most of the boiler failures are due to inadequate maintenance. Inspections of pressure vessels have shown that there is a considerable number of cracked and damaged vessels in workplaces. Cracked and damaged vessels can result in leakage or rupture failures. Potential health and safety hazards of leaking vessels include poisonings, suffocations, fires, and explosion hazards. Rupture failures can be much more catastrophic and can cause considerable damage to life and property. Safe design, installation, operation, and maintenance of pressure vessels in accordance with the appropriate codes and standards are essential to worker safety and health.

Boiler tests should be conducted according to manufacturers' recommendations and applicable codes. Blow-down piping and valves are to remove sludge and other impurities in the boiler water that, if not removed, would seriously impede the efficiency and safety of the boiler (Insurance Institute of America 1990, 44). Tests and inspections should be recorded in a boiler log. When alterations, retrofits, or repairs are necessary on a boiler, they should be made so that the object is at least as safe as the original construction. Alterations, retrofits, and repairs should be done as though they were new construction and should comply with the applicable code or codes. Repairs or alterations by welding should be approved beforehand by an authorized inspector. All welding repairs or alterations must be in accordance with the standards for repairs and alterations to boilers and pressure vessels by welding of the NB code. All welding should be done by a qualified organization.

The design, construction, and maintenance of the boiler room itself play a role in the prevention of boiler fires and explosions. Boiler rooms should be constructed according to building codes ensuring that walls and doors meet applicable fire ratings. Fire protection should be provided. All objects in the boiler room should be located so that adequate space is provided for the proper operation and inspection and the necessary maintenance and repair of the boiler and its controls. An adequate number of exits should be provided. The exits should be clear of obstructions. Ventilation should be provided for the room to permit satisfactory combustion of fuel and ventilation if necessary under normal operations. The minimum ventilation for coal, gas, or oil burners in rooms containing objects is based on the Btus per hour, required air, and louvered area.

CHAPTER QUESTIONS

1. Describe the mechanics of a BLEVE.
2. What is an oxidizer?
3. What are four ways one can prevent boiler explosions?
4. What is an explosion?
5. Describe some of the safety precautions one must take when transporting explosives.
6. Define the various classes of oxidizers.
7. Describe some of the safety precautions one must take when handling ammonium nitrate.
8. Describe some of the more common safety devices found on boilers.
9. Describe some of the safety precautions one must take when using explosives.

REFERENCES

Berthoud, Georges. (2000). Vapor Explosions. *Annual Review of Fluid Mechanics,* *32*: 573–611.

Duval, Robert. (1998). *NFPA Alert Bulletin No: 98-1. LP-Gas BLEVES Result in Fire Fighter Fatalities.* NFPA: Quincy, MA.

Insurance Institute of America. (1990). *Readings in Property Protection.* Malvern, PA: Insurance Institute of America.

National Board of Boiler and Pressure Vessel Inspectors. (2004). *National Board Inspection Code.* Columbus, OH: National Board of Boiler and Pressure Vessel Inspectors.

National Fire Protection Association (NFPA). (1997). *Fire Protection Handbook,* 18th ed. Quincy, MA: NFPA.

NFPA. (1995). *NFPA 430: Code for the Storage of Liquid and Solid Oxidizers.* Quincy, MA: NFPA.

National Safety Council (NSC). (1997). *Accident Prevention Manual for Business and Industry: Engineering and Technology.* Itasca, IL: NSC.

National Transportation Safety Board (NTSB). (1972). *Derailment of Toledo, Peoria and Western Railroad Company's Train No. 20 with Resultant Fire and Tank Car Ruptures, Crescent City, Illinois, June 21, 1970.* NTSB Report Number RAR-72-02, adopted on March 29, 1972.

Occupational Safety and Health Administration (OSHA). (2004). Available at www.osha.gov (accessed June 22, 2005).

Schnepp, Rob, and Paul Gantt. (1999). *Hazardous Materials: Regulations, Response, and Site Operations.* New York: Delmar Publishers.

U.S. Department of Labor. (2004). *Occupational Safety and Health Standards for General Industry, Subpart H: Hazardous Materials, Explosives and Blasting Agents, 29 C.F.R. § 1910.109.* Washington, DC: USDOL.

U.S. Department of Transportation (USDOT). (2003). *Hazardous Materials Regulations: Definitions, 49 C.F.R. § 173.50.* Washington, DC: USDOT.

USDOT. (2003). *Hazardous Materials Regulations: Explosives Placards, 49 C.F.R. § 172.522.* Washington, DC: USDOT.

U.S. Fire Administration. (1973). *America Burning.* Washington, DC: National Commission on Fire Prevention and Control.

Williamson, George. (2002). *Industrial Dust Explosions,* available at www.chemeng.ed.ac.uk/~emju49/SP2001/webpage/index.html (accessed June 22, 2005).

5

Building Construction

The primary reason for studying building construction is that fire protection begins during the preplanning phase of any new building design or remodeling. Construction can affect fire and smoke spread, life safety, and the extent of fire damage that will occur within the building. A well-designed building will consider flame and fire spread, life safety, and smoke spread during the preplanning stage so that construction materials and design features can be selected to reduce or eliminate potential exposures. There are far too many instances of fatalities that have occurred because of the failure to recognize life-safety concerns and fire and smoke spread as they relate to overall building fire safety (Brannigan 1999, 9). Fire in buildings adds to the fire problem for the following reasons (Brannigan 1971 3):

1. The building itself may burn.
2. The contents of the building may be ignited.
3. Occupants of the building may be trapped by the fire.
4. The building structure may make it difficult to attack the fire.
5. The building may collapse in whole or part during the fire.
6. The fire may extend beyond the original point of origin to other buildings.
7. Firefighters may be injured or killed.

BASIC TERMINOLOGY
Some basic terminology needs to be understood when discussing building construction. The following terms provide a better understanding of the concepts in this chapter:

- *Fire resistance* refers to the ability of the material or assembly to resist the effects of the heat and flame from the fire. Therefore, fire-resistant construction would reduce the ease of ignition and flame spread of the building structure (Ladwig 1991, 95). It is equally important to understand that fire resistance is not specifically directed at life safety, smoke control, or dollar losses from a fire (Brannigan 1999, 245).
- *Flame spread* refers to the rate at which a fire will spread from the point of origin to involve an ever-increasing area of combustible material (Ladwig 1991, 373).
- *Noncombustible material* is a material that in the form in which it is used and under the conditions anticipated will not ignite, burn, support combustion, or release flammable vapors when subjected to fire or heat (Brannigan 1999, 41).
- *Dead load* is the weight of the building itself and any equipment permanently attached to or built on the building (Brannigan 1999, 16).
- *Fire load* is the total amount of potential heat in the fuel available to a fire within the building (Brannigan 1999, 29).
- *Safety factor* is the ratio of the strength of a material prior to failure to the safe working stress. For example, a safety factor of ten will occur if the design load is only a tenth of the tested strength (Brannigan 1999, 49).

STRUCTURAL ELEMENTS

In a building fire, three separate elements can be identified (Brannigan 1971, 7):

1. The structural element of the building. A structural element is a member that, if removed, will affect the structural stability of the building.
2. The contents of the building.
3. The nonstructural building elements. These include surface finishes, windows, interior vertical openings, decorative surfaces, air-conditioning systems, and the like.

The major structural elements involved with industrial building construction include beams, columns, trusses, and connectors. A *beam* is defined as a structural element that transmits force in a perpendicular direction to the points of support and is usually thought of as a horizontal member (although this is not always the case) (Brannigan 1999, 52). For example, a *rafter* is structurally a beam that is positioned vertically or diagonally. When a beam is loaded, it deflects or bends downward, with the initial load of its own deadweight plus any additional live load applied. Because of this fact, beams are built with a slight camber so that when the design load is superimposed, the beam will be level. The capacity of a beam increases by the square of its depth as well as the length of the span of the beam. Specifically, the load capacity decreases in direct proportion to increases in span length (Brannigan 1999, 55). There are various types of beams. A simple beam is supported at two points. With simple beam construction, the load is delivered to the two end points, and the rest of the structure renders no assistance in cases of overload. When these two end points are rigidly held in place, the beam is referred to as a *fixed beam*. A *continuous beam* is one that is supported at three or more points. A *girder* is any beam that supports other beams, while a *joist* is one of a series of parallel beams of timber, reinforced concrete, or steel used to support the floor and ceiling loads (Brannigan 1999, 56).

A *column* is a structural member that transmits a compressive force along a straight path in the direction of the member. Columns are typically thought of as vertical structural members, but typically any structural member that is compressively loaded is a column. A *strut* is an example of a nonvertical column (Brannigan 1999, 61). The capacity of a column decreases by the square of the change in column length. For example, a 10-ft. column with a capacity of 10,000 lb. would have a capacity of only 2,500 lb. if its length were increased to 20 ft.

Walls transmit to the ground the compressive forces applied or received at any point on the wall, with the primary function of exterior walls being to protect the interior of the building from the elements (NFPA 1997, 7–18). Walls are classified into two major divisions: *load bearing* or *non–load bearing*. A load-bearing wall carries a load of some part of the structure in addition to the weight of the wall itself. Non-load-bearing walls support their own weight only. There are various types of walls based on their functions. Examples include the following (NFPA 1997, 7–18):

- A *fire wall* is a wall of sufficient fire resistance and stability to withstand the effects of a fire and remain standing despite the possible collapse of the structural framework.

- A *partition wall* is a one-story, interior wall that separates two areas in a building but is not a fire barrier.
- A *curtain wall* is an exterior wall that is supported by the structural frame of the building.

A *truss* is a framework of members that restrains the building through triangular formations. Use of trusses is very common with roof supports. However, where large areas may be column free or where special occupancy requirements may warrant, trusses may be used for purposes other than roof support (NFPA 1997, 7–26).

Connectors transfer the load from one structural element to another and are a very important part of evaluating a building's fire resistance. A building is said to be *pinned* when the elements are connected by simple connectors such as bolts, rivets, or welded joints. In a rigid-frame building, the connectors are strong enough to reroute forces if a member is removed. Connectors are often the weakest link in the structural assembly and are a critical component of structural stability during a fire (Brannigan 1999, 80).

CHARACTERISTICS OF BUILDING MATERIALS

Buildings are constructed of a variety of building materials, each of which influences how that building will be affected during a fire situation. Each material, even different forms of the same material, has certain physical and chemical characteristics that make it more or less desirable for its intended function (Brannigan 1999, 33). All materials can be damaged by fire even if they do not burn because all structural materials used in building construction are adversely affected by the elevated temperatures caused by a fire. The degree and significance of this adverse behavior depend primarily on the function of the elements and the degree of protection afforded. In general, the mechanical properties of strength and stiffness decrease as the temperature rises. Other adverse behavior, such as excessive expansion and accelerated creep, also develop with increases in temperatures. Characteristics of common building materials can greatly influence their structural behavior in a fire.

Steel

In commercial construction, steel is the most common material used, especially with regard to the structure of the building (see figure 5.1). Steel

FIGURE 5.1
Structural steel

is noncombustible and does not contribute fuel to a fire. However, structural steel does have three characteristics that affect its performance when exposed to a fire. The first characteristic is that steel conducts heat, thereby aiding heat transfer. The second is its coefficient of expansion at elevated temperatures. This high coefficient of expansion affects the steel structure because the ends of the structural member are axially restrained and the attempted expansion due to the heat causes thermal stresses to be transferred to the member. This stress, combined with those of normal loading, can cause a quicker collapse. The last characteristic is that steel will lose its strength when subjected to high temperatures. The critical temperature of steel is 1,100°F, at which time its yield stress, or the point at which the steel will fail, is about 60 percent of its value at room temperature (Cote and Bugbee 2001, 149).

The above three characteristics can create serious problems during a fire, with the relative seriousness depending on four factors: (1) the function of the steel element, (2) its level of stress, (3) how the steel member is supported to other structural members, and (4) its surface area and thickness. From a structural viewpoint, the yield stress of steel is the most significant parameter in establishing its load-carrying capacity. Both yield strength and the modulus of elasticity decrease with increasing temperatures.

Due to the fact that unprotected structural steel loses its strength at higher temperatures, it must be protected from the higher temperatures produced during a fire. Often this protection is accomplished by fireproofing that insulates the steel from the heat. The most common methods of insulating steel are to encase the structural steel member or to apply a surface treatment (NFPA 1997, 7–64).

Wood

Wood is combustible, and as it burns, it loses its structural integrity. The important factors that influence the fire endurance of wood are its physical size and its moisture content. As the moisture content in wood increases, so does its ignition temperature, and overall fire spread is reduced. In most cases, the burning of wood produces a charcoal on its surface, which provides a protective coating that insulates the unburned wood from the flame and therefore reduces flame spread (NFPA 1997,

7–70). Because of this fact, heavy timber members (large dimensions) provide much greater structural integrity over the same period of fire exposure than lighter members. It has become increasingly difficult to harvest timbers of such large dimensions, making the use of glued, laminated frames and beams increasingly popular in construction today. These manufactured heavy-timber members also provide reserve strength during a fire and reduce flame spread. Wood-frame construction, which is common in residential construction, utilizes structural members that are considerably smaller than heavy-timber construction; therefore, the fire resistance is considerably reduced. When this type of wood is exposed to fire, it offers little structural integrity, and the fire spreads very quickly, hence its common name "quick burning." Figure 5.2 depicts wood-frame construction.

Fire-retardant treatments may delay ignition and retard combustion when applied to wood. A common fire-retardant treatment of wood is to impregnate the wood with mineral salts. It is important to note that this treatment will reduce the wood's flame spread, but the wood is still combustible.

FIGURE 5.2
Wood-frame construction

Masonry and Brick

Masonry and brick products are quite fire resistant, but they can spall when subjected to elevated temperatures from a fire. With spalling, there is a loss of the surface of the brick and other masonry products. Hollow concrete blocks also generally retain their structural integrity when exposed to a fire but can crack at elevated temperatures. An important consideration regarding the stability of a nonload-bearing masonry or brick wall is the supporting structure of the wall. A steel or wood structure for such a wall could be damaged from a fire, putting the wall at risk of collapse.

Reinforced Concrete

Reinforced concrete is a composite material where steel rods are placed in the concrete. This composite material allows concrete, which naturally has compressive strength, to be combined with steel to provide excellent tensile strength (see figure 5.3). The type of aggregate used in this reinforced concrete, its moisture content, and the fire loading will determine the member's fire resistance. When exposed to a fire, however, the concrete and steel bond can fail, which can result in failures of the reinforced member, as well as spalling and some loss of strength. However, as a general rule, reinforced concrete is very fire resistant, and it is rare to encounter the collapse of a reinforced concrete structure that has been exposed to a fire (NFPA 1997, 7–68).

Gypsum

Gypsum products are very common in construction and include such products as plasterboard and plaster, both of which have overall excellent fire-resistive properties. These properties exist because gypsum has a high portion of chemically combined water, and when it is exposed to a fire, the evaporation of this water requires a great deal of heat energy (Bugbee and Cote 2001, 151).

FIRE-RESISTANCE RATINGS

Fire-resistive barriers are evaluated in testing furnaces by exposure to a fire whose severity follows a time-varying temperature curve known as the *standard time-temperature curve*. The curve was adopted by the American Society for Testing and Materials (ASTM) in 1918 and has been the basis

FIGURE 5.3
Concrete reinforcing steel

for almost all fire-resistance testing ever since. Building materials are provided a rating on their ability to resist the effects of fire without failure, which is typically expressed in hours. Tests used to evaluate the fire resistance of material include Underwriters Laboratories 263: "Fire Tests of Building Construction and Materials," ASTM E119: "Methods of Fire Tests of Building Construction and Materials," and NFPA 251: Standard Methods of Tests of Fire Endurance of Building Construction and Materials (NFPA 2002b, § 2-1). These fire-resistance tests contain detailed test procedures, a guide on the restraint required, if any, and a suggested format for reporting results. The standards also specify the preparation and conditioning of the test specimen and acceptance criteria, which are specific to the element tested. In general, the test continues until failure, which may include any of the following (NFPA 1997, 7–51):

- Failure of test specimen to support a load
- Temperature increase on unexposed surface of 250°F above ambient
- Passage of heat or flame sufficient to ignite cotton waste
- Excess temperature on steel members
- Failure of walls and partitions under hose stream

Information on a building material's fire-resistance rating is available from a variety of sources such as the UL Fire Resistance Directory and Building-Materials Directory. The Fire Resistance Directory provides hourly ratings for a variety of building components, such as beams, columns, and floors. The Building Materials Directory contains a listing and classification for various building materials based on flame-spread ratings (Ladwig 1991, 96).

MAJOR TYPES OF BUILDING CONSTRUCTION
The construction of a building has a significant influence on its fire and life safety and capabilities (NFPA 1997, 7–3). Building construction for life safety includes the layout of the facility, the traffic-flow patterns of the occupants, the types of construction materials used, and their fire-resistance ratings. The design of the facility can aid in preventing the fires from occurring and, once they do, limit the spread of the fire through containment. The NFPA has developed a classification system for building types. All buildings and structures shall be classified according to their type of

construction, which shall be based on one of five basic types of construction designated by Roman numerals as Type I to V, with approved fire-resistance ratings. Table 5.1 illustrates the fire resistance for each of the five types of building construction discussed above and described in NFPA 5000: Building Construction and Safety Code (NFPA 2003b).

Type I buildings, commonly called fire resistive, have structural members such as the frame, walls, floors, and roof that are all noncombustible with a minimum specified fire-resistive rating. In general, these Type I buildings will withstand fire for several hours without structural failure. There are two subclassifications within Type I: Type 443 and Type 332. The basic difference between these two subclassifications is the level of fire resistance specified for the structural frame (NFPA 1997, 7–14). Type I buildings are the best type of construction from a fire-safety perspective, with common building materials used in their construction being concrete, steel, and masonry.

Type II is a construction type in which the structural elements are made entirely of noncombustible or limited-combustible materials, hence the common name noncombustible. Although the building materials are noncombustible, they do not have a sufficient fire-resistance rating to be classified as fire resistant. When exposed to a fire, the structure will not burn or contribute fuel to a fire involving contents, but it can collapse due to structural steel failure. Common building materials include metal frame and metal clad, as well as steel, masonry, aluminum, and mineral fiber. There are three subclassifications of Type II construction. The first subclassification is *Type 222*. With this subclassification, the exterior bearing walls, interior bearing walls, columns, and beams have a two-hour fire resistance. The next subclassification is *Type 111*. With this subclassification, the exterior bearing walls, interior bearing walls, columns, beams, and girders have a one-hour fire resistance. The third subclassification within Type II is *Type 000*, and as the name would imply, this subclassification has exterior bearing walls, interior bearing walls, columns, and girders with no fire resistance (NFPA 1997, 7–15).

Type III, which is commonly called *ordinary construction*, is a construction type where the exterior walls are noncombustible with a minimum two-hour fire resistance, but the interior is constructed of combustible materials. The interior construction is typically made of wood joist and studs; therefore, the entire interior is easily destroyed by fire. Type III con-

Table 5.1 Fire Resistance Ratings for Type I through Type V Construction (hour)

	Type I		Type II			Type III		Type IV	Type V	
	442	332	222	111	000	211	200	2HH	111	000
Exterior bearing walls										
Supporting more than one floor, columns, or other bearing walls	4	3	2	1	0b	2	2	2	1	0b
Supporting one floor only	4	3	2	1	0b	2	2	2	1	0b
Supporting a roof only	4	3	1	1	0b	2	2	2	1	0b
Interior bearing walls										
Supporting more than one floor, columns, or other bearing walls	4	3	2	1	0	1	0	2	1	0
Supporting one floor only	3	2	2	1	0	1	0	1	1	0
Supporting roofs only	3	2	1	1	0	1	0	1	1	0
Columns										
Supporting more than one floor, columns, or other bearing walls	4	3	2	1	0	1	0	H	1	0
Supporting one floor only	3	2	2	1	0	1	0	H	1	0
Supporting roofs only	3	2	1	1	0	1	0	H	1	0
Beams, girders, trusses, and arches										
Supporting more than one floor, columns, or other bearing walls	4	3	2	1	0	1	0	H	1	0
Supporting one floor only	2	2	2	1	0	1	0	H	1	0
Supporting roofs only	2	2	1	1	0	1	0	H	1	0
Floor construction	2	2	2	1	0	1	0	H	1	0
Roof construction	2	1.5	1	1	0	1	0	H	1	0
Interior nonbearing walls	0	0	0	0	0	0	0	0	0	0
Exterior nonbearing walls	0b	0b	0b	0b	0b	0b	0b	0b	0b	0b

Note: H = heavy timber members (see text for requirements).
Source: National Fire Protection Association 2003, *NFPA 5000 Building Construction and Safety Code*.

struction is further divided into two subclassifications. Type 211 has a one-hour fire resistance for the floors and structural elements, while Type 200 has no fire resistance for floors and structural elements (NFPA 1997, 7–15).

Type IV is a construction type in which structural members are basically of unprotected wood with large cross-sectional areas, hence the common name of plank, timber, or mill construction. Bearing walls, bearing portions of walls, and exterior walls must be noncombustible and have at least a two-hour rating. NFPA 200 specifies the minimum size of the heavy timber; for instance, columns must be 8″ × 8″ when supporting floors, wooden floors must be a minimum of 3-in. tongue and groove, and wooden roofs must be a minimum of 2-in. tongue and groove (NFPA 2002b, 5–6). Characteristics of Type IV construction include slow burning with poor heat conduction; for that reason, they are sometimes superior to steel construction of the same load capacity. Although a few large trees of the necessary dimensions exist today, it is not uncommon to see wood laminates being used to provide such structural dimensions today.

Type V construction is a construction type where exterior walls and structural members are primarily made of wood or other combustible materials. As one might expect, Type V construction provides the lowest degree of fire protection. An example is a wood-frame residential home with 2″ × 4″ wood studs, wood siding, wood floors, and a wood roof. Type V construction is subdivided into two subclassifications: Type 111 which has a one-hour fire resistance throughout, including the exterior walls, and Type 000, which has no fire-resistance requirements (NFPA 1997, 7–16).

As one might expect, mixed types of construction are common, and where two or more types of construction are used, it is generally recognized that the requirements for occupancy, size restrictions, or fire protection for the least fire-resistant type of construction will apply. It should be noted, however, that in those cases where each building type is separated by adequate fire walls or area separation walls having appropriate fire resistance, each area may be considered as a separate building (NFPA 1997, 7–17).

FIRE-PROTECTION FEATURES

Fire protection of building elements is provided for two reasons: (1) to prevent the spread of fire within or into the building during an uncontrolled fire, and (2) to ensure that, even under that exposure, the building frame or elements of that frame will not collapse (NFPA 1997, 7–17). Occupant protection in today's buildings improves the safety of people by slowing the spread of smoke and flames. Compartmentation limits the size of the fire. The goals of room compartmentation in confining a fire to the room or suite of rooms of origin are to generally segregate a space with a higher level of fire hazard than the surrounding area and to minimize the risk of loss to an occupant of one space as a result of a fire in a space controlled by another. The most common failure of compartmentation is that a door is left open.

Fire Spread

Fire spread rarely occurs as a result of heat transfer through or structural failure of walls and floor-ceiling assemblies. Important building features that can affect the spread of fire include fire walls, fire doors, fire stops, baffels, fire dampers, and parapets. Fire spread on the inside of a building can occur through one or more of the following methods (Patterson 1993, 11):

1. From occupancy compartment to occupancy compartment
2. Through channels, or void spaces, within the structure
3. Along the outside surface of the building

The common path for flame spread in a building is through open doors, unenclosed stairways and shafts, and unprotected penetrations of fire barriers. Common reasons why fire barriers fail to contain a fire in a building include the following (NFPA 1997, 7–82):

1. *Early failure:* door not closed, opening not protected
2. *Random failure:* faults in the materials or construction
3. *Degradation failure:* wear out of the materials

Factors that influence the spread of fires along the outside of a building include the height of the building, the size and dimension of window openings, and air-flow patterns along the outside of the building.

When properly constructed and maintained, barriers will normally contain fires of the maximum expected severity in light-hazard occupancies. Fire can spread horizontally and vertically from the point of origin through spaces and compartments that do not contain combustibles. This is typical in extended flame movement under noncombustible ceilings, up exterior walls, and through noncombustible vertical openings. This is how fire most commonly travels down corridors and up open stairway shafts. Once a room becomes involved, a fire can travel quickly to adjacent rooms in the absence of fire-separation barriers. Floor-to-floor flame spread is not very common but can occur.

The basic technique to prevent unlimited spread of a fire within a building is to arrange the interior spaces into compartments (Patterson 1993, 11). When designing the building, the fire-resistive qualities of the compartments can be determined. The fire rating of the construction can be achieved through the use of specified building materials and the elimination of openings in the barriers.

Flames can spread in buildings through various spaces and openings. Fires can spread through concealed spaces behind walls, above suspended ceilings, and in utility chases and attics. Fires in concealed spaces burn out of site of the occupants, and detection is usually delayed. Manual fighting of these fires can be very difficult as well.

Unprotected vertical openings have been responsible for many large loss-of-life fires. Vertical sealed spaces act as flues to spread smoke and gases. The products of fire flow upward, then mushroom out horizontally. The following building-design features can prevent or reduce this vertical and horizontal fire spread: fire stops, baffles, fire dampers, parapets, and fire walls.

Fire stops are an important consideration in building design because they act as physical barriers that provide a specific fire resistance and prevent fire and smoke from spreading through concealed horizontal and vertical spaces. Examples may include heating ventilation and air-conditioning, holes and openings in floors, and elevator shafts.

Baffles are physical barriers that are fire resistant and extend between girders and the roof to prevent the spread of fire under the roof. Baffles also play an important role in containing smoke and aid in venting smoke out of the building.

Fire dampers are hinged panels placed inside heating, ventilation, and air-conditioning ducts. When activated, these fire dampers automatically close, reducing the spread of smoke and gases through the system.

Parapets are extensions of an exterior load-bearing wall above the roof. Typically these are at least 36 in. above the roofline, and their primary purpose is to reduce the spread of fire from adjacent buildings, especially in urban areas where buildings are close together.

Fire walls prevent the spread of fire to other adjacent areas. Typically, a fire wall will have a minimum three-hour fire resistance, extend from the foundation through the roof, and have as few openings as possible. Any openings in a fire wall must be protected. Fire walls must maintain their structural stability under fire exposure for their rated duration. Freestanding fire walls are most commonly used in one- and two-story industrial buildings. A freestanding wall is entirely self-supporting and is not directly connected to the building framing. A common example of an opening in a fire wall would be a door opening; therefore, all openings in fire walls should be protected by fire doors.

PROTECTION OF OPENINGS IN FIRE WALLS

Openings in fire walls present a path for smoke, heat, and flames to travel to other areas of an occupancy and therefore must be protected. However, the protection for openings is generally less than that provided by the wall itself. The reasoning behind this is as follows (NFPA 1997, 7–86):

1. Easily ignitable materials are not normally found against doors or other openings in a wall.
2. Fire-extinguishing forces usually extinguish small localized fires that may spread past the wall.

Fire doors, windows, and shutters are the most acceptable means of protecting openings in fire-resistive walls (NFPA 1997, 7–86). The NFPA classifies fire doors based on their fire-resistance rating. The best doors, in terms of fire-resistance rating, are four- and three-hour fire doors. Four- and three-hour fire doors are required in openings in walls separating buildings or dividing a building into different fire areas. Most current codes require only a three-hour fire door when separation walls are required to have a three-hour resistance or more. However, some local municipalities require two three-hour doors, one on each side of the opening, or one four-hour door whenever a wall is required to have a fire resistance of four hours (NFPA 1997, 7–87).

Fire doors with 1.5-hour ratings are required for openings in two-hour enclosures protecting vertical openings, such as stairwells, in buildings. Many codes also permit the use of 1.5-hour fire doors to protect openings in walls separating buildings or dividing buildings into different fire areas when walls are only required to have a fire resistance of 2 hours. Openings in exterior walls that can be subjected to severe fire exposures from outside the building are also commonly protected by 1.5-hour fire doors (NFPA 1997, 7–87).

One-hour fire doors are used for openings in one-hour enclosures or vertical openings in buildings such as stairs and shafts. Forty-five-minute fire doors are commonly used in openings in exterior walls subject to a moderate or light fire exposure from outside the building. These forty-five-minute doors are also used in openings in room partitions and walls around some hazardous areas and are also sometimes permitted in partitions that subdivide the floors of a building. Thirty-minute and twenty-minute fire doors are primarily used for smoke control only (NFPA 1997, 7–87).

IMPACT OF VENTILATION ON BUILDING FIRES AND SMOKE MOVEMENT

The burning rates of materials depend upon the available fuel surface area or the air available for combustion. When ample air is available, the burning rate of fire depends upon the exposed surface area and the properties of the combustible material itself. This is its fuel-surface-controlled rate. When a fire cannot get enough air, it will burn at its ventilation-controlled rate.

Most, if not all, building fires burn at their ventilation-controlled rate at least during the time when containment is possible (NFPA 1997, 7–81). For a fire to burn at its fuel-surface-controlled rate, adequate air must be present. In a $20' \times 20'$ room with an 8-ft. ceiling, more than one-quarter of the wall area must be open to create a fuel-surface-controlled-rate fire (NFPA 1997, 7–81).

Ventilation can also play an important role in the movement and transfer of smoke throughout a building. As mentioned, smoke is the leading cause of death in fires. Therefore, managing smoke in a fire is important for minimizing deaths due to inhalation of toxic fumes and to aid in firefighting efficiency. In terms of ventilation, smoke management aims to do the following (Cote and Bugbee 2001, 160):

1. Maintain means of egress in a useable condition
2. Contain smoke in the environment
3. Maintain a condition outside of the fire area that will assist fire suppression
4. Assist with the protection of life and reduce property damage

INTERIOR FINISH

An important consideration in building construction is the *interior finish*. NFPA 101 § 3.3.112 defines interior finish as those materials or assemblies of materials that form the exposed interior surface of walls and ceilings in a building (NFPA 2003a, 101–29). Examples of interior finish materials include wood, wood paneling, drywall, plastics, fibrous ceiling tiles, and wall coverings. The types of materials used on the interior surfaces of a building, such as floors, ceilings, and wall finishes can have a tremendous influence on smoke and toxic-gas generation and flame spread. Flame spread can simply be described as the speed at which the interior of the building can become involved once ignition has taken place. The most widely used test for flame spread is the Steiner Tunnel Test, which is included within NFPA 255: Standard Method of Test of Surface Burning Characteristics of Building Materials (ASTM E84). This test attempts to stimulate the spread of fire across a plane surface, where radiant heating of the sample from an external heat flux is applied (NFPA 1997, 4–7). Materials are tested based on two reference points for flame spread: asbestos cement board has a value of 0 and red oak has a value of 100. Interior finishes are categorized as Class A, B, and C. *Class A* materials have a flame spread rating from 0 to 25 and are the best in terms of flame spread; in other words, the flame does not propagate as far with these materials as it would with the other classes of materials. *Class B* materials have a flame spread index from 26 to 75, and Class C has a rating from 76 to 200 (Cote and Bugbee 2001, 152).

Interior finish is also important due to its potential for smoke contribution. It is important not only to understand how much smoke is being generated but also to determine if the smoke contains any toxic gases. The interior finish can also increase the combustible load within a building and, thereby, increase the intensity of the fire. One last thing to consider with regard to the fire hazard of interior finish is the combustibility of any adhesive or vapor seals used to apply the interior finish. In some cases the adhesive used can greatly increase the flame spread of the basic interior-finish material (NFPA 1997, 7–37).

BUILDING CONTENTS

In 1973, the U.S. Fire Administration (USFA) found that in terms of design and materials, the environment in which Americans live and work presents unnecessary hazards. The hazards of flames have been studied and regulated to some extent, but recognition of the hazards of smoke and toxic gases came belatedly. The USAF's report *America Burning: The Report of the National Commission on Fire Prevention and Control* recommended that the impact of new materials, systems, and buildings on users and the community should be assessed during the design stages, well before use (1973, ix). However, more than thirty years later, the toxic gases evolved from burning contents and the increased fire loads they create still play a significant role in the extent of fire deaths in the United States.

FIRE LOADING

A relationship has been established between the severity of a fire and its fire load. The fire load is used to predict the fire severity anticipated for various occupancies. It is used to determine the resistance required of fire barriers as well as structural components.

The fire load in a building is the total number of British thermal units that might evolve during a fire in the building or area under consideration and the rate at which the heat will evolve (Brannigan 1971, 27). Fire load is measured as the maximum heat that would be released if all combustibles in a given fire area burned. In a typical building, fire load includes combustible contents, interior floor finishes, and structural elements. Fire load is commonly expressed in terms of the average fire load, which is the equivalent combustible weight divided by the fire area in square feet. *Equivalent combustible weight* is defined as the weight of ordinary combustibles having a heat of combustion of 8,000 Btu per pound that would release the same amount of heat as the combustibles in the room. However, because the fire loads of materials can vary greatly, when estimating the fire load of combustible contents, it is common practice to convert all materials to a "wood equivalent"(Patterson 1993, 6). Table 5.2 illustrates the wood equivalents for selected types of typical building materials (Patterson 1993, 6).

Table 5.2   Wood Equivalents for Selected Types of Building Materials

	Caloric Values	
Materials	BTU/Lb	Lb wood/lb material
Acrylic	11,200	1.40
Coal	13,300	1.66
Nylon	10,000	1.25
Paper	7,000	0.88
Polyester	10,000	1.25
Polyurethane	16,000	2.00
Straw	6,000	0.75

For example, to determine the fire load for an object, 1 lb./sq. ft. of polyurethane releases 16,000 Btu's; 10 lb. of polyurethane releases 160,000 Btu/sq. ft; and 160,000 Btu/sq. ft. per 8,000 Btu/sq. ft. (the ordinary combustible equivalent) yields a fire load of 20 lb./sq. ft.

Although fire load is a representation of the latent energy available in a fire, it is not the complete indication of the severity of a potential fire. The rate at which the fire will progress and the rate at which heat will be released are dependent upon a more comprehensive set of conditions. These include the following (Patterson 1993, 6):

1. The fire load, determined by the nature of the fuel and the amount of the fuel
2. The arrangement of the fuel
3. The size and shape of the room or compartment containing the fire
4. The area and shape of the windows
5. Thermal insulation on the walls and ceiling

OCCUPANCY AND COMMODITY CLASSIFICATIONS

In addition to building construction, it is also important to understand occupancy and commodity classifications because of their potential impact on fire spread. Occupancy and commodity classifications provide a convenient means for categorizing the fuel loads and fire severity associated with certain building operations. The proper occupancy-hazard classification for a given building operation should be determined by carefully reviewing the descriptions of each occupancy hazard and by evaluating the quantity, combustibility, and heat-release rate of the associated contents. This classification system also allows a relationship to be established between the burning fuels and the ability of a sprinkler system to control the associated types of fires. It cannot be overemphasized that proper classification of the occupancy is critical to the overall success of fire-suppression systems. The determination of the type of occupancy hazard influences system design and installation considerations, such as sprinkler-discharge criteria, sprinkler spacing, and water-supply requirements.

NFPA 13: Installation of Sprinkler Systems, Chapter 2, identifies three occupancy classifications (NFPA 2002a, 13–14, 15):

- *Light-hazard occupancies* are occupancies or portions of other occupancies where the quantity or combustibility of contents is low and fires with relatively low rates of heat release would be anticipated. Light-hazard occupancies represent the least severe fire hazard since the fuel loads associated with these occupancies are typically low and relatively low rates of heat release would be expected. Some examples of light-hazard occupancies would include schools, office buildings, and churches.
- *Ordinary-hazard occupancies* are subdivided into two groups. *Ordinary-hazard Group 1* includes occupancies where combustibility is low, quantity of combustibles is moderate, stockpiles of combustibles do not exceed 8 ft., and fires with a moderate rate of heat release would be expected. Examples of Ordinary-hazard Group 1 occupancies would include bakeries and restaurant service areas. *Ordinary-hazard Group 2* includes occupancies where the quantity and combustibility of contents is moderate to high, stockpiles do not exceed 12 ft., and fires with moderate to high rates of heat release would be anticipated. Examples of Ordinary-hazard Group 2 occupancies would include libraries, dry cleaners, and woodworking facilities.
- *Extra-hazard occupancies* represent the potential for the most severe fire conditions and, therefore, present the most severe challenge to fire-protection systems. Like Ordinary-hazard Occupancy classifications, the Extra-hazard Occupancy classification also has two subclassifications. *Extreme Hazard Group 1* includes occupancies where the quantity and combustibility of contents is very high, and dust, lint, or other materials are present, introducing the probability of rapidly developing fires with high rates of heat release but little or no combustible or flammable liquids. Examples of Extra-hazard Group 1 occupancies include printing and saw mills. *Extra-hazard Group 2* includes occupancies with moder-

ate to substantial amounts of flammable or combustible liquids. Examples of Extra-hazard Group 2 occupancies include establishments involved with flammable-liquid spraying and plastic processing.

In addition to understanding the hazards of the occupancies, it is also important to have an understanding of commodity classifications. Commodity classifications provide identification of the type, amount, and arrangement of combustibles and are essential to defining potential fire severity based on a commodity's burning characteristics. Commodity classifications are governed by the types and amounts of materials that are part of a product and its primary packaging. NFPA 13: Installation of Sprinkler Systems, Chapter 2, identifies four commodity classifications, Class I, II, III, and IV (NFPA 2002a, 13–15):

- *Class I* commodities are noncombustible products that meet one of the following criteria: the noncombustible products are placed directly on wooden pallets, placed in a single-layer, corrugated carton, or are shrink-wrapped or paper-wrapped as a unit load with or without pallets.
- *Class II* commodities are noncombustible products that are placed in slatted wood crates, solid wood boxes, multiple-layer corrugated cartons, or a packaging material of equivalent combustibility.
- *Class III* commodities are products made of wood, paper, natural fibers, or Group C plastics with or without cartons, boxes, or crates and with or without pallets.
- *Class IV* commodities are defined as products with or without pallets that meet any of the following criteria: constructed partially or totally of Group B plastics, consist of free-flowing Group A plastic materials, or contain within themselves or their packaging an appreciable amount (5 to 15 percent) of Group A plastics.

As one would expect it is very possible within any facility to have mixed commodities of the above four classes. When mixed commodities are encountered, NFPA 13 §§ 2.2 requires that the storage area be protected by the requirements for the highest-classified commodity and storage arrangement within the facility (NFPA 2002a, 13–14).

UNIQUE RISKS FOR FIRE IN HIGH-RISE BUILDINGS

The NFPA defines a *high-rise building* as a building more than 75 ft. in height as measured from the lowest level of fire department vehicle access to the floor of the highest occupiable story. The fire risk in high-rise buildings has been a special concern to the fire community for as long as there have been high-rise buildings (Hall 2001, 1). Although high-rise buildings account for a very small number of the total buildings within each occupancy class, they account for a large share of the people and property exposed (NFPA 1997, 9–17). Studies indicate that high-rise buildings have a lower risk of fire per square foot of floor area. Sprinklers have also been shown to be beneficial in preventing deaths from fires and significantly reducing property losses (NFPA 1997, 9–18). Some unique features of high-rise buildings make them different from other buildings and thus affect firefighting in the following ways (NFPA 1997, 9-18, 19):

- High-rise buildings affect the fire department's access to the fire. Fire apparatuses have limitations in reaching the upper floors of the exterior of the building.
- The height of the fire affects the number of fire-service personnel required to deliver adequate types and amounts of equipment to the fire. More time and energy are required to deploy forces and equipment to the fire; as a result, these resources could be exhausted before firefighting forces can mount an attack.
- Delays in deploying equipment and firefighters can indirectly affect fire growth, resulting in a fire of greater magnitude.
- The height and location of the building can restrict the fire department's ability to approach the fire at its origin from more advantageous locations.
- Due to building height, egress and people-movement systems within a high-rise are limited.
- Natural forces affecting fire and smoke movement are more significant in high-rise buildings than they are in lower buildings. Due to the height of high-rise buildings, significant stack effects can move large volumes of smoke and heat through a building.
- Due to their design, high-rise buildings significantly increase the occupant, equipment, and material load in a given building. Stacking floors increases the number of occupants and fuel load that could be exposed to a fire compared to lower-height buildings.

BUILDING CODES

When discussing building construction, one must also consider the local building codes. A building code can be defined as a law that sets forth minimum requirements for the design and construction of buildings and structures (NFPA 1997, 1–43). Building codes have been in existence since 1900 BC when King Hammurabi established a form of building codes in Babylonia. These early building codes were very punitive in nature, with a focus on the prevention of building collapse. In the fourteenth century, England established building codes in London for chimney construction to reduce the spread of fire. In the United States, New York developed similar building ordinances for chimney construction, and Boston established building ordinances that required all homes be built of stone with roofs of tile or slate to reduce the spread of fire. The first recommended building code in America was published in 1905 by the National Board of Fire Underwriters and was called the Recommended Building Code.

MAJOR PROVISIONS OF BUILDING CODES

Municipalities adopt and enforce building codes that are typically structured following a model building code. These model building codes are usually a compromise between ideal safety and economic feasibility. The municipality will typically review building plans for compliance with building codes when the building and occupancy permit is issued. The occupancy permit typically identifies the permitted use of the building based on construction type and occupancy. Based on occupancy and construction type, fire-suppression systems and other types of fire-protection systems may be required. Other parts of building codes may address height and area building limitations, and some municipalities have floor limits, such as no buildings shall exceed five stories.

Construction features that are typically covered in building codes include structural integrity, life safety, fire-protection and -suppression systems, mechanical and utility systems, enclosure of vertical openings, and interior finish. These building codes are typically written as either specification or performance codes. A *specification code* spells out in detail what materials can be used, the building size, and how components should be assembled. *Performance codes*, on the other hand, indicate objectives and establish criteria to determine whether they have been met (NFPA 1997, 1–43).

MODEL BUILDING CODES

As was mentioned earlier, municipalities usually adopt or modify model building codes developed by model code organizations. Examples of these model code organizations include Building Officials and Code Administration (BOCA), Southern Building Code Congress, International Conference of Building Officials (ICBO), and the International Code Council. The first building code organization, BOCA, publishes the *National Building Code*, which is very popular in the Midwestern and northeastern United States. BOCA also publishes a plumbing, mechanical, and fire code.

ICBO publishes the *Uniform Building Code*, which is very popular in the western United States. ICBO also publishes a mechanical, plumbing, and fire code. The *Southern Standard Building Code*, published by the Southern Building Code Congress, is very popular in the southern United States. This organization also publishes a plumbing, mechanical, and fire code (NFPA 1997, 1–45).

The International Code Council was established in 1995 with representatives from the three model building code organizations discussed above. The purpose of the International Code Council was to develop one comprehensive set of regulations for building systems that was consistent with the three current model building codes (International Code Council 2003, iii). The International Code Council believed that combining the three codes into one would yield the following substantial advantages (International Code Council 2003, iii):

- Provide one single set of building-code requirements for code-enforcement officials, architects, engineers, designers, contractors, and manufacturers of homes
- Provide uniform education and certification for building-code-enforcement officials.

In 2000, the International Code Council developed the International Building Code, a fire code, a mechanical code, and a plumbing code. This is a relatively new building code, and it will probably be several years before we can determine its rate of adoption by local municipalities across the United States.

CHAPTER QUESTIONS

1. What is fire resistance?
2. What are the three separate elements involved in a building fire?
3. What does a Type 222 subclassification for a building signify?
4. What are three characteristics of steel that can reduce its performance in withstanding a fire?
5. Why does gypsum have excellent fire-resistance characteristics?
6. How does ventilation play a role in the burning rates of materials?
7. Why do high-rise buildings pose a unique fire risk?
8. What is fire loading, and what is it used for?
9. What are some examples of ordinary-hazard occupancies?
10. What are some perceived benefits of having a uniform national building code?

REFERENCES

Brannigan, Francis L. (1999). *Building Construction for the Fire Service*. Quincy, MA: NFPA.

Brannigan, Francis L. (1971). *Building Construction for the Fire Service*. Quincy, MA: NFPA.

Cote, Arthur, and Percy Bugbee. (2001). *Principles of Fire Protection*. Quincy, MA: NFPA.

Hall, John R. (2001). *High-Rise Fires*. Quincy, MA: NFPA.

International Code Council. (2003). *International Building Code—2003*. Country Club Hills, IL: International Code Council.

Ladwig, Thomas H. (1991). *Industrial Fire Prevention and Protection*. New York: Van Nostrand Reinhold.

National Fire Protection Association (NFPA). (1997). *Fire Protection Handbook*, 18th ed. Quincy, MA: NFPA.

NFPA. (2002a). *NFPA 13: Standard for the Installation of Sprinkler Systems*. Quincy, MA: NFPA.

NFPA. (2002b). *NFPA 220: Standard on Types of Building Construction*. Quincy, MA: NFPA.

NFPA. (2003). *NFPA 101: Life-Safety Code*. Quincy, MA: NFPA.

NFPA. (2003b). *NFPA 5000: Building Construction and Safety Code*. Quincy, MA: NFPA.

Patterson, James. (1993). *Simplified Design for Building Fire Safety*. New York: John Wiley and Sons.

U.S. Fire Administration (USFA). (1973). *America Burning: The Report of the*

National Commission on Fire Prevention and Control. Washington, DC: National Commission on Fire Prevention and Control.

USFA. (1987). *America Burning Revisited: National Workshop, Tyson's Corner Virginia, November 30–December 2.* Washington, DC: Federal Emergency Management Agency, USFA.

Life Safety in Buildings

LOSS OF LIFE IN BUILDINGS

Annually, fire claims nearly twelve thousand lives in the United States with industrial fires and explosions claiming approximately two hundred lives each year and injuring over thirty-seven hundred people. Throughout its history, the United States has experienced some of the deadliest fires in the workplace. Some of these fires were the result of inadequate building codes and inadequate life-safety codes for the workplace. Some deadly fires resulted, however, from the company's failure to follow and enforce the life-safety codes that were in effect at the time. Two fires serve as reminders to everyone about the potential for loss of life should a fire hit a company where life-safety measures are not available to the occupants: the Triangle Shirtwaist Factory fire and the Imperial Food Products fire.

TRIANGLE SHIRTWAIST FIRE

The worst industrial fire in U.S. history occurred on March 25, 1911, when fire broke out in the Triangle Shirtwaist Company facility in New York City (Greer 2001). To keep the workers at their sewing machines, the company had locked the doors leading to the exits. As the fire spread rapidly, fed by thousands of pounds of fabric, workers rushed to the stairs, freight elevator, and fire escape. Many died when the rear fire escape collapsed, and many others jumped to their deaths in an effort to escape the burning building (Greer 2001). For all practical purposes, the ninth-floor fire escape in the Asch Building led nowhere, certainly not to safety, and it bent under the weight of the factory workers trying to escape the inferno. Other workers waited at the windows for the rescue workers only to discover that the firefighters' ladders were several stories too short and that the water from the hoses could not reach the top floors (Guthrie 2004). In total, 146 women died. Despite the public outcry, the owners were acquitted of manslaughter charges, although they were ordered to pay $75 to the families of twenty-three victims.

IMPERIAL FOOD PRODUCTS PLANT FIRE

On Tuesday, September 3, 1991, a fire swept through the Imperial Food Products plant in Hamlet, North Carolina. Investigators determined that the cause of the fire had been the ignition of hydraulic oil from a ruptured line only a few feet from a natural-gas-fueled cooker used in preparing chicken (Klem 1992, 30). The fire started in the middle of the processing area of the plant, which was a center room of the facility without windows or doors leading directly to the outside. The structure was a one-story, unsprinklered, noncombustible building (Klem 1992, 29).

The hydraulic fluid ignited immediately, resulting in a fire and thick black smoke that spread quickly throughout the building (Klem 1992, 30). When it was all over, of the approximately ninety workers in the plant that day, twenty-five died, and fifty-four were injured. The state of North Carolina levied $808,150 in penalties against Imperial Food Products for violations, including locked exit doors and inadequate emergency lighting (*Time*, January 1992, 50). Imperial owner Emmett Roe, sixty-five, was sentenced to nineteen years, eleven months in jail as part of a plea bargain that let his son Brad, the plant's operations manager, off scot-free (*Time*, September 1992, 24).

PEOPLE'S BEHAVIORS AND ACTIONS IN A FIRE

Various characteristics of occupants may increase their chances of being victims in a building fire. These characteristics include age, disability, and handicap. Behaviors at the time of a fire that may increase a person's chances of being a victim include panic behaviors and firefighting behaviors.

The death rate from fire among children under five and the elderly over sixty-five is three times that of the rest of the population. Though together these young and old make up only 20 percent of the American population, they account for 45 percent of the fire deaths (U.S. Fire Administration [USFA] 1973, 4).

Three types of human behaviors in fires have been identified. The first behavior, *convergence clusters*, occurs when the occupants in a building that is on fire converge in specific rooms that they perceive as areas of refuge (NFPA 1997a, 8–12). *Panic behavior* occurs when the occupants experience a sudden and excessive feeling of alarm or fear, leading them to undertake extravagant efforts to secure safety (NFPA 1997a, 8–13). In *reentry behavior*, occupants who have successfully exited the building reenter for various reasons. Typically, they do so looking for loved ones, to assist others in exiting, and to assist with firefighting. Occupant firefighting behavior occurs with individuals who have economic or emotional ties to the building. Males predominantly engage in firefighting behavior (NFPA 1997a, 8–15).

ORIGIN AND DEVELOPMENT OF NFPA 101

The object of life safety is to protect life first and property second from the ravages of fire in a building (NSC 1992, 144). Life-safety measures take into account many things, such as building construction, provisions for exits and fire protection, occupant notification, and emergency response. The *National Fire Protection Association* (NFPA) *101: Life-Safety Code* had its origin in the work of the Committee on Safety to Life of the NFPA, which was appointed in 1913. The early codes entailed standards for the construction of stairways, fire escapes, and other egress routes for fire drills in various occupancies and for the construction and arrangement of exit facilities for factories, schools, and other occupancies (NFPA 2003). Major fire losses over the years have resulted in revisions of and additions to the life-safety codes. Examples of major fire losses that resulted in significant life-safety improvements include the Cocoanut Grove Night Club fire in Boston in 1942 and the Our Lady of the Angels school fire in Chicago in 1958.

The Occupational Safety and Health Administration (OSHA) has adopted standards for general industry that address life-safety issues such as emergency lighting, exit signs, and means of egress. Some of the OSHA standards were adopted from existing NFPA life-safety codes, while other standards were promulgated by OSHA. To provide some consistency in federal-building-code and OSHA requirements, in 2002, OSHA decided that an employer who demonstrated compliance with the exit-route provisions of *NFPA 101: Life-Safety Code* would be deemed to be in compliance with 29 C.F.R. § 1910 standards (USDOL 2004b).

BUILDING OCCUPANCIES AND LIFE SAFETY

Life-safety requirements for buildings are determined according to the occupancy classification of the structure or of the area of the structure. An occupancy is the principal use for the structure. The *NFPA 101: Life-Safety Code* classifies occupancies as follows (NFPA 2003):

1. *Assembly occupancy:* an occupancy (1) used for a gathering of fifty or more persons for deliberation, worship, entertainment, eating, drinking, amusement, awaiting transportation, or similar uses, or (2) used as a special amusement building, regardless of occupant load

2. *Educational occupancy:* an occupancy used for educational purposes through the twelfth grade by six or more persons for four or more hours per day or more than twelve hours per week

3. *Other occupancies:* occupancies associated with educational institutions in accordance with the appropriate parts of the life-safety code.

4. *Day-care occupancy:* an occupancy in which four or more clients receive care, maintenance, and supervision by other than their relatives or legal guardians for less than twenty-four hours per day

5. *Health-care occupancy:* an occupancy used for purposes of medical or other treatment or care of four or more persons, where such occupants are mostly incapable of self-preservation due to age or physical or mental disability or because of security measures not under the occupants' control

6. *Ambulatory-health-care occupancy:* A building or portion thereof used to provide services or treatment simultaneously to four or more patients that (1) provides, on an outpatient basis, treatment for patients that renders the patients incapable of taking action for self-preservation under emergency conditions without the assistance of others, or (2) provides, on an outpatient basis, anesthesia that renders the patients incapable of taking action for self-preservation under emergency conditions without the assistance of others

7. *Detention and correctional occupancy:* an occupancy used to house four or more persons under varied degrees of restraint or security, where such occupants are mostly incapable of self-preservation because of security measures not under the occupants' control

8. *Residential occupancy:* an occupancy that provides sleeping accommodations for purposes other than health care or detention and correction

9. *One- and two-family dwelling:* A building that contains not more than two dwelling units with independent cooking and bathroom facilities

10. *Lodging or rooming house:* A building or portion thereof that does not qualify as a one- or two-family dwelling that provides sleeping accommodations for a total of sixteen or fewer people on a transient or permanent basis, without personal care services, with or without meals, but without separate cooking facilities for individual occupants

11. *Hotel:* A building or groups of buildings under the same management in which there are sleeping accommodations for more than sixteen persons and primarily used by transients for lodging with or without meals

12. *Dormitory:* A building or a space in a building in which group sleeping accommodations are provided for more than sixteen persons who are not members of the same family in one room or a series of closely associated rooms under joint occupancy and single management, with or without meals, but without individual cooking facilities

13. *Apartment building:* A building or portion thereof containing three or more dwelling units with independent cooking and bathroom facilities

14. *Residential board and care occupancy:* A building or portion thereof that is used for lodging and boarding of four or more residents, not related by blood or marriage to the owners or operators, for the purpose of providing personal-care services

15. *Mercantile occupancy:* an occupancy used for the display and sale of merchandise

16. *Business occupancy:* an occupancy used for account and record keeping or the transaction of business other than mercantile

17. *Industrial occupancy:* an occupancy in which products are manufactured or in which processing, assembling, mixing, packaging, finishing, decorating, or repair operations are conducted

18. *Storage occupancy:* an occupancy used primarily for the storage or sheltering of goods, merchandise, products, vehicles, or animals

In addition to occupancy requirements, the life-safety codes specify general provisions for means of egress, building facilities, and equipment such as detection and notification systems. The fire-safety requirements in a building under the *NFPA 101: Life-Safety Code* are primarily based upon the type of occupancy, building construction, building contents, and life-safety features. Life-safety features include the presence of panic hardware on doors, fire alarms and detection systems, emergency lighting, and exit lighting, to name a few.

BUILDING CODES AND LIFE SAFETY

Life-safety requirements also tie into the building codes. There are numerous buildings codes in the United States, with their application varying by geographic location. For example, Chicago has its own Chicago Building Codes, while other municipalities may adopt a recognized building code such as the Building Official's and Code Administrator's (BOCA) code. All building codes include life-safety requirements. In 2002, NFPA's Committee on the Building Code prepared the first edition of *NFPA 5000: Building Construction and Safety Code.* NFPA 5000 was developed through a consensus-based procedure covering a range of subjects, including allowable building heights and areas based upon occupancy and construction; protection schemes for vertical openings; means of egress; and the rehabilitation of existing buildings (NFPA 2003). The code covers building systems and features, from energy efficiency to mechanical, electrical, and plumbing systems.

NFPA REQUIREMENTS FOR LIFE SAFETY IN INDUSTRIAL OCCUPANCIES

The *NFPA 101: Life-Safety Code* requirements apply to both new and existing industrial occupancies. Industrial occupancies include factories making products of all kinds and properties used for operations such as processing, assembling, mixing, packaging, finishing, decorating, repairing, and similar operations. Subclassifications of industrial occupancies include the following (NFPA 2003):

1. *General industrial occupancy.* A general industrial occupancy conducts ordinary and low-hazard industrial operations in buildings of conventional design suitable for various types of industrial processes. Also included are multistory buildings where floors are occupied by different tenants or buildings suitable for such occupancy and, therefore, subject to possible use for types of industrial processes with a high density of employee population.

2. *Special-purpose industrial occupancy.* A special-purpose industrial occupancy conducts ordinary and low-hazard industrial operations in buildings designed for, and suitable only for, particular types of operations. Such occupancy is characterized by a relatively low density of employee population, with much of the area occupied by machinery or equipment.
3. *High-hazard industrial occupancy.* A high-hazard industrial occupancy conducts industrial operations that use high-hazard materials or processes or houses high-hazard contents.

Means-of-Egress Requirements

Probably one of the most important aspects of life safety deals with the means of egress. The means of egress consists of three parts: exit access, the exit, and exit discharge (NFPA 1997a, 8–38). The exit access consists of the route one must take through portions of the building that are protected from fire by their design, such as a hallway with a two-hour fire rating. The rated hallway would be considered the exit. The exit discharge is the portion of the exit that separates the exit from the public area. A common exit discharge would be a doorway leading from the building to the outside public walkway. Furnishings, decorations, or other objects shall not obstruct exits or access to them. Doors, clear access widths, floors, and their design shall meet applicable codes. Examples of building criteria include the width of a door, its swing direction, and its construction, such as panic hardware, construction-material ratings, and so forth.

Aspects of the means of egress that should be addressed for life safety include doors and their design, stairs, horizontal exits, ramps, and fixed industrial stairs. The minimum widths, capacity of the means of egress, and the number of means of egress must meet applicable standards. OSHA, for example, requires that not less than two means of egress shall be provided for every story or section and arranged in a manner that minimizes the possibility that both may be blocked by any one fire or emergency.

The occupant load for a means of egress is the maximum number of persons it is intended to serve and is determined by the characteristics of occupancy use (NFPA 2003). The exit doors used as a means of egress must swing in the direction of travel if the room holds more than fifty people or is used in a high-hazard area. Both OSHA and the NFPA require that the means of egress be separated by fire-resistant materials and meet fire-resistance ratings. The exit discharge must lead directly outside or to a street, walkway, refuge area, public way, or open space with access to the outside, and all exit doors must be unlocked; employees must be able to open an exit-route door from the inside at all times without keys, tools, or special knowledge (there are exceptions for mental, penal, or correctional facilities) (USDOL 2004b).

Exit-Route Requirements

Exits in the workplace must meet minimum OSHA requirements when used as a means of egress. An example of a fire escape appears in figure 6.1. Some of these requirements include the following (USDOL 2004b):

1. The ceiling of an exit route must be at least 7' 6" high.
2. Any projection from the ceiling must not reach a point less than 6' 8" from the floor.
3. The width of an exit route must be sufficient to accommodate the maximum-permitted occupant load of each floor served by the exit route, while the exit access must be at least 28 in. wide at all points.
4. Where there is only one exit access leading to an exit or exit discharge, the width of the exit and exit discharge must be at least equal to the width of the exit access.
5. Objects that project into the exit route must not reduce the width of the exit route to less than the minimum width requirements for exit routes.
6. Exit routes must be kept free of explosive or highly flammable furnishings or other decorations.
7. Exit routes must be free and unobstructed.
8. No materials or equipment may be placed, either permanently or temporarily, within the exit route.
9. The exit access must not go through a room that can be locked, such as a bathroom, to reach an exit or exit discharge; nor may it lead into a dead-end corridor.
10. Stairs or a ramp must be provided where the exit route is not substantially level.
11. Safeguards designed to protect employees during an emergency (e.g.,

FIGURE 6.1
Fire escape

sprinkler systems, alarm systems, fire doors, exit lighting) must be in proper working order at all times.

12. Exit discharges should lead building occupants to a safe area outside of the facility. If an exit discharges into a courtyard or other open space, the area should be large enough to accommodate all of the building's occupants.

13. Exit routes must be maintained during construction, repairs, or alterations.

14. During repairs or alterations, employees must not occupy a workplace unless the exit routes required by the OSHA standards are available and existing fire protections are maintained or until alternate fire protection is furnished that provides an equivalent level of safety.

15. Employees must not be exposed to hazards of flammable or explosive substances or equipment used during construction, repairs, or alterations that are beyond the normal permissible conditions in the workplace or that would impede exiting the workplace.

Illumination and Emergency Lighting

Lighting and marking must be adequate and appropriate so that an employee with normal vision can see along the exit route. To assist in evacuation, the life-safety codes require the means of egress to be illuminated with natural lighting that provides the required level of illumination in structures occupied only during daylight hours. In addition to lighting, emergency lighting should also be provided throughout the means of egress. Emergency lighting should be of a sufficient illumination level and should last for at least one and a half hours in the event of the failure of normal lighting. Emergency-lighting illumination levels should be not less than an average of 1 foot-candle and, at any point, not less than 0.1 foot-candle, measured along the path of egress at floor level (NFPA 2003).

Exit Signs

Life-safety codes require that exits, other than main exterior exit doors that are obviously and clearly identifiable as exits, shall be marked by an approved sign that is readily visible from any direction of exit access. The exit signs must be illuminated to a surface value of at least five foot-candles and be distinctive in color. Self-luminous or electroluminescent signs that have a minimum luminance surface value of at least 0.06 foot-lamberts are permitted. Each exit sign must have the word "EXIT" in plainly legible letters not less than 6 in. high, with the principal strokes of the letters in the word "EXIT" not less than three-fourths of an inch wide (USDOL 2004b) (see figure 6.2).

Each exit-route door must be free of decorations or signs that obscure the visibility of the exit-route door. If the direction of travel to the exit or exit discharge is not immediately apparent, signs must be posted along the exit access indicating the direction of travel to the nearest exit and exit discharge. Additionally, the line of sight to an exit sign must be clear at all times. Each doorway or passage along an exit access that could be mistaken for an exit must be marked with the phrase "Not an Exit," with a similar designation, or with a sign indicating its actual use (e.g., "Closet").

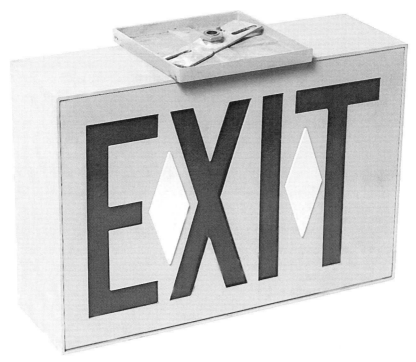

FIGURE 6.2
Exit sign

Sprinkler Systems

The life-safety codes require the installation of sprinkler systems in some occupancies. Where required, sprinkler systems should also meet applicable standards for their installation, maintenance, and testing. Automatic sprinklers are required for new, high-rise industrial occupancies, except for general, low-hazard, or special-purpose industrial occupancies.

Building Contents

Building contents can have a significant impact on the fire loading in a building and greatly affect the spread of smoke and flames; as a result, they are considered an important aspect of life safety. Contents includes objects, goods, or products placed inside a structure for functional, operational, or decorative reasons, excluding parts of the building structure, building service equipment, and items meeting the definition of interior finish (NFPA 2003). The contents of the building provide a fuel source for fire. An evaluation of the contents must take into account the relative probability of the ignition of the combustibles, the spread of flames and heat, the smoke and gases the fire will probably generate, and the possibility of an explosion or building failure that will endanger occupants (NFPA 1997a, 8–35). The interior finish of the building includes the exposed surfaces of interior walls, ceilings, and floors (NFPA 2003). The life-safety codes limit the flame spreads of interior finishes and materials that can be used in the exits, access routes to the exits, and other areas of the building.

Interior Finishes

Interior finishes in industrial occupancies must meet NFPA life-safety requirements for interior wall- and ceiling-finish materials. They must meet the requirements for Class A, B, or C materials in terms of flame spread and smoke development in operating areas and exit enclosures.

Detection, Alarm, and Communications Systems

Detection, alarm, and communications systems assist in identifying fires in their early stages, notifying the building occupants of the potential fire, and notifying the fire department. Chapter 8 provides details on the various types of smoke- and heat-detection systems commonly found in industrial occupancies. OSHA requires a fire alarm system for industrial occupancies, unless the total capacity of the building is under one hundred persons of whom fewer than twenty-five are above or below the level of exit discharge. Alarm initiation shall be made by any of the following means (USDOL 2004b):

1. Manual means
2. An approved automatic fire-detection system plus a minimum of one manual fire alarm box
3. An approved, supervised automatic sprinkler system plus a minimum of one manual fire alarm box

Occupant Notification

OSHA also requires employers to install and maintain an operable employee alarm system that has a distinctive signal to warn employees of fire or other emergencies, unless employees can promptly see or smell a fire or other hazard in time to be adequately warned. In high-hazard industrial occupancies, the fire alarm system should automatically initiate an occupant-evacuation alarm signal.

Building Services

The life-safety codes establish requirements for building utilities and services including heating, ventilating, and air-conditioning equipment. Life-safety codes address ventilation aspects of the building including mechanical ventilation and pressurized stair-enclosure systems, smoke-proof-enclosure mechanical-ventilation equipment, and boiler, incinerator, or heater rooms. Components of the building such as rubbish chutes, incinerators, laundry chutes, elevators, escalators, and conveyors should meet life-safety-protection requirements to prevent the unwanted spread of fires throughout the occupancy.

EMERGENCY-ACTION PLANS

An employer must have an emergency-action plan whenever a specific OSHA standard requires one. For example, OSHA's "Process Safety Management of Highly Hazardous Chemicals" standard (29 CFR 1910.119) requires employers who operate highly hazardous processes to have an emergency action plan in place that meets the requirements of the Emergency Action Plan standard (29 CFR 1910.38). The requirements in this section apply to each such emergency-action plan.

- *Written and oral emergency-action plans.* An emergency-action plan must be in writing, kept in the workplace, and available to employees for review. However, an employer with ten or fewer employees may communicate the plan orally to employees.
- *Minimum elements of an emergency-action plan.* An emergency-action plan must include the following, at a minimum (USDOL 2004c):

1. Procedures for reporting a fire or other emergency
2. Procedures for emergency evacuation, including type of evacuation and exit-route assignments
3. Procedures for employees to follow to determine who will remain to operate critical plant operations before evacuating
4. Procedures to account for all employees after evacuation
5. Procedures to be followed by employees performing rescue or medical duties
6. The name or job title of every employee who may be contacted by employees who need more information about the plan or an explanation of their duties under the plan

Along with the plan, employers must have means to notify the building occupants in the event of a fire. The signal must be distinctive so that workers can distinguish its meaning from other alarms. An important aspect of the emergency-action plan is employee training. For an emergency-action plan to be effective, the employer should designate and train employees to assist in a safe and orderly evacuation of other employees. OSHA requires the employer to review the emergency-action plan with each employee at the following times (USDOL 2004c):

1. When the plan is developed or the employee is assigned initially to a job
2. When the employee's responsibilities under the plan change
3. When the plan is changed

FIRE-PREVENTION PLANS
In addition to the emergency-action plan, OSHA requires employers in certain situations and with certain hazards to have a fire-prevention plan. A fire-prevention plan is required when there is a potential for fire hazards in the workplace. This fire-prevention plan is different from an emer-

gency-action plan. The plan must be in writing, kept in the workplace, and made available to employees for review. Employers with ten or fewer employees may communicate the plan orally to them. The fire-prevention plan must include the following elements (USDOL 2004d):

1. A list of all major fire hazards, proper handling and storage procedures for hazardous materials, potential ignition sources and their control, and the type of fire-protection equipment necessary to control each major hazard
2. Procedures to control accumulations of flammable and combustible waste materials
3. Procedures for regular maintenance of safeguards installed on heat-producing equipment to prevent the accidental ignition of combustible materials
4. The name or job title of employees responsible for maintaining equipment to prevent or control sources of ignition or fires
5. The name or job title of employees responsible for the control of fuel-source hazards

OSHA has identified the following general industry standards that require an emergency-action plan or a fire-prevention plan (USDOL 2004a):

1. Process safety management of highly hazardous chemicals, § 1910.119(n), emergency-action plan
2. Hazardous-waste operations and emergency response, § 1910.120(l)(1)(ii), (p)(8)(i), (q)(1), and (q)(11)(ii), emergency-action plan
3. Portable fire extinguishers, § 1910.157(a) and (b)(1), emergency-action plan and fire-prevention plan
4. Grain-handling facilities, § 1910.272(d), emergency-action plan
5. Ethylene oxide, § 1910.1047(h)(1)(iii), emergency-action plan and fire-prevention plan
6. Methylenedianiline, § 1910.1050(d)(1)(iii), emergency-action plan and fire-prevention plan
7. 1,3-butadiene, § 1910.1051(j), emergency-action plan and fire-prevention plan

CHAPTER QUESTIONS

1. Describe three types of human behaviors in fires.
2. What is an occupancy under the life-safety codes?
3. What three things make up a means of egress?
4. What are the illumination requirements for emergency lighting?
5. When does OSHA require a fire-prevention plan?
6. What are the illumination requirements for exit signs?
7. According to OSHA, does an emergency-action plan always have to be in writing?
8. What occurred at the Imperial Food Products plant?

REFERENCES

Greer, M. E. (2001, October). 90 years of progress in safety. *Professional Safety*, 46(10).

Guthrie, Emily. (2004). *An Information Finder for the Triangle Shirtwaist Factory Fire*, at http://home.earthlink.net/~swade29/frameset.html (accessed December 30, 2004).

Karter, Michael J. (2003). *Fire Loss in the United States during 2002*. Quincy, MA: NFPA.

Klem, Thomas J. (1992, January–February). Twenty-Five Die in Food Plant Fire. *NFPA Journal* 93, no. 1: 29–35.

National Fire Protection Association (NFPA). (1997a). *Fire Protection Handbook*, 18th ed. Quincy, MA: NFPA.

NFPA. (1997b). *NFPA 5000: Building Construction and Safety Code*. Quincy, MA: NFPA.

NFPA. (2003). *NFPA 101: Life-Safety Code*. Quincy, MA: NFPA.

National Safety Council (NSC). (1992). *Accident Prevention Manual for Business and Industry: Engineering and Technology*. Itasca, IL: NSC.

Time. (1992, January 13). Fined. *Time* 151, no. 2: 50.

Time. (1992, September 28). Price of neglect. *Time* 151, no. 13: 24.

U.S. Department of Labor (USDOL). (2004a). *Evacuation Plans and Procedures*, at www.osha.gov/SLTC/etools/evacuation/do_i_need.html (accessed June 23, 2005).

USDOL. (2004b). *Occupational Safety and Health Standards for General Industry, Subpart E: Means of Egress: General Requirements, 29 C.F.R. § 1910.37*. Washington, DC: USDOL.

USDOL. (2004c). *Occupational Safety and Health Standards for General Industry, Subpart E: Means of Egress: Emergency Action Plans, 29 C.F.R. § 1910.38*. Washington, DC: USDOL.

USDOL. (2004d). *Occupational Safety and Health Standards for General Industry, Subpart E: Means of Egress: Fire Prevention Plans, 29 C.F.R. § 1910.39.* Washington, DC: USDOL.

U.S. Fire Administration. (1973). *America Burning: The Report of the National Commission on Fire Prevention and Control.* Washington, DC: National Commission on Fire Prevention and Control.

7

Hazardous Processes

Hazardous processes can be found in industries as part of a variety of operations. The hazards of these processes can include flammable gases, flammable and combustible liquids, reactive gases, toxic gases, and liquefied compressed gases to name a few. The hazards can exist in the chemicals that are being used in the process, in the by-products of a reaction, or in the final process product. Hazards can also be created when problems occur with the process such as in the case of a run-away chain reaction or improper maintenance and repair of process equipment. The end result of any of these situations can include fires, explosions, and the release of hazardous materials.

Major fires and explosions associated with hazardous processes have unfortunately been part of the industrial work environment. During the course of operations at the Phillips Petroleum Houston Chemical Complex in Pasadena, Texas, on October 23, 1989, an explosion and the ensuing fire resulted in 23 deaths and 123 injuries of varying severity. Metal and concrete debris was found as far as six miles away following the explosion (U.S. Fire Administration [USFA] 1990). The explosion occurred in the polyethylene plant when a flammable vapor cloud formed and was subsequently ignited, resulting in a massive vapor-cloud explosion. Following this initial explosion, there was a series of further explosions and fires (Health and Safety Executive 2004). The day before the incident, scheduled maintenance work had begun to clear three of the six settling legs on a reactor. A specialist maintenance contractor was employed to carry out the work. A procedure was in place to isolate the leg to be worked on. During the clearing of a settling leg, part of the plug remained lodged in the pipe work. A member of the team went to the control room to seek assistance. Shortly afterward, the release flammable vapors occurred and approximately two minutes later, the vapor cloud ignited (Health and Safety Executive 2004). The company was fined $6.3 million by the Occupational Safety and Health Administration (OSHA) in 1990 but settled for $4 million.

PROCESSES INVOLVING FLAMMABLE AND COMBUSTIBLE LIQUIDS

A number of industrial processes involve the use of flammable and combustible liquids. These processes pose potential fire hazards to those working nearby. Some of the more typical processes include spray-finishing operations such as electrostatic spray painting, powder-coating processes, dip-tank processes, and oil quenching. Because of the unique hazards of each of these processes, engineering controls and safe work practices must be followed. The National Fire Protection Association (NFPA) has established recommended practices, and OSHA has adopted safety standards designed to minimize the fire hazards associated with these processes.

ELECTROSTATIC SPRAY OPERATIONS

Spray-finishing operations are found in a number of industries. In general, these operations apply materials and coatings to a surface. In many instances, these finishing materials consist of flammable liquids. A common example of a spray-finish operation can be found in the automotive-repair industry, when automobile bodies are spray painted. The process by which the paint is applied to the product can include the use of paint guns and electrostatic spray painting, when the spray material such as paint is negatively charged (while atomized or after having been atomized by the air or airless methods) through the connection of the spraying gun to a generator. The material being painted is positively charged; as a result, the difference in charge leads the particles toward the material to obtain the coating. This type of spray operation is used to reduce overspray, therefore material waste, and makes it possible to obtain very uniform and regular coating layers.

Electrostatic spray operations can be fixed or portable, as with a spray gun. In fixed operations, the parts are typically hung on a conveyor and transported through the spray area. Electrostatic spray equipment used in coating operations must meet design and use standards. The NFPA,

Underwriter's Laboratories, and OSHA have established standards for the use, design, and installation of this type of equipment. Due to the hazards associated with the electrical components used to operate the electrostatic spray equipment, applicable standards should be followed to ensure that potential sources of electrical energy sufficient to ignite flammable vapors are located outside of the spraying area.

Electrostatic spray painting requires the use of high voltage and leads to electrodes. To prevent accidental damage that could result in electrocution, this type of equipment should be properly insulated and protected. Another hazard of using electrostatic atomizing heads is the accidental grounding of the equipment. To prevent this from happening, the electrostatic atomizing heads should be insulated from the ground and adequately supported. In the event that the electrode system is deenergized, an automatic means shall be provided for grounding the electrode system (USDOL 2004b, 29 C.F.R. § 1910.107).

In the application of the coating material, a safe distance of at least twice the sparking distance shall be maintained between goods being painted and electrodes or electrostatic atomizing heads or conductors. The safe distance should be posted near the assembly.

Workers can also be exposed to hazards created by the equipment. To prevent the workers from coming into contact with the equipment, means shall be taken to guard the hazards through the use of railings or guards suitable to maintain a safe distance between the workers and the equipment.

Electrostatic hand-spraying equipment involves equipment that uses electrostatically charged elements for the atomization or precipitation of materials for coatings on articles or for other similar purposes in which the atomizing device is handheld and manipulated during the spraying operation. Equipment used in electrostatic hand spraying should meet applicable design standards. The high-voltage circuits must be designed so as not to produce a spark of sufficient intensity to ignite any vapor-air mixtures or result in an appreciable shock hazard upon coming into contact with a grounded object under all normal operating conditions (USDOL 2004b, 29 C.F.R. § 1910.107). Transformers, power packs, control apparatus, and all other electrical portions of the equipment, with the exception of the handgun itself and its connections to the power supply, shall be located outside of the spraying area or meet safety requirements for this type of environment (NFPA 2003b). To prevent accidental electrocution of users and ignition of vapors, the guns and all equipment should be properly grounded. Additionally, the objects being painted or coated must maintain metallic contact with the conveyor or other grounded support. The hooks shall be regularly cleaned to insure this contact, and areas of contact shall be sharp points or knife edges where possible (USDOL 2004b, 29 C.F.R. § 1910.107).

Ventilation, also a critical element of any spraying operation, is used to keep the concentrations of flammable vapors well below their lower explosive limits. The electrical equipment should be interlocked in a manner that prevents the spraying equipment from operating unless the ventilation system is working (USDOL 2004b, 29 C.F.R. § 1910.107).

SPRAY BOOTHS

Spray booths can be found in a number of industrial facilities. The spray booth is a power-ventilated structure provided to enclose or accommodate a spraying operation. Due to the potential hazards of the flammable vapor concentrations that can be generated in spraying operations, the booth is designed to confine and limit the escape of spray, vapor, and residue and to conduct or direct them safely to an exhaust system. An area containing dangerous quantities of flammable vapors or mists or of combustible residues, dusts, or deposits due to the operation of spraying processes is referred to as the *spraying area*.

To minimize the fire hazards that a spray booth poses for other activities in the industrial occupancy, the spray booth should be separated from other operations by 3 ft. or more, or it should be cordoned off with a partition or wall surrounded by a clear space of not less than 3 ft. on all sides that is kept free from storage or combustible construction (USDOL 2004b, 29 C.F.R. § 1910.107).

To prevent the lighting used in a spray booth from becoming a source of ignition, only approved methods of lighting should be used. When spraying areas are illuminated through glass panels or other transparent materials, only fixed lighting units shall be used as a source of illumination (USDOL 2004b, 29 C.F.R. § 1910.107).

SOURCES OF IGNITION

Due to the fire hazards associated with the flammable and combustible vapors generated in spraying operations, no open flame or spark-producing equipment should be allowed in any spraying area or within 20 ft. of the spraying area unless it is separated by a partition (USDOL 2004b, 29 C.F.R. § 1910.107). Sources of ignition may include electrical sources, mechanical sources, and hot equipment surfaces. Due to the presence of flammable vapors in a sufficient concentration to ignite, electrical wiring on any equipment in or near the spraying areas must meet applicable electrical codes for the hazardous location. Electrical wiring and equipment not subject to deposits of combustible residues but located in a spraying area shall be of the explosionproof type approved for Class I, Group D locations (USDOL 2004b, 29 C.F.R. § 1910.107). Electrical wiring, motors, and other equipment outside of but within 20 ft. of any spraying area and not separated from it by partitions shall not produce sparks under normal operating conditions and shall meet construction requirements for Class I, Division 2 hazardous locations (USDOL 2004b, 29 C.F.R. § 1910.107). Portable lamps approved for Class I, Division 1 locations can be used only in conjunction with cleaning and drying operations. Spray booths, rooms, or other enclosures used for spraying operations should not be used alternately for the purpose of drying by any arrangement that will cause a material increase in the surface temperature of the spray booth, room, or enclosure.

VENTILATION
Spray booths protect the industrial occupancy by preventing harmful vapor concentrations from escaping the booth to areas where they can be accidentally ignited; it plays a big role in removing them from the inside of the booth to a safe location outside the industrial occupancy. The ventilation sweeps the air currents toward the exhaust outlet, where the vapors are ventilated to a safe location outside of the booth. Mechanical ventilation is required at all times while spraying operations are being conducted and for a sufficient time afterward to ensure that vapors are reduced to a nonhazardous level. The exhaust system is intended solely for the spray booth and discharges the vapors to the exterior of the building. Thus, spray-booth ventilation is essential in spray-booth fire prevention. The NFPA's *Standard for Blower and Exhaust Systems for Vapor Removal, NFPA No. 91-1961* establishes the criteria for ventilation systems used in spray-booth operations. This standard has also been adopted by OSHA (USDOL 2004b, 29 C.F.R. § 1910.107).

164

To further prevent the accumulation of paint residues and aid in the movement of air inside the booth, the interior surfaces of spray booths should be smooth and continuous. Baffle plates are also used to ensure an even flow of air through the booth or to collect the overspray before it enters the exhaust duct. OSHA requires that air filters be designed, installed, and maintained so that the average air velocity over the open face of the booth (or booth cross-section during spraying operations) will not be less than one hundred linear feet per minute (USDOL 2004b, 29 C.F.R. § 1910.107). The accumulation of overspray materials can greatly decrease the air velocities in the spray booth; therefore, the air filters should be checked on a regular basis, cleaned, and disposed of properly.

Because the fan and its mechanical parts are a potential ignition source for the vapors, the rotating elements shall be nonsparking. Heat sources such as friction should be eliminated in the fan motor, belts, and other moving parts. The bearings should be of an approved type, typically self-lubricating or lubricated from the outside duct (USDOL 2004b, 29 C.F.R. § 1910.107).

Unless the spray-booth exhaust-duct terminal is from a water-wash spray booth, the terminal discharge point shall be not less than 6 ft. from any combustible exterior wall or roof and shall not discharge in the direction of any combustible construction or unprotected opening in any non-combustible exterior wall within 25 ft. (USDOL 2004b, 29 C.F.R. § 1910.107). Air exhaust from spray operations shall not be directed so that it will contaminate makeup air being introduced into the spraying area or other ventilating intakes; nor shall it be directed so as to create a nuisance. Air exhausted from spray operations shall not be recirculated. Air-intake openings to rooms containing spray finishing operations shall be adequate for the efficient operation of exhaust fans and shall be so located as to minimize the creation of dead air pockets.

FLAMMABLE AND COMBUSTIBLE LIQUIDS: STORAGE AND HANDLING

OSHA limits the quantity of flammable or combustible liquids kept in the vicinity of spraying operations to the minimum required for operations and should ordinarily not exceed a supply for one day or one shift. The liquids should be stored in approved containers or pumped into the spray-finishing room through the use of approved piping and pumping systems.

As discussed in chapter 3, transferring flammable and combustible liquids from one container to another can create fire and explosion hazards. Therefore, transferal of the liquids shall be done using approved equipment and procedures, including the use of bonding wires, adequate grounding, and adequate ventilation. Precautions should also be taken to prevent spills and the presence of unwanted sources of ignition.

In many spraying operations, it is common practice to draw the spray liquid from containers. Provisions for the containers supplying spray nozzles shall meet the following requirements (USDOL 2004b, 29 C.F.R. § 1910.107):

1. They shall be of closed type or provided with metal covers that are kept closed.
2. Containers not resting on floors shall be on metal supports or suspended by wire cables.
3. Containers supplying spray nozzles by gravity flow shall not exceed a 10-gal. capacity.
4. Original shipping containers shall not be subject to air pressure for supplying spray nozzles.
5. Containers under air pressure supplying spray nozzles shall be of limited capacity, not exceeding that necessary for one day's operation; they shall be designed and approved for such use and provided with a visible pressure gauge and a relief valve.
6. Containers under air pressure supplying spray nozzles, air-storage tanks, and coolers shall meet applicable pressure-vessel standards.

FIRE PROTECTION

OSHA requires spray-booth areas, including the interior of the booth, to be protected with either automatic sprinklers or other approved automatic extinguishing equipment (USDOL 2004b, 29 C.F.R. § 1910.107). The sprinkler systems should be properly maintained. To ensure they work properly, sprinklers protecting spraying areas should be kept as free from deposits and buildup of paint and spray material. The sprinkler heads should be cleaned on a regular basis to ensure their proper operation, which may mean cleaning as often as daily. In addition to a fixed extinguishing system, an adequate supply of suitable portable fire extinguishers shall be installed near all spraying areas, and "No smoking" signs in large letters on a contrasting-color background shall be conspicuously posted in all spraying areas and paint-storage rooms.

OPERATIONS AND MAINTENANCE

To reduce the potential for accidental fires involving spraying operations, safety measures should be incorporated into the spraying operations and maintenance procedures. Fires can start from residue material being ignited. To prevent this, housekeeping practices should be followed to clean up overspray residue and the accumulation of deposits of combustible residues. Spraying should take place only in designated areas and never outside of the spray booth. Tools and equipment used in the cleaning of spray booths should be nonsparking. Approved metal waste cans should be provided wherever rags or waste are impregnated with finishing material, and all such rags or waste should be deposited therein immediately after use (USDOL 2004b, 29 C.F.R. § 1910.107). The waste cans should be emptied at least once daily or at the end of each shift.

Because solvents used in the cleaning of the spray booth and equipment can also create a fire hazard, they should have flash points not less than 100°F. Solvents used for cleaning spray nozzles and auxiliary equipment may have flash points not less than the material normally used in spray operations. To remove potentially flammable vapors from the work area during cleaning, ventilating equipment should be operated during cleaning.

DRYING, CURING, AND FUSION APPARATUSES

The drying process and associated equipment can pose potential fire hazards in spray-booth areas. This drying and curing equipment can present potential heat sources and sources of electricity sufficient to ignite vapors that may still be present in the spray booth following the application of coating materials. To prevent potential fires from these sources of ignition, drying, curing, and fusion equipment used in connection with the spray application of flammable and combustible finishes must conform to NFPA 86A: Standard for Ovens and Furnaces (1969) and "drying, curing, or fusion equipment (USDOL 2004b, 29 C.F.R. § 1910.107).

OSHA requires that drying, curing, and fusion units utilizing a heating system that has open flames or that may produce sparks shall not be installed in a spraying area. This type of equipment may be installed adjacent to spraying areas equipped with an interlocked ventilating system. The heating components on drying equipment shall be prevented from starting until the drying space is thoroughly ventilated. The ventilating system should also maintain a safe atmosphere at any source of ignition, and the heating system should automatically shut down in the event that the ventilating system fails.

Spray booths and enclosures used for automobile refinishing may also be used for drying with a portable, electrical, infrared drying apparatus as long as the following conditions are met (USDOL 2004b, 29 C.F.R. § 1910.107):

1. The interior (especially floors) of spray enclosures is kept free of over-spray deposits.
2. During spray operations, the drying apparatus and electrical connections and wiring thereto shall not be located within the spray enclosure or in any other location where spray residues may be deposited.
3. The spraying apparatus, the drying apparatus, and the ventilating system of the spray enclosure shall be equipped with suitable interlocks so arranged that:
   - The spraying apparatus cannot be operated while the drying apparatus is inside the spray enclosure.
   - The spray enclosure will be purged of spray vapors for a period of not less than three minutes before the drying apparatus can be energized.
   - The ventilating system will maintain a safe atmosphere within the enclosure during the drying process, and the drying apparatus will automatically shut off in the event that the ventilating system fails.
   - All electrical wiring and equipment of the drying apparatus conforms with electrical standards, and only equipment of a type approved for Class I, Division 2 hazardous locations is located within 18 in. of floor level.
   - All metallic parts of the drying apparatus shall be properly electrically bonded and grounded.
   - The drying apparatus shall contain a prominently located, permanently attached warning sign, indicating that ventilation should be maintained during the drying period and that spraying should not be conducted in a vicinity where spray will deposit on the apparatus.

AERATED-POWDER COATING OPERATIONS

An aerated powder is any powdered material used as a coating material that shall be fluidized within a container by passing air uniformly from below. It is common practice to fluidize such materials to form a fluidized-powder bed and then to dip the part to be coated into the bed in a manner similar to liquid dipping. Such beds are also used as sources for powder-spray operations. Because the process suspends powder materials in air, a major fire hazard associated with aerated-powder coating operations involves explosions from igniting the suspended particles.

To prevent these explosions, exhaust ventilation shall be sufficient to maintain the atmosphere below the lowest explosive limits for the materials being applied. All nondeposited, air-suspended powders shall be safely removed via exhaust ducts to the powder recovery cyclone or receptacle. Housekeeping measures should be established and followed to prevent the accumulation of powder-coating dusts, and measures should be taken to eliminate sources of ignition from electrical equipment, from equipment that produces heat, and from smoking.

ELECTROSTATIC FLUIDIZED BEDS

An *electrostatic fluidized bed* is a container that holds powder-coating material, which is aerated from below so as to form an air-supported, expanded cloud of such material, which is electrically charged with a charge opposite to the charge of the object to be coated; this object is transported through the container immediately above the charged and aerated materials in order to be coated. Fire hazards with electrostatic fluidized beds involve the ignition of the powder coating, which could result in an explosion. Additionally, the equipment charges the powder material with high voltage, which serves as an additional source of ignition.

To minimize the potential ignition of the powder coating, electrostatic fluidized beds and associated equipment shall be of approved types. The maximum surface temperature of this equipment in the coating area shall not exceed 150°F (USDOL 2004b, 29 C.F.R. § 1910.107). The high-voltage circuits shall be so designed as not to produce a spark of sufficient intensity to ignite any powder-air mixtures or result in an appreciable shock hazard upon coming into contact with a grounded object under normal operating conditions.

Transformers, power packs, control apparatuses, and all other electrical portions of the equipment, with the exception of the charging electrodes and their connections to the power supply, should be located outside of the powder-coating area and meet applicable standards for use in hazardous areas (USDOL 2004b, 29 C.F.R. § 1910.107). All electrically conductive objects within the charging influence of the electrodes shall be adequately grounded. The powder-coating equipment is required to have a permanently installed warning regarding the necessity for grounding these objects. Objects being coated shall be maintained in contact with the conveyor or other support in order to insure proper grounding. Hangers shall be regularly cleaned to insure effective contact, and areas of contact shall be sharp points or knife edges where possible. Electrical equipment should be interlocked with the ventilation system so that the equipment cannot be operated unless the ventilation fans are in operation.

DIP TANKS AND COATING OPERATIONS

Dip-tank and coating operations can pose a fire hazard due to the flammability characteristics posed by the coating material. The fire hazards exist around the tank as well as in the areas where the coating material is draining off of the dipped objects and in the drying areas (see figure 7.1). Examples of operations that can pose fire hazards include dip-tank operations in which objects are painted, dipped, electroplated, pickled, quenched, tanned, degreased, stripped, roll-coated, flow-coated, and curtain-coated. OSHA standards for dip tanks and coating operations apply when a dip tank containing a liquid other than water is used and the liquid in the tank or its vapor is used to do any of the following (USDOL 2004a, 29 C.F.R. § 1910.123):

1. Clean an object
2. Coat an object
3. Alter the surface of an object
4. Change the character of an object

The NFPA also identifies electrical equipment used in areas around dip-tank operations that contain flammable or combustible vapors as a common ignition source for fires involving dip-tank operations. Typically, the electrical equipment found in dip-tank areas is not suited for use in hazardous environments. The vapors from dip-tank operations can also be

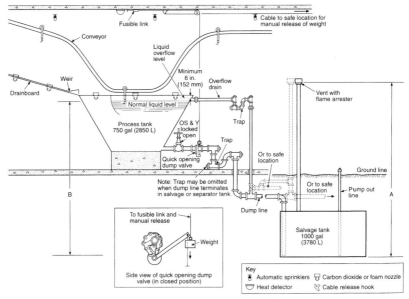

Note: A is greater than B but discharge is at least 12 ft (3660 mm) aboveground.

FIGURE 7.1

Dip-tank operation (Reprinted with permission from 34-2003, *Dipping and Coating Processes Using Flammable or Combustible Liquids*, © 2003, National Fire Protection Association, Quincy, MA. This reprinted material is not the complete and official position of the NFPA on the referenced subject, which is represented only by the standard in its entirety.)

ignited from other sources, such as open flames and sparks generated from welding, cutting and other forms of hot work in the hazardous-environment area. Spontaneous ignition, due to oxidation or exothermic reaction between various coating components, often occurs when excess residue accumulates in work areas, ducts, duct discharge points, or other adjacent areas (NFPA 1997, 3–205). Figure 7.2 depicts a flow-coating operation.

Welding, cutting, and other spark-producing operations can also serve as an ignition source for fires involving dip-tank operations. As a precaution, hot work should not be permitted in or adjacent to a dipping or coating operations area unless hot-work safety precautions have been taken.

As is the case when handling flammable and combustible liquids, static electricity can be generated when the liquid from a container is transferred

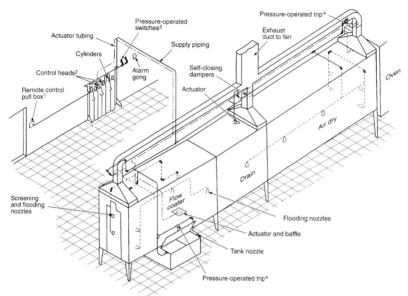

Notes:

1. Normal manual pull-box control and cable.
2. Pneumatic control heads with emergency manual controls.
3. Pressure-operated switches to shut down exhaust fan, pumps, conveyor, and so on, and sound alarm.
4. Pressure-operated trips to release self-closing dampers in exhaust duct and self-closing cover on paint tank.

FIGURE 7.2

Flow-coating operation (Reprinted with permission from 34-2003, *Dipping and Coating Processes Using Flammable and Combustible Liquids*, © 2003, National Fire Protection Association, Quincy, MA. This reprinted material is not the complete and official position of the NFPA on the referenced subject, which is represented only by the standard in its entirety.)

to the dip tank. The static electricity can contain enough energy to ignite the liquids. Proper grounding and bonding should be followed when transferring the liquids. Finally, carelessly discarded smoking materials or matches have been another common ignition source involving dip-tank operations. To prevent fires, smoking should be prohibited around dip-tank, draining, and drying areas, and "No Smoking or Open Flames" signs should be posted at all dipping areas, coating areas, and paint-storage rooms.

Proper layout of dip-tank processes is the first step in preventing fires. Dipping and coating processes shall be separated from other operations, materials, or occupancies by location, fire walls, fire partitions, or other acceptable means. Separating dip-tank process from other parts of the facility will aid in reducing the possibility that sources of ignition will come into contact with the tank and, if a fire does occur, will reduce its potential to spread to other areas.

DESIGN AND CONSTRUCTION OF DIPPING AND COATING EQUIPMENT AND SYSTEMS

Dip-tank fire hazards are controlled by fire-prevention design features on the tanks. Both NFPA standards and OSHA standards stipulate the design and construction features of dip-tank processes. Many of the adopted OSHA standards pertaining to dipping and coating operations are NFPA standards. Dipping and coating equipment shall be constructed of steel, reinforced concrete, masonry, or other noncombustible material and shall be securely and rigidly supported. The supports for dipping and coating tanks that exceed either a 500-gal. capacity or 10 sq. ft. of liquid surface must have a fire-resistance rating of at least one hour.

Overflow Prevention

To prevent the overflow of burning liquid from the dipping or coating tank if a fire in the tank actuates automatic sprinklers, one or more of the following shall be done (NFPA 1997, 3–205):

1. Drain boards shall be arranged so that sprinkler discharge will not flow into the tank.
2. Tanks shall be equipped with automatically closing covers.
3. Tanks shall be equipped with overflow pipes.

Liquid-Level Control

Control of the liquid level of a dip tank is crucial to preventing fires. Accidental overfilling of the tank or release of the liquid from the tank could result in rapidly spreading fire. The liquid in the dipping or coating tank shall be maintained at a level that is at least 6 in. below the top of the tank to allow effective application of extinguishing agents in the event of fire. To prevent accidental overfilling and subsequent spilling of the liquid, dip tanks exceeding a 150-gal. capacity or 10 sq. ft. of liquid surface should be equipped with a trapped overflow pipe leading to a safe location. Depending upon the area of the liquid surface and the length and pitch of pipe, overflow pipes for dipping or coating tanks that exceed a 150-gal.

capacity or 10 sq. ft. of liquid surface shall be capable of handling either the maximum rate of delivery of process liquid or the maximum rate of automatic sprinkler discharge, whichever is greater. The overflow pipe shall have a diameter of at least 3 in. (NFPA 1997, 3–205).

Bottom drains are used on dip tanks to drain the tank in the event of a fire, thus removing the fuel from the fire. The drains automatically open and release the flammable or combustible liquid from the tank and discharge it to a closed, vented salvage tank or a safe location. Dipping or coating tanks that exceed a 500-gal. capacity shall be equipped with bottom drains arranged to drain the tank in the event of fire. Exceptions to this requirement include tanks that are equipped with automatic-closing covers and tanks using liquids in which the viscosity of the liquid at normal atmospheric temperatures makes this impractical. The NFPA has established that acceptable bottom-drain pipe diameters capable of emptying the dipping or coating tank within five minutes are required on these dip-tank operations (NFPA 2003c). When the liquid is evacuated from the dip tank to a salvage tank, the salvage tank must meet design requirements. Some of these requirements include means to pump the released contents from the salvage tank and minimum capacity requirements.

Control of Liquid Temperature

Where dipping or coating liquids are heated, either directly or by the work pieces being processed, procedures shall be followed to prevent excess temperature, vapor accumulation, and possible autoignition (NFPA 2003c). Excess temperature means any temperature above which the ventilation cannot safely confine the vapors generated; in no case shall the temperature exceed the boiling point of the liquid or a temperature that is 100°F less than the autoignition temperature of the liquid. To prevent accidental overheating of the liquid, the dipping or coating tank shall be equipped with approved equipment designed to limit the temperature of the liquid. If excessive temperatures are reached, interlocks designed to shut down the equipment, including conveyor systems, shall be provided.

ELECTRICAL AND OTHER SOURCES OF IGNITION

Dipping and coating process areas where Class I liquids are used, or where Class II or Class III liquids are used at temperatures at or above their flash points, are considered hazardous locations; as a result, electrical equipment used in these areas must meet applicable codes. The hazardous-environment classifications can include the dip-tank area, drain area, and drying areas. Sources of ignition such as open flames and spark-producing equipment shall be prohibited from areas classified as hazardous. Light fixtures used around dip-tank operations shall be approved for use in that area. In order to prevent discharges or sparks from the accumulation of static electricity, all persons and all electrically conductive objects, including any metal parts of the process equipment or apparatus, containers of material, exhaust ducts, and piping systems that convey flammable or combustible liquids, shall be electrically grounded (NFPA 2003c).

VENTILATION

As with spraying operations involving flammable and combustible liquids, ventilation plays an important role in reducing fire hazards in dipping and coating operations as well. Ventilation is intended to maintain the flammable and combustible vapors at safe levels without the ventilation equipment itself serving as a potential ignition source. Ventilating and exhaust systems used with dipping and coating operations should be installed in accordance with *NFPA 91: Standard for Exhaust Systems for Air Conveying of Vapors, Gases, Mists, and Noncombustible Particulate Solids* (NFPA 1999).

The goal of ventilation is to confine the vapor of the dipping and coating process to an area not more than 5 ft. from the vapor source and to remove the vapors to a safe location. If the ventilation system fails, it should be interlocked with the process so that the dipping or coating process automatically shuts down and an alarm sounds. Vapors from the process should be exhausted to a safe location following applicable codes. Because the discharged exhaust could contain flammable vapors, an alarm should be sounded and the dipping or coating process automatically shut down if the concentration of any vapor in the exhaust airstream exceeds 25 percent of the lower flammable limit (NFPA 1999). The exhaust equipment, including ducts, motors, bearings, and belts, should be approved for use with dipping and coating operations so as not to serve as a potential ignition source.

To prevent accidental ignition of vapors from freshly dipped or coated pieces, materials should be dried only in spaces that are ventilated to prevent the concentration of ignitable vapors from exceeding 25 percent of the lower flammable limit (NFPA 2003c). Areas serving as drying areas should be well ventilated in a manner that keeps the concentration of vapors below 25 percent of the lower flammable limit.

STORAGE, HANDLING, AND DISTRIBUTION OF FLAMMABLE AND COMBUSTIBLE LIQUIDS

The storage, handling, and transference of flammable and combustible liquids shall follow accepted practices. Chapter 3 covers flammable- and combustible-liquid handling, transference, and storage. Procedures delimit the maximum quantities to be stored in various containers and cabinets and describe approved containers. The maximum quantity of liquid to be located in the vicinity of the dipping or coating process area—but outside of a storage cabinet, inside storage room, cut-off room or attached building, or other specific process area cut off by at least a two-hour fire-rated separation from the dipping or coating process area—shall not exceed the greater of the quantities given below (NFPA 2003c):

1. A supply for one day
   - 2. 25 gal. of Class IA liquids in containers
   - plus 120 gal. of Class IB, IC, Class II, or Class III liquids in containers
   - plus two portable tanks each not exceeding 660 gal. of Class IB, IC, Class II, or Class IIIA liquids
   - plus twenty portable tanks each not exceeding 660 gal. of Class IIIB liquids.

LIQUID PIPING SYSTEMS

In some instances, flammable and combustible liquids used in dip-tank and coating operations are transferred to the tank through a pump and piping system. Components of the system, including the piping, pumps, and meters, used for transferring liquids through this system must be approved for such use. When the piping system fills the tank from the top, the free end of the fill pipe shall be within 6 in. of the bottom of the tank (NFPA 2003c). If the dip tank uses Class I liquids, the tank and fill pipe shall be electrically connected through a bond wire. Also for Class I liquids, the tank, piping system, and storage tank shall be bonded and grounded to reduce the potential for fires due to static electricity generated during the filling process.

The pumps used to fill the tank must be approved for their use and designed in a manner that prevents the pump from exceeding the design pressures of the system. To prevent the tanks from accidental overfilling, automatic shutoffs must be provided in the tank system. In the event of the activation of the fire-detection system or automatic fire-extinguishing system, the pumping system should be designed to shut down the pump automatically.

FIRE PROTECTION

Fire protection for dip-tank and coating operations includes the use of automatic extinguishing systems and fire-detection systems. Where required in the fire codes, areas in which dipping or coating operations are conducted shall be protected with an approved automatic sprinkler system. Dipping and coating processes can be protected with an approved automatic fire-extinguishing system. The following systems may be permitted (NFPA 2003c):

1. An approved water-spray extinguishing system
2. An approved foam extinguishing system
3. An approved carbon dioxide system
4. An approved dry-chemical extinguishing system
5. An approved gaseous-agent extinguishing system
6. An approved sprinkler system for tanks containing liquids having flash points above 200°F
7. For tanks equipped with a tank cover arranged to close automatically in the event of fire, a sprinkler system that meets NFPA 13

The requirements for fire protection involving dip-tank processes are based upon the size of the process. Small dip-tank processes are those tanks that do not exceed a 150-gal. capacity or do not exceed 10 sq. ft. of liquid surface area. Large dip-tank processes exceed 150 gal. or 10 sq. ft. of liquid surface area. On open, small dip tanks, automatically closing process tank covers or extinguishing systems shall be provided. The tank covers shall close automatically in the event of a fire. The covers and their components shall be constructed of metal and noncombustible materials. When the tanks are not in use, the covers should be kept closed.

On large dip-tank processes, an automatic extinguishing system shall be provided for enclosed processes, for open processes with peripheral vapor containment and ventilation, and for process tanks of a 150-gal. capacity or more or of 10 sq. ft. in liquid surface area or greater. The systems shall be designed to protect the following areas (NFPA 2003c):

1. For dip tanks, the system shall protect the tank, its drain board, freshly coated work pieces or material, and any hoods and ducts.
2. For flow coaters, the system shall protect open tanks, vapor-drying tunnels, and ducts. Pumps circulating the coating material shall be interlocked to shut off automatically in the event of fire.
3. For curtain and roll coaters or similar processes, the system shall protect the coated work pieces or material and open troughs or tanks containing coating materials. Pumps circulating the coating material shall be interlocked to shut off automatically in the event of fire.
4. Approved, automatic-closing process tank covers or fire-protection systems shall be permitted for enclosed systems that do not exceed a 150-gal. capacity or 10 sq. ft. in liquid surface area and for open processes with peripheral vapor containment and ventilation.

OPERATIONS AND MAINTENANCE

In addition to the safety requirements pertaining to the design of dip tanks and coating processes, there are procedure requirements intended to minimize the potential for fires and explosions. Examples of these procedures include the following (NFPA 2003c):

1. Areas in the vicinity of dipping and coating operations, especially drain boards and drip pans, shall be cleaned on a regular basis to minimize the accumulation of combustible residues and unnecessary combustible materials.
2. Use of combustible coverings (e.g., thin paper, plastic) and strippable coatings shall be permitted to facilitate cleaning operations in dipping and coating areas.
3. If excess residue accumulates in work areas, ducts, duct discharge points, or other adjacent areas, then all dipping and coating operations shall be discontinued until conditions are corrected.
4. Approved waste containers shall be provided for rags or waste impreg-

nated with flammable or combustible material, and all such rags or waste shall be deposited therein immediately after use.

5. The contents of waste cans shall be disposed of at least once daily or at the end of each shift.
6. Portable fire extinguishers shall be provided and located in accordance with *NFPA 10: Standard for Portable Fire Extinguishers.*

INSPECTION AND TESTING

Inspections and tests of all process tanks, including covers, overflow pipe inlets, overflow outlets and discharges, bottom drains, pumps and valves, electrical wiring and utilization equipment, bonding and grounding connections, ventilation systems, and all extinguishing equipment shall be made monthly. Any defects found shall be corrected. Periodic inspection by a competent and reliable individual should be made to determine the following (NFPA 2003c):

1. All sprinkler control valves are open.
2. Fire extinguishers are properly charged and in place.
3. Fire-suppression and alarm systems are charged and in operable condition.
4. Electric motors and fan bearings are not overheating.
5. Fan blades are in alignment.
6. Electric wiring has proper overcurrent protection.
7. Guards and globes on lighting fixtures are clean and in place.
8. Overflow and drain systems are in proper operating condition.
9. Cleanliness is being maintained.
10. All operating and safety instructions are being observed.

If repairs or changes are to be made to equipment, care should be taken to see that all residue deposits are removed and the area is kept wetted down with water beforehand to avoid a fire. During such repairs, no dipping or coating operations are to be conducted, all flammable and combustible liquids and portable combustible materials should be removed from the vicinity, and suitable fire extinguishers should be kept readily available.

TRAINING

Personnel involved in dipping or coating processes should receive documented training on the safety and health hazards associated with dip tanks, the operational, maintenance, and emergency procedures required, and the importance of constant operator awareness (NFPA 2003c). Training should also include the use, maintenance, and storage of all emergency, safety, or personal protective equipment that employees might be required to use in their normal work performance. Employees responsible for handling flammable and combustible liquids should be trained.

CHAPTER QUESTIONS

1. How does electrostatic spray painting work?
2. What are acceptable methods of overflow protection on dip tanks?
3. Why is liquid-level control important in dip-tank operations?
4. How does an aerated-powder coating operation work?
5. What is the maximum quantity of flammable or combustible liquids that can be stored in a coating-operation area?
6. When are dipping- and coating-operation areas considered hazardous environments?
7. Describe the type of training workers in dipping and coating operations should receive.

REFERENCES

Health and Safety Executive. (2004). *Hazardous Installations Directorate.* Sudbury, Suffolk, England: Health and Safety Executive, at www.hse.gov.uk/comah/srag tech/casepasadena89.htm (accessed June 23, 2005).

National Fire Protection Association (NFPA). (1997). *Fire Protection Handbook,* 18th ed. Quincy, MA: NFPA.

NFPA. (1999). *NFPA 91, Standard for Exhaust Systems for Air Conveying of Vapors, Gases, Mists, and Noncombustible Particulate Solids.* Quincy, MA: NFPA.

NFPA. (2003a). *Fire Protection Handbook,* 19th ed. Quincy, MA: NFPA.

NFPA. (2003b). *NFPA 33: Standard for Spray Application Using Flammable or Combustible Materials.* Quincy, MA: NFPA.

NFPA. (2003c). *NFPA 34: Standard for Dipping and Coating Processes Using Flammable or Combustible Liquids.* Quincy, MA: NFPA.

U.S. Department of Labor (USDOL). (2004a). *Occupational Safety and Health Standards for General Industry, Subpart H: Hazardous Materials: Dipping and Coating Operations, 29 C.F.R. § 1910.123.* Washington, DC: USDOL.

USDOL. (2004b). *Occupational Safety and Health Standards for General Industry, Subpart H: Spray Finishing Using Flammable and Combustible Materials, 29 C.F.R. § 1910.107.* Washington, DC: USDOL.

U.S. Fire Administration (USFA). (1990). *Technical Report Series: Phillips Petroleum Chemical Plant Explosion and Fire, Pasadena, Texas.* USFA Technical Report Series TR-035. Washington, DC: FEMA, USFA, National Fire Data Center.

Alarm and Detection Systems

A fire alarm system monitors and announces the status of the alarm or supervisory signal-initiating devices, then initiates the appropriate response to the signal. In general, fire alarm systems have three primary functions: (1) to provide an indication and warning of abnormal fire conditions, (2) to alert building occupants and summon appropriate assistance in adequate time to allow egress to a safe place and for rescue operations to begin, and (3) to control fire-safety functions (Moore and Richardson 2002, 52).

Based on the above three functions, a fire alarm system may provide three types of signals: alarm, supervisory, and trouble. An alarm signal will indicate the presence of a fire. A supervisory signal will indicate the operational status of fire-protection systems being monitored, such as an automatic sprinkler system. The trouble signal will indicate a problem or fault with a component or circuit of the alarm system, such as a smoke detector.

An excellent reference for alarm and detection systems is *National Fire Protection Association* (NFPA) *72: National Fire Alarm Code*. This code provides the minimum installation, test, maintenance, and performance requirements for fire alarm systems. It also provides requirements for the application, location, reliability, and limitations of fire alarm components. Examples of components addressed in this code include manual fire alarm boxes, automatic fire detectors, and notification appliances (Moore and Richardson 2002, 3). Equipment that meets the requirements of NFPA 72 must be listed for its specific purpose. This listing will normally identify the permitted use, required ambient conditions, mounting orientation, voltage tolerances, and compatibility. The plans for a fire alarm system should be developed by a qualified person who has working knowledge of NFPA 72 and is experienced in the proper design, application, installation, and testing of fire alarm systems.

NFPA 72 CLASSIFICATIONS FOR FIRE ALARM SYSTEMS

The National Fire Alarm Code has developed a classification system for alarm systems. This classification includes the following four types of alarm systems (NFPA 2002, 1–3.1):

1. *Household fire-warning systems* are alarm systems installed in dwelling units to warn the occupants of a fire emergency so that they can immediately evacuate the building.
2. *Protected-premises fire alarm systems* are designed to warn building occupants to evacuate the premise, actuate the building's fire-protection features, and provide environmental protection.
3. *Supervising-station fire alarm systems* provide a means of communication between the protected premises and a location commonly called a supervising station. There are five types of supervising stations: auxiliary fire alarm systems, remote supervising-station fire alarm systems, proprietary supervising-station systems, central-station fire alarm systems, and municipal fire alarm systems.
4. *Public fire alarm reporting systems* transmit alarms from street locations to a public emergency-service communication center. There are two types of public fire alarms systems: the local energy type and the shunt type.

POWER SUPPLIES FOR ALARM SYSTEMS

Fire alarm systems need to have at least two independent and reliable power supplies that have an adequate capacity for their specific application. The first power source is commonly referred to as the primary power source and is usually provided by electrical service from a commercial electrical distributor. The primary power service must be on dedicated branch circuit(s) that is mechanically protected, and all electrical wiring and equipment must be in accordance with the *NFPA 70: National Electrical Code.*

The secondary power supply serves as a backup to the primary supply and must automatically supply electrical energy to the system within thirty seconds after failure of the primary supply. This secondary supply must also have a capacity that will allow the alarm system to operate for twenty-four hours (Bunker and Moore 1999, 72-21). Two examples of secondary supplies include storage batteries and an engine-driven generator. An excellent reference for generators as secondary power supplies is *NFPA 110: Standard for Emergency and Standby Power Systems.*

INITIATING DEVICES

An initiating device includes all types of sensors, ranging from manually operated fire alarm boxes to switches, that detect the operation of a fire-suppression system (NFPA 2002, 55) (see figure 8.1). These initiating devices do not respond to the fire itself but to some change in ambient conditions as a result of the fire such as elevated temperatures or smoke. Important considerations for initiating devices include installation location, selection of the type of device, and temperature classifications for heat-sensing devices.

FIGURE 8.1
Fire alarm pull station

BASIC CONSIDERATIONS FOR INSTALLATION

In general, where possible, initiating devices should be installed throughout the entire facility, including uninhabited spaces such as closets and
storage areas. Possible references for installation of devices include the
device manufacturer, local building codes, and NFPA 72. In some situations, the term *total complete coverage* is used regarding coverage of initiating devices. Total complete coverage implies coverage in all rooms, halls,
storage areas, basements, attics, lofts, spaces above suspended ceilings,
other subdivisions and accessible spaces, the inside of all closets, elevator
shafts, enclosed stairways, dumbwaiter shafts, and chutes (Moore and
Richardson 2002, 101). It is important to note that inaccessible areas need
not be protected by detectors when total complete coverage is applied.
Another common term applied regarding coverage is *partial coverage*. Partial coverage implies that initiating devices are placed in all common areas,
work spaces, and other unoccupied spaces where the environments are
suitable for proper detector operation. In all cases, initiating devices must
be installed so that they are accessible for periodic maintenance and testing (Moore and Richardson 2002, 103).

An important consideration regarding the placement and spacing of
smoke and heat detectors is the transfer of combustion products, such as
heat and smoke, from the fire to the detector. This transfer of smoke,
aerosol, or heated combustion-product gases and air can be described
through a set of physical principles generally called a *fire plume* (NFPA
1997, 1–86). Specifically a fire plume is the buoyant column of flame and
heated combustion products rising above the fuel. This buoyancy occurs
as a result of density differences. Density is inversely proportional to temperature; therefore, the hotter gases associated with the plume cause an
upward force on the hot gases relative to the cooler surrounding air. This
basic principle is behind the requirement that most detectors be placed on
the ceiling or within 12 in. of the ceiling.

SELECTION OF INITIATING DEVICES

The two most important considerations in selecting an alarm system are
the need for speed and accuracy of response to a fire with minimal chances
for false alarms. Therefore, it is critical to select the proper type of initiating device for each application. This selection process requires a thorough
understanding of how each type of detector operates and the environment

in which it will operate. Environmental factors to consider include the kinds of potential fires expected, the quantity and types of fuel sources, potential ignition sources, and the range of ambient air temperatures (NFPA 1997, 5–20). There are three general types of fire detectors to choose from: smoke, heat, and flame. In general, heat detectors have the lowest rate of false alarms, but they also have the slowest response time. In contrast, flame detectors offer the fastest response time but the highest rate of false alarms.

HEAT-SENSING FIRE DETECTORS

A heat detector responds to an increase in the ambient temperature in its immediate vicinity. Specifically, the increase in temperature of the sensing element of the heat detector is due to the absorption of heat from fire. There are three basic principles for detecting heat: fixed temperature, rate compensation, and rate of rise. Fixed-temperature detectors are set to activate when the operating element reaches a set temperature. A rate-of-rise detector activates in response to a rate of temperature change such as 15°F in one minute. Rate-compensation detectors activate when the surrounding air reaches a set temperature (Bugbee and Cote 2001, 245).

The performance of a heat detector depends on two parameters: its temperature classification and its time-dependent thermal-response characteristics. It is critical to select a detector that will be stable in the environment in which it is installed. For this reason, all heat-sensing fire detectors must be marked with their operating temperature and thermal-response coefficient. As a general rule, the temperature rating of the detector should be at least 20°F above the maximum expected temperature at the ceiling. A temperature difference less than this may cause false alarms, while selecting a temperature significantly higher will increase response time. Traditionally, the temperature classification has been the principal parameter used in selecting the proper detector for a given area. Heat-sensing fire detectors of the fixed-temperature or rate-compensated type are classified by the temperature of operation and marked with a color code, as specified in table 8.1 (Moore and Richardson 2002, 111).

LOCATION OF HEAT-SENSING FIRE DETECTORS: SPOT VERSUS LINE DEVICES

Each heat-sensing fire detector can be installed as either a spot-type or a line-type device. As the name implies, spot-type devices occupy a specific

Table 8.1   Temperature Classification and Color Code

Temperature Classification and Color Code	Temperature-Rating Range (°F)
Low: uncolored	100–134
Ordinary: white	135–174
Intermediate: blue	175–249
High: red	250–324
Extra high: green	325–399
Very extra high: orange	400–499
Ultra high	500–575

spot or point, while line devices extend over a distance, sensing temperature along their entire length.

NFPA 72 requires that spot-type heat detectors be located on the ceiling not closer than 4 in. from the sidewall or on the sidewalls between 4 and 12 in. from the ceiling. Line-type heat detectors are to be placed on the ceiling or on the sidewalls not more than 20 in. from the ceiling (Moore and Richardson 2002, 113).

The distance between the detectors must not exceed their listed spacing. The listed spacing for a heat detector is determined using a number of variables, such as anticipated fire size, fire growth rate, ambient temperature, ceiling height, and thermal-response coefficient. NFPA 72 also required that all points on the ceiling have a detector within a distance equal to 0.7 times the listed spacing (0.7S). It should also be noted that the listed spacing is useful for comparing two heat detectors to each other, but it cannot be used to predict when a given detector will respond (Moore and Richardson 2002, 117).

SMOKE-SENSING FIRE DETECTORS

A smoke detector responds to the presence of smoke in the air in its immediate vicinity. The sensitivity of a smoke detector in responding to smoke is based on the percent of obscuration required to produce a signal. This sensitivity is expressed as the percent per foot obscuration and must be identified on the detector (Moore and Richardson 2002, 137). For most fires, smoke detectors respond much faster than either automatic sprinklers or heat detectors because smoke does not dissipate as quickly as heat in large, open areas. The difference in the speed of response becomes even more dramatic with low-energy smoldering fires.

LOCATION AND SPACING OF SMOKE DETECTORS

In general, the placement of smoke detectors is based on the premise that in order for a smoke detector to respond, the smoke must travel from the point of origin to the detector (see figure 8.2). This flow of smoke is based on the fire plume, discussed previously, as well as on building and site characteristics, such as ceiling shape and surface, ceiling height, configuration of contents in the area to be protected, burning characteristics of the combustible materials present, and ventilation (Moore and Richardson 2002, 137).

The location and spacing of smoke detectors is based on the effect of the above site-specific characteristics on the flow of smoke from these early-stage, low-energy-output fires. The design process begins by locating detectors so that they will provide general area protection with additional detectors added to take into account known building characteristics that may affect smoke movement. Some general guidelines provided by NFPA 72 for the spacing of smoke detectors are that spot-type smoke detectors be located on the ceiling not closer than 4 in. from a sidewall or, if placed on a sidewall, between 4 and 12 in. from the ceiling. On smooth ceilings, spacing of 30 ft. is permitted to be used as a guide and all points on the ceiling shall have a detector within a distance equal to 0.7 times the selected spacing (Moore and Richardson 2002, 141–42). It is important to

FIGURE 8.2
Smoke detector (photo courtesy of Kidde Products)

note that these are general guidelines, and the manufacturer's recommendations or the local building codes, whichever are more stringent, should take precedence for smoke-detector placement.

RADIANT-ENERGY-SENSING FIRE DETECTORS

A radiant-energy-sensing fire detector responds to the influx of radiant energy that has traveled from the fire to the detector. The radiant-energy-sensing fire detector can be classified as either a flame detector or a spark or ember detector. In each case, either heat, smoke, or light travels from the fire to the detector before the device initiates the alarm signal. The selection of these detectors is more precise than that of the other types because the designer must match the spectral response of the detector to the spectral response of the fire to be detected and minimize the possibility of nuisance alarms from nonfire sources (Moore and Richardson 2002, 161–62). Some extraneous sources of radiant emissions that have been identified as interfering with the stability of flame detectors include sunlight, lightning, X rays, and ultraviolet radiation from arc welding. Radiant-energy-sensing fire detectors are commonly used in environments that are unsuitable for heat or smoke detectors, such as the following:

- Open-spaced buildings with high ceilings, such as warehouses
- Outdoor areas where winds can prevent smoke and heat from reaching a heat or smoke detector
- Areas where rapidly developing, flaming fires can occur, such as aircraft hangers

There are three basic types of flame detectors. First, there are ultraviolet flame detectors that use a vacuum photodiode Geiger-Muller tube for detecting ultraviolet radiation from a flame (Moore and Richardson 2002, 158–59). The second type of flame detector is a single-wavelength, infrared flame detector, which uses different photocell types to detect the infrared emissions in a single-wavelength band that are produced by a flame. In concept, because these flame detectors respond to specific, single wavelengths, they can be fuel specific. A similar type is the multiple-wavelength infrared flame detector, which, as the name implies, senses radiation at two or more narrow bands of wavelengths. The third type of flame detector is the ultraviolet/infrared flame detector, which is a combination of the first two types. Specifically, this detector senses ultraviolet radiation with a vacuum photodiode tube and a selected wavelength of infrared radiation with a photocell and uses this combined signal to indicate a fire (NFPA 1997, 5–19, 20).

The second broad classification of radiant-energy-sensing fire detectors includes spark or ember detectors, which use a solid-state phototransistor to sense the radiant energy emitted by embers. The embers are typically between 0.5 and 2.0 in normally dark environments. As a general rule, these detectors are extremely sensitive and can have response times in the microseconds (Moore and Richardson 2002, 160).

LOCATION AND SPACING OF RADIANT-ENERGY-SENSING FIRE DETECTORS

Radiant-energy-sensing fire detectors must be located and spaced consistently with their listing or manufacturer's recommendation. Simply stated, a flame detector cannot detect what it cannot "see." Therefore, the number of detectors should be based on the detectors being positioned so that no point requiring detection in the hazard area is obstructed or outside the field of view of at least one detector. Some general considerations for the location and spacing of radiant-energy-sensing fire detectors are size of the fire that is to be detected, the fuel involved, the sensitivity of the detector, the distance between the fire and the detector, and the field of view of the detector.

The field of view of the detector is based on the fact that the greater the angular displacement of the fire from the optical axis of the detector, the larger the fire must become before it is detected. This principle establishes the field of view of the detector (Moore and Richardson 2002, 163).

SPRINKLER-WATER-FLOW ALARM-INITIATING DEVICES

In many facilities, the sprinkler system is used as both a suppression system and a detection system. Specifically, a sprinkler-water-flow alarm initiates an alarm signal when the flow of water through the system is greater than that from a single sprinkler head of the smallest orifice size. NFPA 72 recommends that the water-flow alarm be adjusted so that it is initiated within ninety seconds of a sustained flow equal to or greater than that of a single sprinkler (smallest orifice) that can be installed in a system (Moore and Richardson 2002, 172).

In most sprinkler systems, this water-flow alarm will provide a signal locally, either in the immediate vicinity of the riser or throughout the entire facility. The signal can also be transmitted off premise to a supervising station.

In a wet-pipe sprinkler system, the water-flow-alarm initiating device is either a hydraulically operated alarm check valve commonly called a *water motor gong* or an electrically operated, vane-type water-flow alarm. Water-flow alarms that can be used for dry-pipe, preaction, and deluge sprinkler systems include hydraulically operated water motor gongs and drop-in-pressure water-flow alarms. An electrically operated, vane-type water-flow alarm is not permitted on these types of sprinkler systems (NFPA 2003, 9–47).

In a large wet-pipe system with large sprinkler risers, the flow from a single head can be hard to detect, depending on the amount of trapped air in the piping. The air in the piping acts as a gas cushion, allowing pulsating variations in water pressure within the riser when a single head discharges. These variations in water pressure can prevent either the vane of a vane-type water-flow switch or the clapper of an alarm check valve from opening for long enough to initiate the alarm signal. Therefore, it is not uncommon to install an excess pressure pump and pressure-drop alarm-initiating devices in large wet-pipe systems to reduce the effects of pressure variations in the system and to minimize response time (Moore and Richardson 2002, 173).

SIGNAL ANNUNCIATION

The primary purpose of fire alarm system annunciation is to enable responding personnel to identify the location of a fire quickly and accurately and to indicate the status of emergency equipment or fire-safety functions that might affect the safety of the occupants in a fire situation (Moore and Richardson 2002, 73). NFPA 72 requires all protected premise systems to indicate fire alarm, supervisory, and trouble signals distinctively.

Supervisory signals can be used to monitor the functions of a sprinkler system, such as the water-control valve and the water pressure and level in the system. Trouble signals with the alarm system indicate a fault in a monitored circuit or component (NFPA 2002, 72-22).

The fire alarm annunciation system must be specific enough to identify the origin of a fire alarm signal as quickly as possible to reduce response time. For the purpose of alarm annunciation, each floor of the building must be considered as a separate zone. However, if a floor area exceeds 20,000 sq. ft., additional zoning should be considered. In addition, if the alarm system serves more than one building, each building must be indicated separately on the signal-annunciation panel (Moore and Richardson 2002, 74).

NOTIFICATION DEVICES

The primary purpose of a notification device is to convey information to building occupants during a fire emergency. This may be as simple as notifying building occupants to evacuate or alerting fire and emergency brigades of appropriate extinguishment strategies. In general, notification devices should be sufficient in quantity, audibility, intelligibility, and visibility so as to reliably convey the intended information. To guide the designers and installers of fire alarm systems so that the system will deliver audible and visible information with appropriate intensity, the device nameplate must state the capabilities of the appliance, as determined through tests conducted by the listing organization. This may include electrical requirements and rated audible or visible performance (Moore and Richardson 2002, 270). The proper location of notification devices is critical to ensure that they operate as intended. Where possible, wall-mounted devices should be placed above the finished floors at heights no lower than 80 in., and below the finished ceiling, at heights no lower than 6 in. (NFPA 2002, 72-58).

AUDIBLE AND VISIBLE CRITERIA OF NOTIFICATION DEVICES

A notification device is only effective if it is heard or seen. Therefore, specific audible and visual criteria have been established by NFPA 72. Audible notification devices intended for operation in the public mode must have a sound level of at least 75 dBA at 10 ft., or a sound level at least 15 dBA above the average-ambient-sound level, or 5 dBA above the maximum sound level, having a duration of at least sixty seconds (Moore and Richardson 2002, 277–78). These sound levels should be measured 5 ft. above the floor in the area in which the device is installed. Emergency voice/ alarm communications systems used as part of the alarm system must be capable of reproducing prerecorded, synthesized, or live messages intelligibly. NFPA 72 defines an intelligible system as one that has a measured value equivalent to a Common Intelligibility Scale (CIS) value of 0.7 or greater using the guidelines in Annex A of IEC 60849, "Sound Systems for Emergency Purposes" (Moore and Richardson 2002, 276).

Visible-signaling notification devices are often used to supplement audible devices; however, they are required when the average sound-pressure level exceeds 105 dBA because it could be harmful to occupants to try to overcome such a high sound level with audible fire alarm signals. Figure 8.3 depicts a typical fire alarm.

In general, there are two methods of visible signaling. The first involves the identification of an emergency condition by direct viewing of an illuminating appliance, such as a strobe light. Currently both NFPA 72 and 101 recognize only strobe lights as visible-signaling devices. NFPA 72 requires that the flash rate not exceed two flashes per second and that the maximum pulse duration be 0.2 seconds. In addition, the light-source color shall be clear or nominal white and not exceed 1,000 candlepower. The second method of visible signaling involves illumination of the surrounding area. With this method, an illumination of 0.0375 foot-candles

FIGURE 8.3
Fire alarm

in all occupied spaces requiring visible notification meets the minimum light-intensity requirements according to NFPA 72 (NFPA 2002, 72-58-60).

REPORTING SYSTEMS

The primary purpose of a fire alarm reporting system is to send a signal or communication to an outside agency regarding a fire emergency. In general, these reporting systems can be classified as public fire alarm systems, proprietary supervising systems, central-station systems, and remote supervising systems.

PUBLIC FIRE ALARM SYSTEMS

A public fire alarm reporting system allows the general public to initiate a fire alarm signal from manual fire alarm boxes. Such an alarm system may also be used to transmit other signals or calls of a public emergency nature as long as the transmission does not interfere with the transmission and receipt of fire alarms. The manual fire alarm boxes must be located where they are conspicuous and accessible. One way of accomplishing this is to mount the boxes on support poles that are identified by distinctive colors or signs placed at least 8 ft. above the ground and visible from all directions, wherever possible. Indicating lights of a distinctive color can also be used to make the manual fire alarm boxes more conspicuous. The boxes must also have operating instructions plainly visible, and the actuating device must be designed to make its use readily apparent (NFPA 2002, 72-77-78).

CENTRAL-STATION FIRE ALARM SYSTEMS

A central-station fire alarm system receives fire alarm, supervisory, and trouble signals from a protected premise. These stations are controlled and operated by a person, firm, or corporation whose business is the furnishing of such systems. Such a company will have obtained specific listing from a nationally recognized testing laboratory as a provider of central-station service (NFPA 1997, 5–7, 8).

Central-station components typically include the central-station physical plant, exterior communications channels, subsidiary stations, and signaling equipment located at the protected premises. At the protected premise, the central station will be involved with the installation, testing, maintenance, and runner servicing of the alarm system. At the actual central station, the monitoring of the system and signals will occur, as will the retransmission of signals to the appropriate emergency-response service and record keeping.

The exterior communications channels between the protected premise and the central station must have two independent means for retransmitting a fire alarm signal to the designated public emergency-response center (Moore and Richardson 2002, 324). Today, it is not uncommon for computer-based automation systems to manage the receipt and retransmission of signals. When such systems are used, the central station must automatically record the time and date of the retransmission of signals.

The central station must have a minimum of two trained operators on duty at all times to monitor signals. According to NFPA 72, all alarm signals must be treated as positives. This standard requires that the operators of central stations take the following actions for all alarm signals (Moore and Richardson 2002, 325–27):

- Immediately retransmit the alarm to the public fire-service communications center
- Dispatch a runner to the protected premises to arrive within one hour after receipt of a signal if equipment needs to be manually reset by the prime contractor
- Immediately notify the subscriber
- Provide notice to the subscriber, the authority having jurisdiction, or both

PROPRIETARY SUPERVISING-STATION SYSTEMS

A proprietary supervising station is very similar to a central-station system, except this system is located at the protected property or at another property belonging to the same owner. Such a system is owned and operated by the property owner and receives signals from one or more properties under the same ownership. Where more than one building exists, the alarm signal must identify the specific building in which the signal originates. For large facilities, the floor, section, or other subdivision of the building must be designated at the proprietary supervising station or at the building that is protected (Moore and Richardson 2002, 334). These systems transmit fire alarm signals, as well as supervisory and trouble signals, to the station. The actual proprietary station must be located in a fire-resistive, detached building or in a cutoff room not exposed to the hazardous areas of the properties that are to be protected. This station must have an automatic emergency-lighting system that has a power source independent of the primary lighting source and capable of providing illumination for a minimum of twenty-six hours. There must be two different means for alerting the operator when each signal is received. The maximum elapsed time from sensing a fire alarm at an initiating device circuit until it is recorded or displayed at the proprietary supervising station must not exceed ninety seconds (Moore and Richardson 2002, 336).

All communications and transmission channels between the proprietary supervising station and the protected premise control panel must be tested either manually or automatically once every twenty-four hours to verify operation. In addition, all operator controls at the proprietary supervising station must be tested at each change of shift.

All personnel at the proprietary supervising station must be trained, competent, and in constant attendance so that appropriate action can be taken when necessary. It is generally recommended that at least two operators be on duty at all times, with one of the operators acting as a runner to the alarm location if an alarm is activated.

REMOTE-SUPERVISING-STATION FIRE ALARM SYSTEMS

A remote-supervising-station system provides a means for transmitting alarm, supervisory, and trouble signals from the protected premises to a remote supervising station. Such systems normally transmit alarm signals to a public fire-service communications center, community emergency-response center, or other constantly attended location acceptable to the authority having jurisdiction. These types of systems are typically selected when management does not believe it needs the level of protection offered by a central-station or proprietary supervising system.

The remote supervising station must have a minimum of two operators on duty at all times to monitor signals. When a signal is received at the station, the operator on duty must notify the owner or the owner's designated representative immediately. All controls at the remote supervising station must be tested at the beginning of each shift or change in personnel. The signal-receiving equipment at the remote station must indicate each signal both audibly and visibly. In addition, a trouble signal must be received when the system or any portion of the system at the protected premises is placed in a bypass or test mode. As with the other systems, a record must be maintained of all signals received, including time, date, location, and any system restorations (Moore and Richardson 2002, 343–44).

INSPECTION, TESTING, AND MAINTENANCE OF FIRE ALARM SYSTEMS

The owner of an alarm system is responsible for the testing and maintenance of the system. In general, this inspection, testing, and maintenance should follow the requirements specified in NFPA 72, conform to the alarm manufacturer's recommendations, and also be completed in such a way as to verify the proper operation of the alarm system.

All personnel working on the system must be qualified and experienced in the inspection, testing, and maintenance of fire alarm systems. An example of a qualified person would be one who is factory trained and certified by the state or local municipality or by an agency such as the International Municipal Signal Association (Moore and Richardson 2002, 430).

A specification for the inspection, testing, and maintenance of an alarm system should identify the procedures to be performed, how they are to be performed, the type of data to be recorded, and the frequency of testing, inspection, and maintenance. An example of a procedure is notifying all persons and facilities receiving alarm, supervisory, or trouble signals and all building occupants of testing to prevent unnecessary response.

Examples of documents recommended by NFPA 72 for testing and maintaining a system include the fire alarm system record of completion, point-to-point wiring diagrams, individual device interconnection drawings, as-built (record) drawings, copies of original equipment submittals, operational manuals, and manufacturer's proper testing and maintenance requirements (Moore and Richardson 2002, 432).

NFPA 72 also provides a detailed listing of the recommended frequencies for testing alarm system components. In almost all cases, testing is required initially after installation and then at intervals ranging from weekly to yearly. In situations where automatic testing is performed at least weekly by a remotely monitored fire alarm control unit, the manual testing frequency is permitted to extend to yearly. The following are some examples of NFPA 72 recommended testing frequencies after installation (NFPA 2002, 72-87):

- *Annual testing:* emergency voice/alarm communications equipment and remote annunciators
- *Semiannual testing:* batteries in fire alarm systems
- *Quarterly testing:* control equipment used in building systems not connected to a supervising station
- *Monthly testing:* engine-driven generators and batteries used in central-station facilities

All records on the maintenance, inspection, and testing of alarm systems must be retained until the next test and for one year following. This record must identify, at a minimum, the following information (Moore and Richardson 2002, 462–63):

- Date
- Test frequency
- Name and address of property
- Name of person performing inspection, maintenance, tests, or combination thereof, as well as affiliation, business address, and telephone number
- Name, address, and representative of approving agencies
- Designation of the detector(s) tested
- Functional test of detectors
- Functional test of required sequence of operations

CHAPTER QUESTIONS

1. T/F Fire alarm systems need to have at least three independent and reliable power supplies that are of adequate capacity for their application.
2. T/F Radiant-energy-sensing fire detectors respond to an increase in the ambient temperature in their immediate vicinity.
3. T/F Visible signaling is required when the average ambient-sound-pressure level exceeds 105 dBA.
4. T/F In a proprietary supervising station, three operators are required

to be on duty at all times so that there are always two people at the station when one is sent as a runner to an alarm location.

5. T/F The primary purpose of a fire alarm reporting system is to send a signal or communication to an inside agency regarding a fire emergency.

6. The trouble signal, within a fire alarm system, indicates:

   a. The operational status of the fire-protection systems being monitored

   b. The presence of a fire

   c. A problem or fault with a component or circuit of the alarm system

   d. None of the above

7. Secondary power supplies serve as backup to the primary supply. This power supply must have enough capacity to allow the alarm system to operate for how many hours?

   a. 12

   b. 24

   c. 36

   d. 48

8. For most fires, _____ detectors responds much faster than automatic sprinklers or _____ detectors.

   a. smoke; heat

   b. heat; radiant energy

   c. spark; smoke

   d. flame; smoke

9. The fire rating for rooms containing remote-supervising-station equipment should be:

   a. 1 hour

   b. 2 hours

   c. 3 hours

   d. 4 hours

10. Engine-driven generators and the batteries used in central-station facilities need to be tested how often?

   a. Annually

   b. Semiannually

   c. Quarterly

   d. Monthly

11. List and describe the three functions of an alarm system.
12. Explain what factors need to be considered when selecting an alarm system.
13. What is the primary purpose of signal annunciation?
14. Maintenance, inspection, and testing records must be retained until the next test and for one year thereafter. What information must be provided in these records?
15. What is a zone, and what are its criteria?

REFERENCES

Bunker, Merton W., and Wayne D. Moore. (1999). *National Fire Alarm Code Handbook.* Quincy, MA: NFPA.

Cote, Arthur, and Percy Bugbee. (2001). *Principles of Fire Protection.* Quincy, MA: NFPA.

Moore, Wayne D., and Lee Richardson. (2002). *National Fire Alarm Code Handbook,* 4th ed. Quincy, MA: NFPA.

National Fire Protection Association (NFPA). (1997). *Fire Protection Handbook,* 18th ed. Quincy, MA: NFPA.

National Fire Protection Association (NFPA). (2003). *Fire Protection Handbook,* 19th ed. Quincy, MA: NFPA.

NFPA. (2002). *NFPA 72: National Fire Alarm Code.* Quincy, MA: NFPA.

9

Fire Extinguishment

The four components the fire tetrahedron—fuel, oxygen, a heat source and a chain reaction—can be used as attack points to extinguish a fire. Since fires can occur only if all four of the tetrahedron components are present in sufficient concentrations, removal of any one of the four will result in no fire. All fire-extinguishing methods used in firefighting apply techniques designed to attack one or more of the four components of the fire tetrahedron. The equipment used to remove a piece of the fire tetrahedron and extinguish the fire can range from a portable fire extinguisher to a fixed sprinkler system. Examples of the various approaches and the area of the tetrahedron they influence appear in table 9.1.

CLASSIFICATIONS OF FIRES

Fires can be classified by the type of material involved in the combustion process. This classification system is useful in determining the most appropriate type of extinguishing agent to use. The five classes of fires are as follows:

Table 9.1 Extinguishing Methods

Extinguishing Method	Tetrahedron Component
Water spray	Heat (cooling) and, to a lesser extent, the water spray removes the oxygen from the fuel surface
Carbon dioxide	CO_2 removes the oxygen from the fuel surface and, to a lesser extent, cools the surface of the burning material
Dry chemical fire extinguisher	This interrupts the chemical reaction
Fire break cut in a forest fire	This removes fuel from the fire

1. *Class A:* combustible materials (wood, paper)
2. *Class B:* flammable liquids (oils, petroleum products)
3. *Class C:* electrical fires
4. *Class D:* combustible metals
5. *Class K:* combustible cooking media

In Class C, electrical fires, the material actually involved in these fires may be Class A, ordinary combustible materials, or Class B, flammable liquids. The special classification for electrical fires is to provide an extinguishing agent that is not electrically conductive.

EXTINGUISHING AGENTS

The agent used to extinguish a fire can range from water to dry-chemical compounds to carbon dioxide. Some extinguishing agents are preferred over others based upon their characteristics and the characteristics of the burning material.

WATER

Of all the extinguishing materials available, water is the most widely used and available for many reasons; it is inexpensive, abundant, and effective in fire suppression (NFPA 1997, 6-5). Water is considered a good extinguisher because of its physical properties (NFPA 1997, 6-5):

1. Water is a heavy and relatively stable material.
2. Water can absorb a great deal of heat.
3. When water is converted to a vapor, its volume increases about sixteen hundred times, displacing an equal volume of air around the fire.

Water can extinguish a fire by removing heat and, in some instances, oxygen. In order for a material to sustain combustion, the surface of the material must be heated to its fire point. Water extinguishes a fire primarily by cooling the surface of the materials below the temperature necessary to support combustion. Water can also extinguish a fire by removing oxygen from the surface of the burning material, thereby smothering the fire. Steam can be generated from the water hitting the material; thus, the steam displaces the air around the material.

Water can also extinguish a fire through dilution. Water-soluble mate-

rials may be diluted in water. Ethyl and methyl alcohol fires may be put
out by dilution (NFPA 1997, 6-7). One problem is that a large amount of
water may be needed; thus, the water and alcohol could exceed the holding capacity of the container.

To improve the performance of water, man-made additives have been
designed. These additives prevent the water from freezing or corroding
piping and improve its ability to penetrate burning material. There are
many instances in which water is used as an extinguishing agent where
environmental conditions expose the agent to possible freezing. This is
most common when using water in fixed extinguishing systems in areas
such as building attics and uninsulated storage areas. Additives like glyc-
erin or proylene glycol are used to lower the freezing point of water in the
sprinkler system, thus preventing the water from freezing and breaking
the piping. To prevent the water in a sprinkler system from corroding the
piping, additives like calcium chloride with a corrosion inhibitor are
added to the water.

A characteristic of water that reduces its ability to extinguish fires is its
surface tension. Surface tension is the force acting on the surface of a liquid, tending to minimize the area of the surface; quantitatively, it is the
force that appears to act across a line of unit length on the surface (NFPA
1997, 6-7). Water has a relatively high surface tension, which slows its ability to penetrate burning combustibles, as well as its spread through closely
packed or baled materials. To lower the surface tension of water and
improve its ability to penetrate materials, wetting agents can be added.
Wet water agents should not be used on electrical equipment because of
the increased conductivity of the solution.

Another characteristic of water that limits its use as an extinguishing
agent is its ability to conduct electricity. When water is applied to electrical
equipment, a continuous circuit is formed that can conduct the electrical
charge back to the person applying the water. The electrical conductivity
of water in firefighting is most important to firefighters applying water
streams in a fire. Water can be used in certain situations on electrical fires
as long as the minimum distances established for the use of water streams
on electrical equipment and the minimum distances for applying fixed
water systems to live, uninsulated electrical equipment are adhered to.
Some factors that influence the conductivity of water when it is used as an
extinguishing agent include the voltage of the electrical equipment, the

nozzle design, the purity of the water, the length and area of the water stream, and the resistance of the person's body, depending upon if it is wet or dry (NFPA 1997, 6-8). The minimum safe distances to live electrical equipment are influenced by the type of nozzle used and the voltage of the equipment.

WATER USE ON SPECIAL HAZARDS

While water has been found to be an ideal extinguishing agent for many types of fires, in some situations water may make the fire problem worse. For example, certain chemicals, such as carbides and peroxides, can react with water, releasing flammable gases and heat. Combustible metals such as titanium, magnesium, and sodium will react with water, releasing energy. Radioactive metals pose a hazard with water not from a fire standpoint but from a contamination standpoint in which the water can become irradiated and spread the hazardous material. While water can be effective in cooling the surface of flammable and combustible liquid fires, it can also cause the fire to spread due to burning liquid floating on the surface of the water.

CARBON DIOXIDE

Carbon dioxide is a noncombustible, nonreactive gas that has been used for many years as an extinguishing agent. It extinguishes fires primarily by displacing the oxygen surrounding the surface of the burning material. As a result, the oxygen levels are reduced below the point required to sustain combustion. While it is commonly identified as the agent for electrical fire suppression, carbon dioxide will also work as an extinguishing agent on most materials except cellulose materials. Carbon dioxide extinguishes fires primarily by eliminating oxygen, but cellulose materials have an available oxygen source present due to the nature of their composition, making it difficult to extinguish the fire using carbon dioxide (see figure 9.1). Carbon dioxide can be used for combustibles and flammable and combustible liquids if applied properly. A downside of using carbon dioxide on flammable-liquid fires is that when air is reintroduced over the surface of the liquid, the fire can reignite.

In some instances, carbon dioxide can also aid in extinguishing a fire by cooling if it is applied directly on the surface of the burning material. Examples of this use in industry include liquid-filled dip tanks protected

FIGURE 9.1
Carbon dioxide extinguisher (photo courtesy of Kidde Products)

by carbon dioxide systems that can discharge the gas directly onto the burning surface of a liquid-filled dip tank.

Some characteristics of carbon dioxide that may limit its use as an extinguishing agent include the fact that it can suffocate not only the fire but also people. The carbon dioxide concentration levels necessary to extinguish a fire can produce unconsciousness and death in people; so, as a precaution, carbon dioxide should not be used in normally occupied areas unless a warning can be given before the material is discharged (NFPA 1997, 6-371).

HALOGENATED AGENTS

Halogenated materials use a hydrocarbon material with an atom of the halogen series: fluorine, bromine, chlorine, or iodine. By adding this halogen atom, the gas has nonflammability characteristics and increased flame extinguishability. Halon 104, or carbon tetrachloride, was first used as an extinguishing agent in 1900; in 1910, it was used in portable fire extinguishers. Because carbon tetrachloride was toxic, deaths occurred. New forms of halogenated extinguishing agents were developed. The most widely used are Halon 1301 and Halon 1211. The U.S. Army Corps of Engineers developed the numbering system for halogenated agents. The digits represent the chemical composition of the agent as follows:

- *Digit 1:* number of carbon atoms in the chemical
- *Digit 2:* number of fluorine atoms
- *Digit 3:* number of chlorine atoms
- *Digit 4:* number of bromine atoms
- *Digit 5:* number of iodine atoms, if any (if omitted, none are used)

Halogenated agents are commonly used in handheld fire extinguishers and fixed extinguishing systems protecting electrical equipment and electronics. Halon agents vaporize quickly in a fire and leave no corrosive or abrasive residue. Because of this property, halon extinguishing agents do not damage the electrical components like dry-chemical agents; as a result, they became very popular in industry. Although they have been very effective extinguishing agents, Halon 1301, 2402, and 1211 were identified in the Montreal Protocol on Substances that Deplete the Ozone Layer as ozone-depleting substances. Halons are bromated chlorofluorocarbons and are very effective at destroying the earth's ozone layer. As a result, their use is being phased out.

To replace halon, new extinguishing agents have been developed with the same firefighting characteristics as halon. Examples of two new extinguishing agents replacing halon are Halotron, manufactured by Halotron, and FE-36, manufactured by Dupont. Inergen is another environmentally friendly fire-suppression agent manufactured by Ansul. Inergen is a blend of three naturally occurring gases, nitrogen, argon, and carbon dioxide, and does not deplete the ozone layer.

DRY CHEMICALS

Dry chemicals are commonly used extinguishing agents. They can be found in both fixed systems and portable fire extinguishers (see figure 9.2). There are different types of dry-chemical products on the market. Examples of dry-chemical agents include sodium bicarbonate, potassium bicarbonate, potassium chloride, and monoammonium phosphate. The most widely used dry-chemical agent is monoammonium phosphate. Ex-

FIGURE 9.2
Multipurpose dry-chemical extinguisher (photo courtesy of Kidde Products)

tinguishers filled with this material are referred to as triclass dry-chemical extinguishers. The designator "triclass" refers to the fact that the agent can be used on Class A, B, or C fires. The dry-chemical agents purple K (potassium bicarbonate) and sodium bicarbonate are useful on Class B and C fires.

The manner in which dry-chemical agents extinguish a fire varies. For example, sodium bicarbonate, when heated by fire, releases CO_2 and smothers the fire. Monoammonium phosphate, on the other hand, forms a sticky film that smothers the fire. Dry-chemical agents can also extinguish a fire by interrupting the fire's chemical chain reaction by preventing the particles of combustion (free radicals) from coming together and continuing the reaction (NFPA 1997, 6-342).

Dry-chemical agents are very popular because of their versatility. However, there are some downsides to their use. Generally, the materials are nontoxic; however, when inhaled in heavy concentrations, they can be irritants. Dry chemical agents can be used on combustible materials, on electrical fires because they are nonconductive, and on flammable-liquid fires, but they should not be used in areas where there is delicate electrical equipment. The agents can be slightly corrosive, resulting in damage to the electrical equipment.

FOAM EXTINGUISHING AGENTS

Firefighting foam is an aggregate of gas-filled bubbles from a water-based solution. The gas used in the bubbles is typically an inert gas. Since the foam is lighter than liquids, it will float on top of flammable and combustible liquid, producing a layer that excludes oxygen, cools, and produces a vapor seal. The foam agent is produced by mixing a concentrate with water, then aerating the mixture. Foams are defined by their expansion ratio, which is the volume of foam after air is added to the volume of the foam before it is added. The classifications of foam extinguishing agents are as follows (Cote and Bugbee 2001, 197):

1. *Low-expansion foam:* 20:1
2. *Medium-expansion foam:* 20 to 200:1
3. *High-expansion foam:* 200 to 1,000:1

Flammable- and combustible-liquid fires use foam as the only permanent extinguishing agent. In a fire, foam will break down, and the water content will vaporize; therefore, foam must be applied in sufficient concentrations. Aqueous-film-forming foam (AFFF) is a synthetic agent that produces a foam layer on top of a liquid. It is used on flammable-liquid fires, including gasoline and kerosene fires. When foams are used to extinguish a fire, the more gently the foam is applied, the more rapid the extinguishment and the less foam required. The rate at which the foam is applied will also determine the successful extinguishment of the fire.

COMBUSTIBLE METAL EXTINGUISHING AGENTS

Fires involving combustible metals, such as sodium, magnesium, and potassium, pose special fire hazards. Water-based extinguishing agents are reactive with these metals, and common dry-chemical extinguishers are ineffective on fires involving these materials. Specially formulated dry-chemical agents have been developed for fires involving combustible metals, and there are only a few acceptable agents that have been approved as extinguishing agents. Met-L-X powder, for example, is suitable for use with fires involving magnesium, sodium, potassium, and sodium-potassium alloy. Na-X is a suitable extinguishing agent for use on low- or non-chlorine-containing sodium fires. These powders are available in pails and are spread on the burning material.

PORTABLE FIRE EXTINGUISHERS

The first fire extinguisher was patented by Alanson Crane on February 10, 1863 (http://inventors.about.com/library/inventors/blfiresprinkler.htm) and has since become the most common method of extinguishing fires. The fire extinguisher has evolved in terms of design and function over its 140 years of existence. Early versions of portable fire extinguishers worked using a pump to generate pressure inside the cylinder. Other fire extinguishers, referred to as inverting type, required the user to tip the extinguisher upside down, causing baking soda to create pressure from the generated carbon dioxide inside the cylinder. Early types of fire extinguishers, now considered obsolete and therefore ineffective and dangerous, include any extinguisher having a shell construction of copper or brass joined by soft solder and/or rivets; inverting-type extinguishers such as soda acid; and foam, water-cartridge, and loaded stream cartridge extinguishers. An inverting-type fire extinguisher required the user to turn it upside down in order to create pressure inside the cylinder. Today's modern portable fire extinguishers use either a stored-pressure cylinder or a cartridge. The user needs to hold the extinguisher, pull the pin on the handle, and squeeze the handle.

Because different classes of materials can be involved in a fire, portable fire extinguishers are designed to extinguish materials based upon their class. The fire extinguishers are classified according to the types of materials they may be used on. Table 9.2 summarizes the various classes of fire extinguishers and the extinguishing agents more commonly used in ordinary building protection.

LABELING

Fire extinguishers are labeled so that users can quickly identify the classes of fire on which the extinguisher will be effective. The marking system combines pictographs of both recommended and unacceptable extin-

Table 9.2   Summary of the Types of Portable Fire Extinguishers

Fire Extinguisher Class	Types of Materials	Extinguishing Agents
Class A	Ordinary combustibles, wood, paper,	Water, aqueous film-forming foam, multipurpose dry chemical (ammonium-phosphate), halogenated agents*
Class B	Flammable and combustible liquids, oils, grease	Carbon dioxide, aqueous film-forming foam, multipurpose dry chemical (ammonium-phosphate), halogenated agents*
Class C	Electrical fires	Carbon dioxide, multipurpose dry chemical (ammonium-phosphate), halogenated agents*
Class D	Metal fires	Special dry powder agents such as Met-L-X and NA-X

*Halogenated agents may include Halon 1301 and Halon 1211. "Halogenated type agents" include Halotron® I (American Pacific Corporation) and FE-36TM (DuPont).

guisher types on a single identification label. Figure 9.3 depicts examples of typical labels (NFPA 2002a):

FIRE EXTINGUISHER RATING SYSTEMS

The classification and rating system described in this standard is that of Underwriters Laboratories and Underwriters Laboratories of Canada; it is based on the extinguishing of preplanned fires of determined size and description as follows (NFPA 2002a).

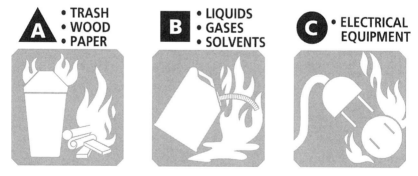

FIGURE 9.3
Standard labeling for fire extinguishers (Kidde Products)

1. *Class A rating:* wood
2. *Class B rating:* 2-in. (5.1-cm) depth *n*-heptane fires in square pans
3. *Class C rating:* no fire test; agent must not conduct electricity
4. *Class D rating:* special tests on specific combustible-metal fires
5. *Class K rating:* special tests on cooking appliances using combustible cooking media (vegetable or animal oils and fats)

The classification and rating are found on the label affixed to the fire extinguisher.

For example, a fire extinguisher is rated and classified 4-A:20-B:C. This imparts the following information:

1. It should extinguish approximately twice as much Class A fire as a 2-A-rated [2.5-gal. (9.46L) water] fire extinguisher.
2. It should extinguish approximately twenty times as much Class B fire as a 1-B-rated fire extinguisher.
3. It is suitable for use on energized electrical equipment.

Currently, laboratories classify fire extinguishers for use on Class A fires with the following ratings (NFPA 2002a): 1-A, 2-A, 3-A, 4-A, 6-A, 10-A, 20-A, 30-A, and 40-A. Effective June 1, 1969, fire extinguishers classified for use on Class B fires have the following ratings: 1-B, 2-B, 5-B, 10-B, 20-B, 30-B, 40-B, 60-B, 80-B, 120-B, 160-B, 240-B, 320-B, 480-B, and 640-B. Ratings from 1-A to 20-A and from 1-B to 20-B, inclusive, are based on indoor fire tests; ratings at or above 30-A and 30-B are based on outdoor fire tests.

Ratings of 4-B, 6-B, 8-B, 12-B, and 16-B, previously used to classify individual fire extinguishers for use on Class B fires, were not used for new fire extinguishers after June 1, 1969. Existing fire extinguishers having these ratings are acceptable if they have been properly inspected and maintained in accordance with NFPA 10.

For Class B fires, it should be recognized that the amount of fire that can be extinguished by a particular fire extinguisher is related to the degree of training and experience of the operator.

For fire extinguishers classified for use on Class C fires, no number is used since Class C fires are essentially either Class A or Class B fires involving energized electrical wiring and equipment (NPFA 2002a). Except when discharged from an extinguisher, water-based agents are conductive, and agent pooling after discharge might present additional hazard concerns.

The size of the different suitable fire extinguishers installed should be commensurate with the size and extent of the Class A or Class B components, or both, of the electrical hazard being protected.

No number is used for fire extinguishers classified for use on Class D fires. The relative effectiveness of these fire extinguishers for use on specific combustible-metal fires is detailed on the fire extinguisher nameplate (NPFA 2002a).

Fire extinguishers that are effective on more than one class of fire have multiple-letter and number-letter classifications and ratings.

FIRE EXTINGUISHER USE IN THE WORKPLACE

Employers have a critical decision to make regarding the use of fire extinguishers in the workplace. Because firefighting can be a dangerous activity, some employers may decide that immediate evacuation is the best for employees in the event of a fire. Others employers may find themselves in situations in which fire services in the area are limited or take an extremely long time to reach the facility. In those cases, some employers may decide to have employees use fire extinguishers and standpipe hose systems to fight the fire; others may establish a fire brigade. Depending upon the company's policy, Occupational Safety and Health Administration (OSHA) standards will be applied differently; however, OSHA does not require any employer to assign firefighting duties to an employee. The employer may choose to adopt as its policy that all employees are required to evacuate the building immediately. In that case, the policy must be implemented by adopting a comprehensive emergency-action plan and a fire-prevention plan, both of which meet OSHA criteria. Where extinguishers are provided but are not intended for employee use and the employer has an emergency-action plan and a fire-prevention plan stating so, then fire extinguisher training is not required.

In situations where the employer provides fire extinguishers for general employee use, OSHA standards specify requirements for their distribution, placement, design, testing, and maintenance and for employee training in their use. In situations where designated employees are authorized to use fire extinguishers, OSHA standards specify requirements for their design, testing, and maintenance and for employee training in their use.

FIRE EXTINGUISHER DISTRIBUTION AND MOUNTING

Portable fire extinguishers should be mounted in such a manner that they are readily accessible. They should be selected based upon the anticipated size and class of any fires. OSHA requires that portable fire extinguishers be distributed so that maximum travel distances to get to the extinguishers are met. These travel distances are based upon the class of fire. For Class A fires, the travel distance for employees to an extinguisher should be 75 ft. or less. Instead of fire extinguishers, the employer may provide uniformly spaced standpipe systems or hose stations. For Class B fires, portable fire extinguishers should be distributed so that the travel distance to any extinguisher is 50 ft. or less. For Class C fires, the employer shall base the travel distances upon the existing Class A or Class B hazards. Class D fire extinguishers or powder containers shall be distributed so that the travel distance from the combustible-metal working area to any extinguishing agent is 75 ft. or less. Portable fire extinguishers for Class D hazards are required in those combustible-metal working areas where combustible-metal powders, flakes, shavings, or similarly sized products are generated at least once every two weeks (USDOL 2004).

MAINTENANCE, INSPECTION, AND TESTING

The employer is responsible for ensuring that all portable fire extinguishers are maintained in a fully charged and operable condition and kept in their designated places. The employer is also responsible for the inspection, maintenance, and testing of all portable fire extinguishers in the workplace. Visual inspections of fire extinguishers or hoses used in lieu of extinguishers shall be conducted monthly. Annually, the employer should assure that portable fire extinguishers are subjected to a maintenance check. The annual maintenance checks should be recorded and the records maintained by the employer. The maintenance check records must be kept for one year after the last recorded inspection or the life of the useful extinguisher shell, whichever is less.

In addition to the monthly visual inspections and annual maintenance checks, fire extinguishers must also go through a hydrostatic test. Hydrostatic testing of portable fire extinguishers is done to protect against unexpected in-service failure. This can be caused by internal corrosion, external corrosion, and damage. The employer shall ensure that fire extinguishers go through the appropriate hydrostatic testing at the prescribed intervals based upon the type of extinguisher. Additional hydrostatic testing on cylinders is required in the following circumstances (USDOL 2004):

1. When the unit has been repaired by soldering, welding, brazing, or use of patching compounds
2. When the cylinder or shell threads are damaged
3. When there is corrosion that has caused pitting, including corrosion under removable nameplate assemblies
4. When the extinguisher has been burned in a fire
5. When a calcium chloride extinguishing agent has been used in a stainless steel shell

Hydrostatic testing of extinguisher hoses that are equipped with a shut-off nozzle at the discharge end of the hose must also be tested at the same test intervals as the extinguisher. Records pertaining to hydrostatic testing of fire extinguishers shall be maintained by the employer as well.

TRAINING

If employees are required to use fire extinguishers in the event of a fire, then they must receive annual training on the proper use of fire extinguishers. The training program should cover topics such as proper selection of an extinguisher, how to use the extinguisher, and the hazards of fires and firefighting. The training should be conducted when employees are initially assigned to a job where they may have to use an extinguisher and then at least annually thereafter (USDOL 2004).

WATER-BASED SPRINKLER SYSTEMS

From 1852 to 1885, perforated-pipe systems were used in textile mills throughout New England as a means of fire protection. However, they were not automatic systems; they did not turn on by themselves. Inventors first began experimenting with automatic sprinklers around 1860. The first automatic sprinkler system was patented by Philip W. Pratt of Abington, Massachusetts, in 1872. Henry S. Parmalee of New Haven, Connecticut, is considered the inventor of the first practical automatic sprinkler head. Parmalee improved upon the Pratt patent and created a better sprinkler system. In 1874, he installed his fire sprinkler system into the piano factory that he owned (http://inventors.about.com/library/inventors/blfiresprinkler.htm).

Until the 1940s, sprinklers were installed almost exclusively for the protection of commercial buildings, whose owners were generally able to recoup the expense with savings in insurance costs. Over the years, fire sprinklers have become mandatory safety equipment, and building codes require that they be placed in hospitals, schools, hotels, and other public buildings.

IMPACT OF SPRINKLER SYSTEMS ON FIRES

Sprinkler systems can be classified according to their design and operation. The most common types of sprinkler systems are wet-pipe systems, dry-pipe systems, preaction systems, and deluge systems. The selection of the type of sprinkler system is based upon the type of environment in which it will be used. For example, wet-pipe systems are the most versatile system found in a variety of occupancies, including business, residential, and industrial occupancies. Wet-pipe systems can be used to protect against a variety of fire hazards. In a wet-pipe system, water is present throughout all of the piping in the facility, from the riser to the sprinkler head. As sprinkler heads open, water is discharged immediately. If properly working, a sprinkler system should contain a fire to an area that can be covered by one sprinkler head. If the fire spreads beyond the one head, additional heads will open as needed until the fire is extinguished.

Dry-pipe systems are used in areas of buildings that are susceptible to freezing. In a dry-pipe system, water is only present in the system up to the check valve at the riser. Between the check valve and the sprinkler, air is in the system. As the sprinkler heads are opened from the fire, air escapes, then water fills the riser, cross-mains and branch lines, ultimately discharging at the opened sprinkler head.

In a preaction system, sensors in the area of the fire are activated; these in turn open the water valve to the sprinkler system, allowing water to flow through to the affected area. In a deluge system, all sprinkler heads in the system are open at all times. When the deluge system is activated, water flows through the piping and is discharged through all sprinkler heads.

WET-PIPE SYSTEMS

A wet-pipe sprinkler system comprises many components (see figure 9.4). In order for such a system to work properly and extinguish a fire, an adequate, unobstructed water supply must be provided in sufficient volume. This requires an adequate water supply, proper water pressure, and cor-

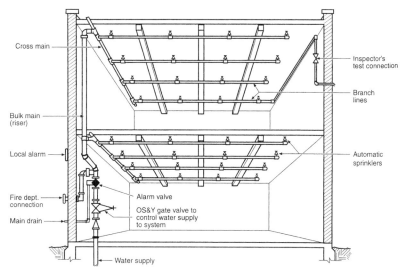

FIGURE 9.4

Basic components of a wet-pipe sprinkler system (reprinted with permission from the *National Fire Protection Handbook*, 19th ed., © 2003, National Fire Protection Association)

rect sprinkler piping and sprinkler heads. This section describes the components of a typical water-based sprinkler system along the water-flow path through the system from where it enters the building to the point of water discharge at the sprinkler head.

WATER SUPPLY AND DISTRIBUTION

The *water-supply system* is the source where the water is actually found. The *water-distribution system* is the portion of the water system that actually delivers the water to the consumer connections and the fire hydrants. Water supply can come from two main sources: the ground-water supply and the surface-water supply. Ground water is stored in the ground. Surface supplies are from lakes, streams, and the like. Surface supplies are more influenced by the weather and rainfall.

Two major types of water-distribution systems are gravity systems and direct-pumping systems (Klinoff 2003, 346). A true gravity system provides water to the source without the use of pumping equipment. A gravity system is extremely reliable because it does not require the use of mechanical equipment to provide the flow of water. Pumping systems are located at the source of the water. They are used to overcome the friction loss in the supply system and to provide adequate working pressures in the distribution system.

PIPING

Various types of pipes are used in fire service. Two of the most common types of piping are PVC pipe and steel pipe. Each has unique characteristics and is selected for use based upon the type of environment in which it will be used. When piping is laid for fire-protection systems, some rules should be adhered to in order to ensure an adequate and reliable water source for fire protection. For starters, incoming piping should have a diameter of at least 6 in. when used for fire service. Because the diameter of the piping is directly related to the volume of water available to the sprinkler system, a smaller-diameter piping where the water enters the building may greatly hinder the water density at the sprinkler head. The pipe should also be laid at an adequate depth to protect it from freezing. In general, it is advisable to avoid running piping under buildings, and when a pipe passes through a wall or foundation, it should be protected from fracture. When the pipe is backfilled, the backfill material should be placed around the pipe so that at least 2 ft. of cinderfree material is in place around the pipe, as cinders, ashes, and other such material in dirt cause the pipe to corrode.

In a typical wet-pipe system, water enters the building at a determined pressure through municipal water lines. Depending upon the jurisdiction, these water lines could be part of the domestic water lines to the building, or they could be a separate, dedicated water line serving only the sprinkler system. If the water line feeding the sprinkler system is a dedicated line, post-indicator valves may be placed outside the building to allow the water to the sprinkler system to be shut down. The post-indicator valve states whether the valve is open or closed and the section of the system that the valve controls. Control valves are placed in the water-distribution system to allow for sections of the system to be shut down (see figure 9.5).

As the water line to the sprinkler system enters the building, backflow preventers are placed in the piping somewhere before the sprinkler riser. If there are significant decreases in water pressure, the backflow preventers prevent water from being sucked out of the sprinkler system into the

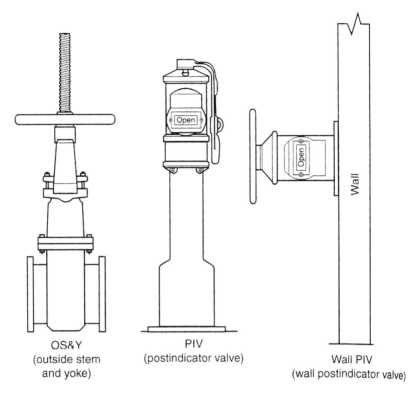

FIGURE 9.5
Sprinkler-system control valves (reprinted with permission from the *National Fire Protection Handbook*, 19th ed., © 2003, National Fire Protection Association)

municipal water system. Water from sprinkler-system piping could contaminate water supplies if this were allowed to occur. Requirements for the installation of backflow preventers and their maintenance and inspection are established by local ordinances and the Environmental Protection Agency.

OUTSIDE STEM AND YOKE VALVES

The sprinkler system is typically provided with outside stem and yoke (OS&Y) valves on both sides of the backflow preventers. These valves allow the building owner to shut off the water to the sprinkler system inside the property. To close the OS&Y valve, a handwheel is turned on the valve, causing the stem, or screw, portion of the valve to lower and seal the valve closed. An OS&Y valve is in the open position when the stem is visible. To prevent unwanted closing of the OS&Y valves and thus shutting off of the water to the sprinkler system, the handwheels may be locked and chained in the open position or equipped with a valve supervisory switch that will alert the monitoring service when there is a potential problem with the sprinkler system.

WATER-FLOW ALARMS

The vertical section of piping from the water supply is referred to as the riser. At the base of the riser piping, a water-flow-alarm check valve may be present. The water-flow check valve serves two purposes. First, in a wet-pipe system, if there is a drop in water pressure below the check valve, the clapper will remain seated and keep the water in the sprinkler-system piping above the clapper valve. The second purpose of the check valve is to activate a water-flow alarm in some systems. The water-flow alarm alerts the building occupants that water is flowing in the sprinkler system. When water begins to flow, the clapper valve will be raised from its seated position. The actual activation of a water-flow alarm may be accomplished by various means. A mechanical water gong alarm can be activated by the moving water rotating a wheel inside the riser pipe. The rotating wheel causes a striker to hit a gong. Water-flow alarms may also be electrically operated. With this type of water-flow alarm, the water-flow may be detected by electrical switches incorporated into a pressure or water-flow device (NFPA 1997, 5-30).

In wet-pipe systems, water-pressure gauges are located above and below the clapper valve. These pressure gauges will alert the inspector of potential problems in the water lines, such as a loss in pressure of water entering the system. Located below the sprinkler-system water-flow check valve are a 2-in. pipe and valve, which allow the inspector to conduct a 2-in. main-drain test. During this test, the valve located at the base above the water-flow-alarm check valve is closed to ensure the water above the main clapper valve remains in the system. Opening the 2-in. main-drain valve allows water to flow from the municipal supply through the 2-in. pipe and into a drain. The water-pressure gauge located below the clapper valve indicates the water pressure that would be available to the sprinkler system should it be activated. The 2-in. main-drain test will alert the inspector of potential water-supply problems, such as inadequate water pressure and the presence of debris or obstructions in the water-supply line. To run the 2-in. main-drain test, the inspector closes the main supply valve below the water-flow-alarm check valve. The inspector opens the 2-in. drain fully and checks and records the water pressure. There should not be a significant drop in water pressure when the 2-in. drain is open. If there is, there may be a blockage in the supply line. The inspector then closes the 2-in. drain valve. The pressure should return to approximately normal. The inspector then restores the water supply to the sprinkler system.

DRY-PIPE SYSTEMS

Dry-pipe systems are used in facilities where the sprinkler system could be subject to freezing temperatures. In a dry system, air is under pressure in the system above the water-flow-alarm clapper valve. An air compressor keeps the system under pressure. When the sprinkler head opens, air rushes out, releasing the clapper valve. Water then rushes into the pipes and puts the fire out. In a dry-pipe system, it is very pertinent that the clapper be maintained in its seated position. Sometimes it is possible to "trip" the valve. Water then leaks into the pipes unnoticed. The 2-in. main-drain test and the inspector's test are performed in virtually the same way as described above. One must be sure to drain all of the water out of the system and reseat the main clapper. Reseating the clapper valve may require removing the cover from the valve and manually closing the valve inside.

In a dry system, air pressure is taken at the top of the main clapper, and water pressure is taken at the bottom. There is a difference between the air and water pressures. It used to be standard for the water pressure to be 5 to 6 times greater than the air pressure. If the water pressure is 100 psi, then $100/6 = 17$ psi of air is needed; however, to prevent accidental tripping, an additional 15 to 20 psi is used.

CROSS-MAINS AND BRANCH LINES

The cross-mains and branch lines lead out from the riser. The cross-mains are the horizontal, larger-diameter pipes feeding the branch lines. The sprinkler heads are mounted onto the branch lines. The remotest sprinkler head in the sprinkler system is the head that is the farthest in distance from the water supply. At the end of the branch line containing this

remotest head is the inspector's test valve. The inspector's test simulates
the opening of the remotest sprinkler head in the system. Opening this
valve should activate the water-flow alarm in the same manner as an
opened sprinkler head would. On some systems, a water gauge is present
so that the inspector can verify the water pressure at the remotest sprinkler
head (see figure 9.6). The inspector's test, also referred to as a *trip test,* will
identify problems with the water-flow alarm and inadequate water pressure due to poor water supply and blocked or restricted pipes. To run the
test, the inspector opens the inspector's test valve and notes the water-
pressure reading. A slight decrease in pressure should be observed. The
water-flow alarm should be activated, and the fire department should
receive a signal that the fire alarm has been activated. There should be a
short delay between the time when the water begins to flow and the activation of the alarm, but the delay should not be any greater than ninety
seconds. If the alarm activates immediately after the valve is opened, the
valve may be susceptible to false alarms due to slight changes in water-
level in the riser. When the test has been completed, the inspector's valve
is closed, and the alarm system is reset.

FIGURE 9.6
Sprinkler head

Sprinkler piping should be maintained to prevent corrosion and blockage. Foreign material can get into the system as a result of broken water mains. Small debris like rocks can lodge in the nozzle of the hose or sprinkler head and clog it. Silt and sand buildups can totally obstruct the branch lines. If the system does have blockage, it must be cleaned.

SPRINKLER HEADS

The termination point of a sprinkler system is the sprinkler head. In a typical wet-pipe system, sprinkler heads are designed to open when the temperatures around the head exceed a predetermined level. There are two major types of sprinklers, bulb sprinkler heads and fusible sprinkler heads. With bulb sprinklers, there is a glass bulb with a liquid inside. There is also an air bubble. As the liquid heats up, it expands, the air bubble disappears, and the glass bulb shatters, releasing a fitting that was holding back the water in the branch line. In a fusible-link sprinkler head, a piece of metal that was holding the fitting on the sprinkler head melts.

The temperature at which the sprinkler head will operate is identified by a color-coded system. The colors may be painted in the arm of a eutectic metal sprinkler head, or the color of the liquid inside a bulb-style sprinkler head will signify its operating temperature. For other styles of sprinkler heads, operating temperatures are stamped on their arms. The National Fire Protection Association (NFPA) has established a uniform color-coding system for sprinkler heads. Table 9.3 identifies the temperature ratings and color codes for sprinkler heads (NFPA 1997, 6-146).

Sprinkler heads are uniformly spaced throughout the area they are to protect according to code. The spacing of the heads ensures uniform, overlapping water coverage on the floor. A deflector plate on the sprinkler

Table 9.3   Ratings of Fire Sprinkler Heads

Temperature Rating (°F)	Temperature Classification	Color Code	Glass Bulb Color
135–170	Ordinary	Uncolored or black	Orange or red
175–225	Intermediate	White	Yellow or green
250–300	High	Blue	Blue
325–375	Extra high	Red	Purple
400–475	Very extra high	Green	Black
500–575	Ultra high	Orange	Black
650	Ultra high	Orange	Black

head creates the water-fall pattern. The deflectors may create a circular water-distribution pattern, or they may deflect the water in a particular direction, as is the case with a sidewall sprinkler head.

In addition to the temperature at which a sprinkler head is designed to operate, sprinkler heads also differ in their design. The early sprinkler systems were nothing more than piping drilled with holes. Today, sprinkler heads are specially engineered components designed to ensure uniform water coverage throughout the area they protect. Variations in sprinkler heads include the size of the nozzle orifice, whether they are mounted on top of the branch line, as in the case of upright sprinkler heads, or on the bottom of the branch line, as in the case of pendant sprinkler heads.

To ensure their proper operation, sprinkler heads should not be painted. Doing so could seal the cap shut, preventing the flow of water, or increase the temperature at which they will activate. Maintaining clearance below the sprinkler head should ensure adequate water coverage. OSHA standards for general industry require a minimum clearance of 18 in. below sprinkler heads in areas where ordinary combustible materials are stored and of 36 in. below sprinkler heads where flammable and combustible liquids are stored.

FIRE DEPARTMENT CONNECTIONS

In addition to the water supply coming into the building, a sprinkler system may also be equipped with an additional fire department connection. The purpose of the connection is to allow the fire department to add additional water sources to the sprinkler system, thus increasing the water flow or to provide water flow that may be missing to the sprinkler system. To ensure that fire department connections are in proper working order, the caps should be in place. Inspections should be conducted to ensure that foreign objects have not been placed in the piping, posing a potential clog in the sprinkler-system water-supply line. Figure 9.7 shows an example of a fire department connection.

SPRINKLER-SYSTEM INSPECTIONS

The NFPA has developed *NFPA 25: Standard for the Inspection, Testing, and Maintenance of Water-Based Fire Protection Systems* to serve as a guide for the inspection, testing, and maintenance of sprinkler systems. OSHA, as well as local building codes, has established standards for the inspection

FIGURE 9.7
Sprinkler-system connection

and testing of these systems. In addition to meeting OSHA requirements for sprinkler systems (fixed extinguishing systems), various agencies will also conduct inspections on sprinkler systems, including the fire department, insurance carriers, sprinkler contractors, and fire alarm service companies.

Tests to conduct on a regular basis include the inspector's test, the 2-in. main-drain test, water-flow alarm tests, and fire department–connection tests. The following lists additional items that should be inspected on a sprinkler system (NFPA 1997, 6-264):

1. Test all alarms at least once a year.
2. All piping should be subjected to a hydrostatic test and checked for leaks.
3. Care and maintenance of the extinguishing system requires more than just inspection.
4. Water-based extinguishing systems are subject to deterioration problems and impairment through neglect.

5. The systems need to be inspected and routinely maintained to ensure that they will function properly.

6. In springtime, run trip tests, clean and reset dry-pipe valves, and test the antifreeze solution in the system.

7. Check drains and dry-pipe valves to ensure that they are not leaking.

8. Check the building for problems with insulation and potential sources of freezing.

9. Sprinklers made prior to 1920 should be replaced.

10. When sprinklers are subjected to corrosion or loading (accumulation of foreign material), they should be inspected frequently.

11. Accumulations of foreign materials, such as paint, on sprinkler heads will affect their ability to discharge water and may increase the rated temperature at which they are activated.

12. Corrosion can damage sprinkler heads to the point that they are inoperative. The corrosion can be so bad that it wakens or destroys the sprinkler head. There are corrosion-resistant sprinkler heads approved for hazardous locations where corrosive conditions are present.

FIRE HYDRANTS

There are two major types of fire hydrants used in the United States, the dry barrel and the wet barrel (see figure 9.8). The dry-barrel fire hydrant is used when temperatures get below freezing. The dry-barrel hydrant has its valve located below the frost line. A drain valve located at the base of the hydrant allows residual water to drain out. The wet, or "California," barrel is used in warmer climates. These hydrants have valves at each outlet.

There is no single standard for the placement of fire hydrants. The Insurance Services Office has guidelines set for insurance rating purposes. They suggest that hydrants be spaced around a building with a distance no greater than 800 ft. between hydrants. When the hydrants are used for hose connections, they should be arranged so that the hose lengths needed to fight fire are no greater than 250 ft. The NFPA has recommended standards for color-coding hydrants according to their rated flows in gallons per minute. The top operating nut and the caps are painted accordingly.

STANDPIPE AND HOSE SYSTEMS

The fire-protection system that provides a fire-hose-attachment station on each floor of a building is called a *standpipe system* (Klinoff 2003, 373).

FIGURE 9.8
Barrel-type fire hydrant

Standpipe hose systems provide a fixed means for transporting water for firefighting from a reliable water supply to designated areas of a building (see figure 9.9). These systems provide water for manual firefighting purposes. Standpipe systems vary in terms of their design and expected users. The three classes of standpipe hose systems are as follows (Klinoff 2003, 373):

1. *Class I.* 2.5-in. hose connections at designated locations in buildings to be used for full-scale firefighting by fire department personnel. Class I systems are generally required in sprinklered and unsprinklered buildings more than three stories high. They reduce the need for firefighting personnel to lay extended lengths of hose.
2. *Class II.* 1.5-in. hose connections intended to be used as first aid measures by occupants and fire brigades to battle a fire before the fire department gets to the scene. With Class II systems, a hose, nozzle, and a rack are typically installed on each hose connection.
3. *Class III.* Provided for both first aid response and full-scale firefighting.

FIGURE 9.9
Standpipe hose case

Class III systems are provided with both Class I and Class II connections. The connection is made with a 2.5-in. adaptor.

Because of the hazards posed by untrained personnel and occupants' handling hoses, Class II and III systems are becoming less frequent.

There are different methods for determining the location of standpipe hose systems in a building. The actual-length method requires that standpipes be arranged in a manner so that 100-ft. lengths of hose with an average water discharge of 30 ft. will reach all sections of the building. According to the exit-location method, standpipe stations are located at exit stairs and horizontal exits. Since exits must be reasonably distributed, it is assumed that hoses will be adequately distributed. Also, the exit-location method in Class I systems enables the fire department to attach their hoses to the stations before entering the building.

The basic components of the standpipe system are the hose, the piping, and the hose case or station. The piping in a standpipe system is commonly made of steel. The water for the standpipes can come from a variety of sources. The water can be provided from a municipal supply that is always present. Some standpipe systems are dry, meaning that the fire department must connect its water supply to the standpipe system, typically through connections located outside the building.

The hoses used on standpipe systems must meet the standards for standpipe use. Preconnected hoses are usually limited to lengths of 100 ft. to minimize problems untrained people may have using them. On Class II and Class III systems, a hose must be provided, and the hoses must be lined. Unlined hoses are no longer acceptable because they have a tendency to rot and deteriorate. On Class I systems, most often the fire department brings the hose. Table 9.4 lists items that should be included in a program designed to ensure the proper care and maintenance of standpipe stations (NFPA 2002b):

CHAPTER QUESTIONS

1. What does the main-drain test indicate in a wet-pipe system?
2. What does an inspector's test test for in a wet-pipe system?
3. What is a Class B fire, and what type of extinguishing medium is appropriate?
4. How does a bulb-style sprinkler head work?

Table 9.4   Standpipe and Hose Systems

Component/Checkpoint

Hose connections
Cap missing
Fire-hose-connection damaged
Valve handles missing
Cap gaskets missing or deteriorated
Valve leaking
Visible obstructions
Restricting device missing
Manual, semiautomatic, or dry standpipe: valve does not operate smoothly

Piping
Damaged piping
Control valves damaged
Missing or damaged pipe support device
Damaged supervisory devices

Hose
Inspect
Remove and inspect the hose, including gaskets, and rerack or rereel
Mildew, cuts, abrasions, and deterioration evident
Replace with listed, lined, jacketed hose
Coupling damaged
Gaskets missing or deteriorated
Incompatible threads on coupling
Hose not connected to hose-rack nipple or valve
Hose test outdated

Hose nozzle
Hose nozzle missing
Gasket missing or deteriorated
Obstructions
Nozzle does not operate smoothly

Hose storage device
Difficult to operate
Damaged
Obstructed
Hose improperly racked or rolled
Nozzle clip in place and nozzle correctly contained?
If enclosed in cabinet, will hose rack swing out at least 90 degrees?

Cabinet
Check overall condition for corroded or damaged parts
Difficult to open
Cabinet door will not open fully
Door glazing cracked or broken
If cabinet is break-glass type, is lock functioning properly?
Glass-break device missing or not attached
Not properly identified as containing fire equipment
Visible obstructions
All valves, hose, nozzles, fire extinguisher, etc., easily accessible

5. In what types of situations are dry-pipe sprinkler systems most suitable?

6. Describe the three different classes of standpipe hose systems.

7. What is the purpose of a fire department connection?

8. What are the two major types of fire hydrants used in the United States?

9. What is the purpose of the water-flow check valve in a sprinkler system?

REFERENCES

Cote, Arthur, and Percy Bugbee. (2001). *Principles of Fire Protection*. Quincy, MA: NFPA.

Klinoff, Robert. (2003). *Introduction to Fire Protection*. Clifton Park, NY: Delmar Learning.

Lab Safety Supply. (2004). *Use, Placement, Maintenance and Testing of Portable Fire Extinguishers, Document Number: 135*. Janesville, WI: Lab Safety Supply.

National Fire Protection Association (NFPA). (1997). *Fire Protection Handbook*, 18th ed. Quincy, MA: NFPA.

NFPA. (2002a). *NFPA 10: Standards for Portable Fire Extinguishers*. Quincy, MA: NFPA.

NFPA. (2002b). *NFPA 25: Standard for the Inspection, Testing, and Maintenance of Water-Based Fire Protection Systems*, 2002 ed. Quincy, MA: NFPA.

U.S. Department of Labor (USDOL). (2004). *Occupational Safety and Health Standards for General Industry, Subpart L: Fire Protection: Portable Fire Extinguishers, 29 C.F.R. § 1910.157*. Washington, DC: USDOL.

Fire-Program Management

INTRODUCTION

In today's highly competitive marketplace, few companies can survive a major loss from a fire or other emergency incident. Over the years, it has become clear that organizations can substantially reduce these losses by developing and implementing effective fire-risk-management programs. Such programs focus on the identification, evaluation, and control of hazards in order to protect employees, the public, the environment, and company assets from loss due to fire or other emergency incidents. This process includes the following primary steps (Schneid and Collins 2001, 1–4):

1. Identification of the fire and emergency hazards or events that could lead to significant loss
2. Quantification of the risk (probability of a fire or emergency event's occurrence and loss consequences)
3. Development and evaluation of alternative prevention and protection strategies to reduce fire and emergency risk
4. Measurement to determine the effectiveness of the strategies in reducing the fire and emergency risk associated with the implemented alternatives

A thorough risk assessment, using these four steps, will provide decision makers with a fundamental knowledge of the potential risks present at a facility and its survivability following a fire or other emergency. It is understood that every organizational structure and its culture are different; therefore, the actual responsibilities of a safety professional in this process will vary. These four areas will address some of the safety professional's more common responsibilities.

HAZARD IDENTIFICATION

Hazard identification is the process of recognizing hazards that can pose significant, undesirable losses. This identification of hazards should start during the preplanning stages with the evaluation of new materials, processes, and production modifications and should continue during the inspection of existing facilities. The safety professional will be responsible for providing the technical knowledge related to the fire codes and standards that may be used to identify actual or potential fire hazards. These fire codes could be the National Fire Protection Association (NFPA) codes or local building codes. Typically, the standards we are referring to will be primarily the Occupational Safety and Health Standards contained within 29 C.F.R. § 1910 and 1926. Other types of standards that may be relevant include applicable insurance standards, such as those of Factory Mutual. References, such as the NFPA's *Industrial Fire Hazards Handbook*, many NFPA codes, and insurance publications can be used to describe fire hazards in major industries and special-process hazards based on current technology and past loss experience.

The safety professional must have knowledge not only of these standards and codes but also of how they should be applied in particular situations. For example, with new construction, the safety professional may want to evaluate the site under consideration for any of the following (Schneid and Collins 2001, 1–4):

- Exposure to natural disasters such as floods or exposures from adjacent facilities and processes
- Availability of adequate water supply for fire protection
- Acceptability of local emergency support forces, such as a fire department
- Presence of impediments to site access such as traffic, terrain, or other buildings
- Incorporation of building design factors such as fire-resistant building materials, fire areas and segregation for high-value or high-hazards areas, alarm and automatic suppression systems, and sufficient exits

QUANTIFICATION OF RISK

Once we have identified a fire hazard, we need to assess the risk. The type and level of risk-assessment conducted will depend on cost and time limitations, the significance of the decision, and the complexity of the problem. For example, routine code-compliance problems many times can be handled by making simple choices. However, complex problems involving new technologies or high-hazard operations will require application of more detailed risk-assessment methods.

A basic risk assessment involves identifying the probability and severity of potential fire losses.

With both of these factors, an element of uncertainty must be recognized. Two approaches for determining the probability values for fire-event occurrence include objective and subjective estimation. Objective estimation develops probability values for the risk by using available data on loss-event frequencies. Therefore, it is critical to make sure that this data is both reliable and valid. Subjective estimation develops probabilities for fire risk by using inferential judgment based on available loss-trending information, such as equipment failures, human error, ignition sources, loss-control elements, and damageability factors. A good source for such information is the NFPA Fire Analysis and Research Division. In recent years, there has been an increase in the use of formalized risk-assessment methods to support decisions on fire-safety issues. Increasingly, predictive methods that integrate statistical data, deterministic models, and expert opinion are being used (NFPA 2000a, 10-151–10-152).

When addressing the severity of a fire risk, it is important to consider both direct and indirect loss potentials. Direct losses include damage to buildings, equipment, and contents. Indirect losses include business interruption, liability for injury or death, environmental contamination, and damage to company image. For most quantification studies, loss potential is expressed in equivalent monetary terms.

Once we have the probability and severity of the fire risk, this data is used to make a decision about the acceptability of the risk. If the risk is acceptable, no immediate action may be necessary. However, we may still need to monitor the risk for changes that could render it no longer acceptable. If the risk is unacceptable, then decisions must be made about how to deal with it. Some general options available for handling fire-risk exposure include the following (NFPA 2000a, 10-152–10-154):

1. Avoiding the risk by not completing the activity
2. Transferring the risk by purchasing insurance to cover potential losses or making alternate risk-transfer arrangements such as self-insurance

3. Providing loss-control improvements
4. Developing a risk-management program that includes a combination of the above

The latter two options are common responsibilities of a safety professional and are integral to the third step in the risk-assessment process: development of fire-protection and -prevention strategies.

FIRE-PROTECTION AND -PREVENTION STRATEGIES

Safety professionals will be directly responsible for recommending the appropriate fire-prevention and -protection strategies to an organization. There are two broad categories for these strategies: engineering and administrative controls. Engineering controls are typically the first priority for a safety and health professional because these controls can eliminate the risk of a fire or explosion. Examples of engineering controls may include any of the following: substitution of a nonflammable liquid for a flammable liquid, pressure-relief devices, explosionproof electrical wiring, and ventilation in a spray-painting booth. These engineering controls eliminate the fire or explosion risk by eliminating the ignition source, preventing excessive pressure buildup, or reducing the concentration of flammable gases or vapors to below their flammable limits. It is worth noting that some engineering controls do not eliminate the risk but minimize damage after a fire starts. The most common example is an automatic sprinkler system. Such a system does not prevent a fire but will minimize the damage it causes once it starts. Related to this responsibility of recommending appropriate strategies is the need for the safety professional to coordinate inspection, testing, and maintenance of these fire-suppression systems once they have been installed.

The fourth option for risk control discussed above was the development, implementation, and monitoring of fire-risk-management programs. The safety professional will be very involved in the development of many of these programs, all of which should be in writing and define the program's specific purpose or objective and scope.

Employee training is an important part of many fire-risk-management programs. Employee training might include training in the use of fire extinguishers, emergency response, and participation in a fire brigade if one is used at the establishment. The U.S. Fire Administration, which is part of the Federal Emergency Management Agency (FEMA), is an excellent source for fire-safety training.

The last responsibility of a safety professional within fire-program management is the development and evaluation of fire-response strategies. In light of the events of September 11, 2001, these responsibilities have become increasingly more important and have expanded beyond simple fire-response plans to include emergency-response plans.

Once a risk-management decision has been made that involves loss-control improvements, it may be necessary to conduct a cost-benefit analysis. Determining the cost of fire-loss-control alternatives, which includes design, installation, system maintenance, and training expenses, is usually a very straightforward process. However, evaluating the benefit or the amount of risk reduction is a much more difficult task. Determining this benefit involves assessing the reduced probability of fire occurrence, reducing the severity of losses, or both. Estimating the fire risk is not an exact science and requires considerable judgment. However, valuable information may be available about loss experience provided by insurance reports and the National Fire Incident Reporting System. In addition, fire-protection engineering analysis can also help in estimating fire risk after control strategies have been implemented. Finally, another tool available to the safety professional for risk assessment is computer modeling, which integrates deterministic fire-hazard modeling, probabilistic modeling, and risk-profile (loss-data) information (NFPA 2000, 10-153).

MEASUREMENT OF THE EFFECTIVENESS OF FIRE STRATEGIES

In essence, this last step reevaluates the probability of the fire risk after the strategies have been implemented. If they have been implemented successfully, the probability will be reduced to the level identified in the cost-benefit study discussed above. This measurement of effectiveness is important with all strategies but especially those directed at fire-risk-management programs.

It cannot be overemphasized that a written program is only as effective as its implementation. The safety professional's responsibility to measure and evaluate a program is critical to insuring that the program is properly implemented and effective in reducing fire risk.

In conclusion, a properly conducted risk assessment will provide management with an idea of the relative degree of risk that a facility may be vulnerable to, the facility's level of preparedness to handle a fire or other emergency, and its ability to survive the emergency situation and remain in business.

EMERGENCY-RESPONSE PLANS

An emergency-response plan is essentially a standard operating procedure for handling emergency situations. Twenty years ago emergency-response plans focused on fire and natural emergencies. Such a narrow scope is no longer acceptable, with today's emergency risks evolving substantially. Emergencies now encompass areas such as cyberterrorism, product tampering, biological attacks, and ecological terrorism, threats that were virtually unheard of fifteen years ago. The results of these risks can be just as devastating to an organization as a fire or natural emergency, and the preventative and proactive measures taken are substantially different. Appropriate planning and preparedness before a emergency happens are essential to minimizing the risks and resulting damages (Schneid and Collins 2001, i–ii).

Reaction after the emergency must be coordinated in order to minimize damage as well as to avoid further damage to remaining assets. This planning and preparedness through the development of an emergency-response plan is a very important responsibility of the safety professional. To assist the safety professional in meeting this responsibility this section does the following:

- Provides an overview of federal regulations that have emergency-response requirements
- Discusses preplanning activities necessary for developing a response plan
- Provides suggestions for the elements to include in a response plan

FEDERAL REGULATIONS RELATED TO EMERGENCY RESPONSE

On a federal level, there are three primary governmental agencies with regulatory responsibilities related to emergency response. For the public sector, the primary governmental agency is FEMA; in the private sector, the two primary agencies are the Occupational Safety and Health Administration (OSHA) and the U.S. Environmental Protection Agency (EPA) (Schneid and Collins 2001, 29–30). The following is a summary of some of the FEMA, OSHA, and EPA regulations impacting emergency response within an organization. This list is not meant to be all-inclusive and is only a summary of the regulations. Safety professionals must review the full text of the regulations to determine their application and specific requirements. Compliance with the applicable regulations is essential in order to avoid potential penalties, as well as to ensure a complete and thorough emergency-response plan.

FEMA

FEMA's responsibilities for national preparedness to emergencies include development of federal-program policy guidance and plans to insure that governments at all levels can cope with and recover from emergencies. This includes the development of concepts, plans, and systems for the management of resources for a variety of national emergencies. FEMA also supports state and local governments in fulfilling their emergency-response responsibilities by providing funding, technical assistance, services, supplies, and equipment.

Another important responsibility of FEMA in emergency management is mitigating the effects of emergencies through research. These research efforts typically focus on increasing the nation's capability to predict, prevent, respond to, and recover from emergencies (Vulpitta 2002, 6–7).

OSHA

OSHA has established standards for the development of emergency-action plans and fire-prevention plans, as well as standards for emergency responders. The following is a summary of some of these standards:

OSHA Employee Emergency Plans and Fire Prevention Plans: 29 C.F.R. § 1910.38

This OSHA standard details requirements for emergency-action plans required by any other section of OSHA standards. Emergency and fire-prevention plans must be in writing, kept in the workplace, and available to employees for review. However, OSHA does permit an employer with ten or fewer employees to communicate the plan orally to them.

At a minimum, OSHA standards require that the emergency-action plan address the following (USDOL 2004a, 29 C.F.R. § 1910.38):

- Procedures for reporting fires and other emergencies
- Procedures for emergency escape and assignment of emergency escape routes
- Procedures to be followed by employees who remain to operate critical plant operations before they evacuate
- Procedures to account for all employees after emergency evacuation has been completed
- Procedures to be followed by employees performing rescue or medical duties
- Identification of the names or regular job titles of persons and departments to contact for further information or explanation of duties under the plan
- Procedures for maintaining an alarm system that has a distinctive signal for each purpose and that complies with 29 C.F.R. § 1910.165
- Procedures for designating and training a sufficient number of persons to assist in the safe and orderly emergency evacuation of employees
- Procedures for reviewing the emergency-action plan with each employee covered by the plan when the plan is developed, the employee is initially assigned to a job, the employee's responsibilities under the plan change, or the plan is changed

OSHA standards also provide specific requirements for fire-prevention plans. The purpose of the fire-prevention plan is to prevent a fire from occurring in a workplace. As with the OSHA emergency plan, the fire-prevention plan must be in writing, kept in the workplace, and made available to employees for review. However, OSHA does allow an employer with ten or fewer employees to communicate the plan orally to them. At a minimum, OSHA requires the fire-prevention plan to include the following (USDOL 2004b, 29 C.F.R. § 1910.39):

- A list of all major fire hazards, proper handling and storage procedures for hazardous materials, identification of potential ignition sources and procedures for their control, and the type of fire-protection equipment necessary to control each major hazard

- Procedures to control accumulations of flammable and combustible waste materials
- Procedures for regular maintenance of safeguards installed on heat-producing equipment to prevent the accidental ignition of combustible materials
- Identification of the name or job title of employees responsible for maintaining equipment to prevent or control sources of ignition or fires
- Identification of the name or job title of employees responsible for the control of fuel-source hazards
- Procedures for informing employees upon initial assignment to a job of the fire hazards to which they are exposed and of those parts of the fire-prevention plan that are necessary for their self-protection

Two definitions are important to understanding OSHA's requirements for fire-prevention plans. An *incipient fire* is a fire in the initial stage that can be extinguished by portable fire extinguishers. *Interior structural fires* are fires that are beyond the incipient stage and therefore cannot be controlled by portable fire extinguishers (USDOL 2003, 29 C.F.R. § 1910.155). Because of the costs associated with implementing a fire brigade, many organizations may develop fire strategies to address only incipient stage fires and allow the municipality to handle interior structural fires. If such a strategy is implemented, all employees who are involved in fighting incipient stage fires must be trained annually in the general principles of using portable fire extinguishers as well as the hazards involved in incipient-stage firefighting. It is important to note that the designated employees must also receive hands-on training in the use of portable fire extinguishers on an annual basis.

**OSHA Hazardous-waste Operations and Emergency
Response: 29 C.F.R. § 1910.120**
   This OSHA standard was initially developed in response to the EPA's Superfund Amendments and Reauthorization Act (SARA) Title III Emergency Planning and Community Right-to-Know Act, but it tends to have a much broader application within industry. Even though an organization may not be covered under this act, it may have to comply with this regulation if its employees are required to respond to a hazardous-material release or spill. Therefore, it is important to review all of this OSHA regu-

lation, as well as the Emergency Planning and Community Right to Know Act discussed later in this section, before developing an emergency-response plan. The following general requirements of this OSHA standard are specifically related to emergency response (USDOL 2004d, 29 C.F.R. § 1910.120):

- Development of a safety and health program designed to identify, evaluate, and control safety and health hazards and provide for emergency response.

- A preliminary evaluation of the site's hazards prior to entry by a trained person to identify potential site hazards and to aid in the selection of appropriate employee-protection methods.

- Training of employees before they are allowed to engage in hazardous-waste operations or emergency response that could expose them to safety and health hazards. Persons completing specific training for hazardous-waste operations shall be certified.

- Medical surveillance at least annually and at the end of employment for all employees exposed to any particular hazardous substance at or above established exposure levels or those who wear approved respirators for thirty days or more on site. Such surveillance will also be conducted if a worker is exposed to unexpected or emergency releases.

- An emergency-response plan to handle possible on-site emergencies prior to beginning hazardous-waste operations. Such plans must address personnel roles; lines of authority, training, and communications; emergency recognition and prevention; safe places of refuge; site security; evacuation routes and procedures; emergency medical treatment; and emergency alerting.

- An off-site emergency-response plan to better coordinate emergency-action by the local services and to implement appropriate control action.

OSHA Chemical Process Safety Management: 29 C.F.R. § 1910.119

This OSHA standard was developed in response to Clean Air Act amendments and applies to companies in certain chemical-processing and -handling fields. The primary purpose of the Chemical Process Safety Management standard is to eliminate or minimize the consequences of catastrophic releases of toxic, reactive, flammable, or explosive chemicals.

This standard is similar to the EPA's Risk Management Programs for Chemical Accident Release Prevention Standard, which focuses primarily on community safety rather than employee safety. Provisions of the chemical-process safety standards that are related to emergency management include the following (USDOL 2004c, 29 C.F.R. § 1910.119):

- Development of a written emergency-action plan for the entire facility that must be kept at the workplace and made available for employee review
- Review of the emergency-action plan with employees when it is developed, when duties or responsibilities change, or when the plan is changed
- Audits of the emergency-action plan at least once every three years

OSHA Fire Brigades: 29 C.F.R. § 1910.156

One of the first OSHA requirements for the establishment of a fire brigade is the development of an organizational statement. This statement is basically a required policy statement that addresses the existence of the brigade, the number of members, a description of the fire brigade's function, and the type, amount, and frequency of training (USDOL 2004e, 29 C.F.R. § 1910.156). A fire brigade may perform the following duties during a fire emergency:

- Sound the alarm and aid in employee evacuation
- Shut off machinery and utilities and ensure that fire-suppression systems are working properly and fire doors are closed
- Move motor vehicles away from plant
- Direct firefighters to the scene of a fire
- Stand by at sprinkler valves
- Extinguish the fire and maintain a fire watch after the fire is extinguished
- Assist with salvage operations and put fire-protection equipment back into service

OSHA standards require that all brigade members be physically capable of performing the duties assigned to them. The OSHA standard identifies no specific testing or examination to determine if a person is physically capable. For this reason, during the examination, all the functions and duties

associated with being a member of the fire brigade, including requirements for personal protective equipment (PPE), must be made clear to
the physician. It should also be noted that the requirement for the brigade
members to be physically capable of performing their duties only applies
to those members performing interior structural firefighting (USDOL
2004e, 29 C.F.R. § 1910.156).

Another major requirement of OSHA standards on fire brigades is the
training of members. OSHA standards require that training of brigade
members be provided before they perform fire-brigade activities and at
least annually thereafter. In addition to the annual training required by
OSHA, members conducting structural firefighting must receive education or training quarterly. The quality of training is expected to be comparable to that offered by state fire academies and schools mentioned in the
OSHA standards. Training content must be commensurate with the duties
performed by brigade members and must be hands-on. Examples of training content include principles and practices of firefighting and the handling of other emergencies. Members should get experience with all firefighting equipment. A review of emergency plans and procedures,
equipment operation, special fire hazards, fire drills, and coordination and
communication with community emergency-response agencies are also
recommended training topics (USDOL 2004e, 29 C.F.R. § 1910.156).

OSHA requires that the employer maintain and inspect, at least annually, all firefighting equipment to assure its safe operation. Portable fire
extinguishers and respirators must be inspected at least monthly. Firefighting equipment that is damaged or unserviceable must be removed
from service and replaced (USDOL 2004e, 29 C.F.R. § 1910.156).

OSHA standards also require that the employer shall provide to all
employees involved in the fire brigade, at no cost, the necessary personal-
protection equipment. It is also the responsibility of the employer to
assure that all fire-brigade members wear the personal-protection equipment when engaged in interior structural firefighting. Specifically, the
employer shall ensure that the protective clothing protects the head, body,
and extremities and consists of at least the following components (USDOL
2004e, 29 C.F.R. § 1910.156):

- *Foot and leg protection.* Such protection can be achieved either through
  fully extended boots that provide protection for the legs or through protective shoes or boots worn in combination with protective trousers,

both of which must meet requirements for Class 75 footwear, be water resistant for at least 5 in. from the bottom, and equipped with slip-resistant outer soles.

- *Body protection.* Such protection shall be coordinated with foot and leg protection to insure full body protection for the wearer. This can be achieved through the wearing of a fire-resistant coat in combination with fully extended boots or protective trousers. In either case, the fire-resistant coat or trousers must meet the NFPA 1971 "Standard on Protective Ensemble for Structural Fire Fighting."

- *Hand protection.* Such protection shall consist of protective gloves or glove systems that provide protection against cuts, punctures, and heat penetration. All gloves or glove systems shall be tested in accordance with the test method contained in the National Institute for Occupational Safety and Health's "The Development of Criteria for Firefighters Gloves."

- *Head, eye, and face protection.* Head protection shall consist of a protective head device with earflaps and chin straps that meet the performance-construction testing requirements of the National Fire Safety and Research Office of the National Fire Prevention and Control Administration. Protective eye and face devices shall be used by fire-brigade members when performing operations in which the hazards of flying or falling materials that may cause eye and face injuries are present. Protective eye and face devices provided as accessories to protective head devices are permitted when such devices meet the requirements of 29 C.F.R. § 1910.133.

- *Respiratory protection.* The employer shall provide at no cost to employees and ensure the use of respirators that comply with 29 C.F.R. § 1910.144. An approved, self-contained breathing apparatus with a full face piece or with approved helmet or hood configurations must be worn by fire-brigade members involved in interior structural firefighting or when in confined spaces where toxic products of combustion or oxygen deficiency is present.

EPA

Superfund Amendments and Reauthorization Act Title III Emergency Planning and Community Right-to-Know Act of 1986

The Emergency Planning and Community Right-to-Know Act has two major purposes: (1) to increase public knowledge of and access to information on the presence of toxic chemicals in communities, the release of toxic chemicals into the environment, and waste-management activities involving toxic chemicals; and (2) to establish requirements for federal, state, and local governmental agencies and many business facilities regarding emergency response to environmental emergencies (EPA 2004b). At the state level, this act requires all states to establish a state emergency-response commission (SERC), which approves districts or areas where local emergency-planning communities (LEPCs) will be formed. The LEPCs must develop a local emergency-response plan based on an evaluation of available resources for preparing for and responding to potential hazardous-material incidents. The plan should include the identification of facilities, transportation routes, response and notification procedures, evacuation plans, training programs, and designation of a community coordinator (Vulpitta 2002, 8–9).

The following general requirements of the Emergency Planning and Community Right-to-Know Act apply specifically to emergency response (EPA 2004b):

- Both a written safety and health program and an emergency-response plan must be in place.
- A facility emergency coordinator must be appointed to work with the LEPC to ensure that the emergency-response plan is compatible with and integrated into a community emergency-response plan. Figure 10.1 depicts a HazMat response.
- Evaluation of the site characteristics by a trained person must include a list of extremely hazardous substances around which planning is carried out and provide a hazardous-chemical inventory to the state and local fire department. Facilities required to have a material safety data sheet (MSDS) available under OSHA must submit the MSDS or a list of MSDS hazardous materials to the state commission, local planning committee, and local fire department.
- Training and certification, as well as annual medical surveillance, must be provided for all involved personnel.

Another important aspect of this act is the creation of the EPA's Superfund Emergency Response program. This program provides quick response to the release, or threatened release, of hazardous substances

FIGURE 10.1
HazMat decontamination (EPA website)

wherever and whenever they occur. This is one of two major components of the Superfund Response program designed to protect human health and the environment from the multiple threats posed by hazardous substances. The program has three main priorities (EPA 2004b):

- Readiness to respond twenty-four hours per day to a release incident
- Response with whatever resources are required to eliminate immediate dangers to the public and the environment
- Community relations that can be used to inform the public about a release, response activities, and the substances involved

Resource Conservation and Recovery Act

The Resource Conservation and Recovery Act (RCRA) is primarily an environmental regulation that covers facilities having hazardous waste; however, this act does have requirements for written contingency plans that a safety professional may need to comply with. As a general rule, most emergency plans developed to comply with the previous OSHA standards will be acceptable under RCRA. The following is a summary of some of the requirements under RCRA related to emergency management (EPA 2004a, 40 C.F.R. § 264):

- Personnel training related to emergency management must be provided by a person trained in hazardous-waste management and must include instruction in hazardous-waste procedures and contingency-plan implementation. All personnel must be able to respond effectively to emergencies that require them to be familiar with emergency procedures, equipment, and other systems.

- Emergency equipment related to internal communications or alarm systems must be provided. This would include a device for summoning community emergency assistance, as well as extinguishment equipment to include, at a minimum, an adequate supply of water for firefighting, portable fire extinguishers, fire-control equipment, spill-control equipment, and decontamination equipment.

- Planning with local responding agencies must be completed to insure that all agencies are familiar with the facility layout, the properties of the hazardous waste handled and associated hazards, places where people will be working, and facility access and evacuation routes. This planning should also extend to state emergency-response teams, contractors, and equipment suppliers, as well as local hospitals.

- Contingency plans must be developed for each facility in order to minimize the hazards to human health or the environment from fires, explosions, or unplanned releases of hazardous wastes. These contingency plans should describe the actions plant personnel will take in response to emergencies. The plan should include a list of the names, addresses, and phone numbers of all qualified emergency coordinators, as well as a list of all emergency equipment at the facility, its location, a physical description of each item, and a brief outline of the equipment's capabilities.

- Emergency procedures must be developed, outlining the responsibilities of the emergency coordinator. Examples of responsibilities include activating the facility alarm; notifying appropriate state or local agencies; identifying the character, source, amount, and extent of the release of hazardous waste; assessing the health and environmental hazards from the release; taking all reasonable measures to control and stop the emergency; monitoring for leaks, pressure buildup, and other problems; and

providing for postemergency treatment, storage, or disposal of recov-
ered waste.

NFPA 1600: RECOMMENDED PRACTICE FOR
EMERGENCY MANAGEMENT

This NFPA standard provides recommendations for the minimum criteria
for emergency-management planning for both private and public organizations. Specifically, this standard recommends the following five core
planning areas (NFPA 2002b, 4-7):

- *Assessment and mitigation:* the types of hazards that make the organization vulnerable to emergencies and steps that can be taken to prevent or
  reduce the effects of the emergency
- *Preparedness:* the activities, programs, and systems developed prior to an
  emergency that are used to support the facility's response program
- *Response:* the activities that will help to stabilize and control the emergency
- *Recovery:* the activities that will help to return the facility to a functional
  status
- *Training and evaluation:* training activities based on duties and responsibilities and an overall review and evaluation of the plan on a regular
  basis

The National Response Team (NRT), which is chaired by the EPA, is made
up of sixteen federal agencies, each with responsibilities and expertise in
various aspects of emergency response to pollution incidents. Prior to an
incident, the NRT provides policy guidance and assistance. During an
incident, the NRT provides technical advice and access to resources and
equipment from its member agencies. The NRT also helps the private sector with prevention, preparedness, and response efforts by encouraging
innovation and collaboration to increase the effectiveness and reduce the
cost related to compliance with response regulations. This interagency
planning and coordination framework is replicated at the regional, subre-
gional, and local levels. There are thirteen regional response teams, one
for each of the ten federal regions, to help ensure that appropriate federal
and state assistance will reach an incident scene quickly and efficiently
when needed (USNRT 2004).

In June 1996, the NRT published the Integrated Contingency Plan (ICP). Rather than being a regulatory initiative, the ICP document provides guidance. It presents a sample contingency-plan outline that addresses the requirements of the following federal regulations: the Clean Water Act; the EPA's Risk Management Program Regulation, Oil Pollution Prevention Regulation, and RCRA Contingency Planning Requirements; and OSHA's Emergency-Action Plan Regulation, Process Safety Management Standards, and Hazardous Waste Operations and Emergency-Response Regulation. The ICP has three primary objectives (EPA 2004d, 6-7):

- Provide a mechanism for consolidating multiple facility response plans into one plan that can be used during an emergency
- Improve coordination of planning and response activities within the facility and with public and commercial responders
- Minimize duplication of effort and unnecessary paperwork burdens and simplify plan development and maintenance

The ICP sample format is based on the Incident Command System (ICS), which allows the plan to dovetail with established response-management practices. The NRT intends to continue promoting the use of the ICP guidance by regulated industries and encourages federal and state agencies to rely on the ICP guidance when developing future regulations (EPA 2004d, 7).

PLANNING AN EMERGENCY-RESPONSE STRATEGY

The development of an effective emergency response starts with planning. Facility management is responsible for seeing that an emergency-response program is implemented and that it is frequently evaluated and updated (Vulpitta 2002, 14). The input and support of all employees, as well as the community, must be obtained to ensure an effective program. Therefore, an important part of the planning process starts with developing an emergency-response committee. This committee will be responsible for coordinating the emergency-response plan's development, as well as its implementation, including training, emergency drills, equipment, and plan evaluation. Members of this committee should actually be involved with responding to the emergency and, at a minimum, include membership from community emergency-response agencies and facility personnel, including representatives from management, maintenance, engineering, transportation, safety, and human resources. The involvement of community emergency-response agencies is an absolute necessity in maintaining ongoing relationships and communications between the facility and the local community.

One of the first activities of the emergency-response committee is to identify the potential risks, assess their viability, evaluate the probability of their occurring, and appraise the potential damage. Such a survey will focus on the following:

- *Facility operations, processes and raw materials.* The emergency-response planning committee must assess facility operations, processes, and materials to determine if they pose substantial potential emergency risks or if the facility is located near other operations or facilities posing such risks (Stringfield 2000, 18–20). Although the risks from emergencies will vary from operation to operation, risks are often classified as man-made or natural. Natural risks are inherent but are often overlooked when assessing potential risks. The emergency-response planning committee needs to determine if the facility is located near any natural risks, such as an earthquake fault, volcano, hurricane zone, heavy snow area, flood zone, or forest-fire area. Man-made risks include those associated with fire and explosions, hazardous-material incidents, aircraft crashes, shipwrecks, and railroad and truck accidents. The committee must also consider emerging risks such as workplace violence, terrorism, bioterrorism, and cyberterrorism. Workplace violence, for example, has become the leading cause of work-related deaths in some retail industries, opening an expanding area of potential liability against those employers who fail to safeguard their workers.
- *Prevention and preparedness level of the facility.* The emergency-response planning committee must assess the prevention activities, procedures, programs, and plans that currently exist to prevent the risk of emergencies (Stringfield 2000, 26–27). This includes having knowledge of the fire-protection systems in a building, of how these systems operate, and of the actions necessary to supplement these systems. Preincident planning must determine not only whether these systems exist but whether they are adequate for the building occupancy. The committee will also

have to evaluate the capability of the facility to respond to an emergency situation. Life-safety considerations should be the first priority for pre-incident planning. A facility that has a good training program, instructing employees and conducting drills in emergency procedures, will mitigate life-safety risks.

Based on the above, the committee will need to review facility information regarding drawings, process-flow diagrams, phone lists, rosters, material-safety datasheets, evacuation plans, training records, community emergency plans, and so forth. This type of information should be available not only to emergency responders within the facility but also to community emergency-response agencies that may be involved.

It is critical that the emergency-response committee properly identifies and assesses each facility on an individual basis to identify the actual or potential risk of emergencies. Based on this assessment, a customized emergency-response program should be developed and implemented to address the specific risks for each facility.

Another important decision in planning a response strategy is determining the extent to which the organization is willing to commit time and money to developing and implementing an emergency-response plan. The emergency-response committee must know the time and resource commitments at their disposal so that it can plan accordingly. Examples of costs include PPE, fire and other emergency equipment and supplies, medical costs, and training costs. This training will include conducting drills regularly for all employees and community emergency-response agencies. This is both expensive and very time-consuming. Part of this commitment also includes taking on the increased risk of injury to employees involved in emergency-response activities. In some organizations, where this increased risk of injury may be unacceptable, employees' only emergency-response strategies may be simply to evacuate.

Once the emergency-response committee has completed the risk assessment and determined the organization's level of support, it is then time to evaluate emergency support at the local, regional, and state levels.

An evaluation of the support and capability of local community emergency-response agencies may take into account whether an agency is a paid or volunteer organization, the type of equipment it has available, its expected response times, and the training of its members. Since many facilities have hazards that community emergency-response agencies may not recognize, a list of all the hazards and emergency risks that the responders may come in contact with is crucial for planning purposes. The emergency-response team may also want to draw on the expertise of the LEPC to assess the capabilities of community response agencies (Schneid and Collins 2001, 39–41).

Part of this planning step may also include developing formal agreements with nearby organizations, such as restaurants, hospitals, and schools, to provide food, shelter, and medical assistance in the event of a major emergency. The emergency-response plan will want to specifically identify the organization, a contact name, the phone number and address, and the travel distance. All of this planning with the community will allow the emergency-response committee to develop an inventory of key resources and equipment that will be needed during an emergency and to show the amount of equipment and number of resources that may also be available within the community. This might include communications equipment, food and drink, lighting, medical supplies, material-handling equipment, power tools, spill cleanup materials, rescue equipment, and traffic-control supplies.

The last aspect of the planning process that the emergency-response committee may want to consider is communication with the community and media during an emergency. At the very least, this committee needs to determine the best way to communicate with the community, employees, local and state emergency-response agencies, federal and state regulatory agencies, and the media. All employees involved will want to know what has happened, as will the local community, and it is critical that the facility determine the best way to communicate this information accurately.

In conclusion, when preincident planning by the emergency-response committee is successful, everyone benefits. Both internal and external emergency-response agencies can more effectively manage their response activities, which results in a safer response and minimizes property loss.

This preincident planning is a continuous process, and all facility changes must be evaluated to determine their effect on emergency risks and responses. Keeping up with changes in a facility requires a high level of commitment, communication, and cooperation among all organizations involved in emergency response.

DEVELOPING THE WRITTEN EMERGENCY-RESPONSE PLAN

After completing the risk assessment and reviewing applicable regulations, the emergency-response committee is now ready to develop the written draft emergency-response plan. Various model emergency-response plans are available for the committee to use as a starting point; however, it is recommended that companies use the ICP as a benchmark. This plan was developed collaboratively by the EPA, the U.S. Coast Guard, the Minerals Management Service, the Research and Special Programs Administration, and OSHA. The ICP is intended to provide guidance to facility management in the preparation of a single emergency-response plan that will eliminate the need for the multiple emergency-response plans that facilities may have prepared in the past to comply with various regulations (EPA 2004d, 1). The structure of the ICP guidance is based on the National Interagency Incident Management System (NIIMS) ICS, a nationally recognized system that allows for effective interaction among response personnel and that is currently being used by numerous federal, state, and local organizations (EPA 2004d, 8). The ICP format is organized into three main sections: an introductory section, a core plan, and a series of supporting annexes. The core plan is intended to reflect the essential steps necessary to initiate, conduct, and terminate an emergency-response action: recognition, notification, and initial response, including assessment, mobilization, and implementation. The core plan should reflect a hierarchy of emergency-response levels. The use of response levels by an organization allows response personnel to match the emergency and its potential impacts with the appropriate resources, personnel, and emergency-response actions. The consideration and development of response levels should be consistent with similar efforts that may have been taken by the LEPC or mutual-aid organization. The concept of these response levels should be considered in developing checklists or flowcharts designed to serve as the basis for the core plan. The annexes are designed to provide key supporting information for conducting an emergency-response under the core plan, as well as document compliance with regulatory requirements not addressed elsewhere in the ICP. Annexes 1 to 3 are not meant to duplicate information that is already contained in the core plan but to provide more detailed, supporting information on response actions that are specific to the hazards encountered. The ICP encourages the use of checklists or flowcharts wherever possible to capture these emergency-response actions in a concise, easy-to-understand manner. Annexes 4 through 8 are dedicated to providing information that is noncritical at the time of a response, such as cross-references to demonstrate regulatory compliance and background planning information (EPA 2004d, 7–12). The ICP appears in appendix A of this book.

In conclusion, an emergency-response plan is the foundation for operations during an emergency. A good plan provides important information that assists the incident commander in implementing appropriate strategies and tactics for managing the incident. Use of the ICP model emergency plan is not required to comply with federal regulatory requirements, and facilities can continue to maintain multiple plans for compliance if they so desire. However, an emergency-response plan prepared in the ICP format is the federally preferred method of response planning. The ICP model will also minimize duplication in the preparation and use of emergency-response plans at the same facility and will improve economic efficiency for both the regulated and the regulating communities. Facility expenditures for the preparation, maintenance, submission, and update of a single plan should be much lower than for multiple plans. The use of a single emergency-response plan per facility will eliminate confusion on the part of facility first responders, who must often decide which plan is applicable to a particular emergency. Use of a single, integrated plan should also improve coordination between facility response personnel and local, state, and federal emergency-response personnel (EPA 2004d, 4–7).

EMERGENCY MEDICAL CARE

Emergency-response plans must include provisions for emergency medical care. During most emergencies, injuries and illnesses that require emergency medical care can reasonably be expected to occur; response time is a crucial factor in minimizing these injuries and illnesses. Emergency-response planning would start with a survey of local medical facilities regarding medical capabilities and response times; then, arrangements would be made to handle emergencies based on facilities' capabilities. Ambulance services need to be familiar with a facility's location and access routes in advance (Vulpitta 2002, 28–29).

OSHA standard 29 C.F.R. § 1910.151 sets forth three general requirements regarding emergency care:

- The employer shall ensure the ready availability of medical personnel for advice and consultation on matters of plant health.
- Where the eyes or body of any person may be exposed to injurious corrosive materials, suitable facilities for quick drenching or flushing of the eyes and body shall be provided within the work area for immediate emergency use.
- In the absence of an infirmary, clinic, or hospital in near proximity to the workplace, which is used for the treatment of all injured employees, a person or persons shall be adequately trained to render first aid. Adequate first aid supplies shall be readily available.

Three key terms in the above standard are *near proximity*, *adequately trained*, and *adequate first aid supplies*. OSHA Letters of Interpretation addresses each of these as follows (USDOL 2002):

- *Near proximity.* In areas where accidents resulting in suffocation, severe bleeding, or other life-threatening or permanently disabling injuries or illnesses can be expected, a three- to four-minute response time, from time of injury to time of administering first aid, is required. In other circumstances (i.e., where a life-threatening or permanently disabling injury is unlikely), a longer response time, such as fifteen minutes, is acceptable.
- *Adequate training.* OSHA's "Guidelines for Basic First Aid Training Programs" recommends the following topics for first aid training: teaching methods, responding to a health emergency, surveying the scene, basic adult cardiopulmonary resuscitation (CPR), basic first aid intervention, universal precautions, first aid supplies, trainee assessments, and program update. Refresher training to maintain the CPR and first aid certificates must be conducted annually for CPR and every three years for first aid. An OSHA directive also indicates that persons with a current training certificate in the American Red Cross Basic, Standard, or Advanced First Aid Course shall be considered adequately trained to render first aid (USDOL 1976).
- *Adequate first aid supplies.* OSHA has often referred employers to ANSI Z308.1, "Minimum Requirements for Workplace First Aid Kits," for guidance in the minimum requirements for first aid kits; however, it should be noted that OSHA has not adopted this ANSI standard, which

is therefore not mandatory. OSHA cannot provide a list of exact requirements for first aid supplies that will apply to every workplace. Therefore,
each workplace must be evaluated on a case-by-case basis, taking into
account the types of injuries and illnesses that are likely to occur. To
assist in this evaluation, a safety professional may want to consult with
the local fire and rescue department or a licensed health-care provider.

Another aspect of medical services related to emergency-response teams is
preplacement medical examinations and medical surveillance. Specifically,
before assigning personnel to these teams, the employer must ensure that
employees are physically capable of performing the duties that may be
assigned to them.

TRAINING

Training is absolutely critical to the effectiveness of an emergency plan.
When addressing training, OSHA uses two distinct terms: *education* and
training. OSHA defines education as the process of imparting knowledge
or skill through systematic instruction. Training, on the other hand, is the
process of making trainees proficient through instruction and hands-on
practice in the operation of equipment that is to be used in the performance of assigned duties. Before implementing an emergency-action plan,
a sufficient number of people must be trained to assist in administrating
the critical elements of the plan. All other employees need to be trained in
how to respond to each type of emergency. In addition to the specialized
training for key people, other employees should be trained in the following (Vulpitta 2002, 22):

1. Emergency escape procedures, exit-route assignments, and alarm identification
2. Procedures for employees who remain to operate critical plant operations or to shut down equipment before they evacuate
3. Procedures to account for all employees after emergency evacuation
   has been completed
4. Rescue and medical duties for those employees who are to perform
   them
5. Preferred means of reporting emergencies

Emergency-response training needs to be completed initially when the plan is developed and for all new employees. Refresher and supplemental training should be given at least annually, as well as when new equipment, materials, or processes are introduced, when procedures have been updated or revised, or when a drill or actual emergency event indicates that an improvement needs to be communicated to employees (Vulpitta 2002, 22). After training, the employer should certify that workers have received and successfully completed the specified training.

A very important part of emergency-response training is the use of emergency drills, which also serve as a tool to measure planning effectiveness. As a general rule, these drills should be held at random intervals and at least once annually. A well-designed drill allows all participants, including outside response agencies, to practice responses they have been trained to perform. Recording drill details, such as the time that alarms were sounded and employees' and emergency responders' responses, will help facility management and community response agencies evaluate the effectiveness of both the plan and the training (Vulpitta 2002, 23). In buildings or industrial parks with several places of employment, the emergency plans should be coordinated with other companies and employees in the building or industrial park.

PERSONAL PROTECTIVE EQUIPMENT

PPE is a consideration in fire-program management, especially in the area of emergency-response planning. Effective personal protection is essential for anyone who may be exposed to potentially hazardous substances during an emergency incident (Vulpitta 2002, 26). In emergency situations, employees can be exposed to a variety of hazardous circumstances, including any of the following:

- Fire, smoke, and electrical hazards
- Chemical splashes or contact with toxic materials
- Explosion hazards such as flying particles
- Unknown atmospheres that may have inadequate oxygen levels or contain toxic gases, vapors, and mists

It is extremely important that employees be adequately protected in these situations, and these employees must also receive medical clearance to wear PPE.

MEDIA CONTROL

As mentioned in the ICP model emergency-response plan, it is critical to plan for the communication of information to the outside world through the media during an emergency. All areas of possible information flow must be addressed to ensure that the organization is putting the best "spin" on an already bad situation. Some suggested measures for addressing the media as part of the overall emergency-response plan include the following (Schneid and Collins 2001, 84–86):

- Designate a safe area that is away from the flow of emergency traffic for all media vehicles and for all media communications.
- Maintain security in the designated media area and prohibit media representatives from accessing the emergency area.
- Identify a specific member of management to be the spokesperson for the company, and allow no other employees to talk to the media. The person selected should have experience in public relations and dealing with the media.
- Send the media to appropriate areas to acquire video footage when necessary.
- Provide informational packets with company information to the media.
- Have legal counsel review all information prior to its presentation to the media, and keep questions from the media to a minimum.

If the emergency involves environmental spills, a possible source of help is the EPA's Community Relations Program. This program has three primary objectives (EPA 2004c):

- To provide information to the community on the health and environmental effects of the release and the response actions under consideration
- To encourage citizens to provide information about the site and its surrounding areas and to express any concerns about the actions being undertaken
- To include citizen comments and concerns in the decision-making process at an emergency-response site

An official EPA spokesperson is appointed for each emergency-response action to keep the public informed and to respond to any questions. Meeting with citizens in the community, responding to inquiries from the media, and providing local officials with site-status information are some of the activities that the EPA is likely to undertake.

RECOVERY AFTER AN EMERGENCY

An effective plan for the recovery of your organization after an emergency incident must be a part of an emergency-response plan. Business recovery starts immediately after the emergency phase of the incident is over. Business recovery has expanded its focus over the past fifteen years to include recovery of the entire business, including all technology, people, and processes, and is intended to ensure the continuity of a business after an incident occurs. An emergency incident can cause lost production, invoices not going out, wages not being paid, suppliers not being paid, orders missed or lost, and loss of customer confidence. Therefore, failure to have a formal business-recovery plan puts the organization at much higher risk of not recovering and consequently going out of business (Stringfield 2000, 43).

Entire books and a variety of computer software programs have been written on business-recovery plans, and both can be helpful in the development of a business-recovery plan. In general, there are four essential steps in the development of a recovery plan. The first step is to identify an individual(s) responsible for the development and implementation of a business-recovery plan. This individual(s) will be assigned to work with agencies and organizations pertaining to business-recovery activities (Stringfield 2000, 47).

The second step is to complete a business-impact assessment to identify the operational and financial impact of an inoperable business function on the organization's ability to conduct its critical business processes. This assessment provides the basis for formulating the organization's business-recovery strategy related to restoring operations within the required time frames. Information regarding the effect of an incident and its impact on a unit's downtime is collected through interviews with management (Government Information Technology Agency 2004). This information is analyzed and business, operational-impact, and financial-impact analyses are developed for each function.

A *business analysis* identifies and describes critical business functions and the high-level resources that support these functions, along with the customers served by these functions. Such an analysis can also determine the relative value of important business processes and help management determine what measures should be taken to avoid downtime. The *operational-impact analysis* identifies the organizational implications associated with the loss of access to or use of a facility or loss of the facility all together. It highlights which functions may be interrupted by an incident and the consequences to customers of such interruptions. The *financial-impact analysis* identifies the economic losses that could result from an incident and the downtime of a business unit. The results of this analysis may provide cost justification for the implementation and maintenance of specific recovery strategies (Government Information Technology Agency 2004).

The third step is the development of a business-recovery strategy that defines the specific resources necessary for the performance of each critical business-unit function, then sets a recommended strategy for the recovery of those resources if downtime were to occur. This strategy will provide the specific guidelines by which the plan will be implemented. These guidelines are developed in consultation with business-unit managers by identifying the specific resources required for full and partial operation of various business units. These resources are then organized into logical categories with similar recovery needs. It is also important for the guidelines to describe recovery alternatives for each category identified above. Once this information is received, one can then select the approach from each set of alternatives that will most effectively meet the organization's continuity and budget requirements.

The fourth and last step is the implementation and evaluation of the business-recovery plan, which includes the documentation of the procedures and plans for each of the business units, as well as the administration of the overall plan, describing high-level contingency-management procedures. Most organizations' recovery strategies will depend on certain internal and external contracts and arrangements as tools for recovery. Therefore, any instructions needed to take advantage of these contracts should be documented in the plan. Business-unit managers should be heavily involved in this phase to ensure their ownership of the program once the implementation is complete (Government Information Technology Agency 2004).

INVESTIGATION OF EMERGENCY INCIDENTS

To prevent future loss incidents, it is critical to investigate every incident that results in, or could have reasonably resulted in, a major release, fire, or explosion accident. One of the most important reasons for investigating loss incidents is to determine the causes so that preventive measures can be taken to prevent future occurrences.

As a general rule, incident investigations should be initiated as soon as possible after the emergency phase of the incident. All investigators should have plant and process knowledge, as well as training in loss incident investigation. The organization must develop a formal, written, loss-incident investigation form that, at a minimum, includes the following information: date of incident, date of investigation, name(s) of investigators, description of incident, causal factors, and resulting recommendations. These loss-incident reports should be reviewed by appropriate personnel within the facility.

Fire investigations have four primary objectives: review of structural damage, fire-ignition sequence, fire development, and fire casualties. The actual investigation of the fire typically will start with a review of the exterior of the structure to document any fire damage or other damage that may have been caused by firefighting. Next, the investigator will review the interior of the structure to document any fire damage or other damage caused by firefighting.

Once the review of the exterior and interior is complete, the investigator will attempt to reconstruct the fire. The focus here is to try to identify the fire's progression, starting with its origin and the location of combustibles or other fuels. The investigator will examine the ignition sequence by identifying the heat source, combustible material, and the act that brought the heat source in contact with the combustible material. In evaluating the progression of the fire, the contents of the building, such as ordinary combustibles, are examined because of their influence on both fire growth and smoke and gases produced. Structural features of the building, such as compartmentation, fire walls, interior finish, concealed spaces, and so forth, will also be investigated to determine their effect on fire development (Cote and Bugbee 2001, 114–16).

After the fire has been reconstructed, the investigator will then focus on interviewing witnesses and firefighters at the scene. The investigator seeks witnesses' observations about conditions, such as flame spread, heat generated, smoke volume and color, property damage, security issues, and unusual activities. Based on the reconstruction of the fire and the interviews, the investigator may need to conduct laboratory tests on the materials to evaluate such things as burn characteristics of materials, composition of residues, or possible failures of mechanical equipment like heaters. If failure of equipment is a possibility, the investigator may need to review the service and maintenance records of the suspect equipment.

Once all of this information is collected, the investigator will analyze it to determine incident causes. Here, the focus should be on both surface and underlying causes. Surface causes are typically related to unsafe acts and or conditions, while underlying causes are related to management-system deficiencies that allowed the unsafe acts and conditions to exist. All causes must be identified and appropriate recommendations developed if we hope to prevent future incidents. It should also be pointed out that we need to investigate incidents so that accurate information and documentation can be provided for insurance and legal reasons. Recommendations will address the causes identified, focusing on engineering controls first, then on administrative controls. All good investigations include a follow-up on recommendations to make sure that they have been effective in reducing or eliminating the causes of fire. It should be noted that if fire casualties occur or if arson is suspected, fires are typically investigated by the local fire marshal or police department (Cote and Bugbee 2001, 116).

The remainder of this chapter will cover other common safety-professional responsibilities in the area of fire-program management, specifically, the maintenance of fire-protection systems, fire inspections, and hot-work-permit programs.

MAINTENANCE OF FIRE-PROTECTION SYSTEMS

As discussed in chapter 9, fire-protection systems play a vital role in the reduction of fire losses in industrial facilities. Unfortunately, large fire losses stemming from malfunctioning fire-protection equipment continue to occur for a variety of reasons, such as closure of sprinkler water-control valves and inoperative fire pumps, fire detectors, alarm systems, and sprinkler heads. The maintenance requirements for fire-protection systems have been addressed in earlier chapters; therefore, this chapter focuses on the development of procedures to follow when any fire system is inoperable as a result of maintenance, renovation, equipment failure, or an emergency incident. Effective procedures during fire-system shutdown are critical in reducing the possibility of fire losses. These procedures should be in writing and, at a minimum, do the following:

- Assign responsibility and authority to control the shutdown of fire systems to one individual, such as a maintenance supervisor or a plant engineer, who must be notified immediately of any shutdowns to fire-safety systems
- Provide training and education for all those involved in the shutdown procedures
- Limit the area affected by the shutdown
- Supplement manual fire protection, such as portable fire extinguishers in the shutdown area, with automatic fire-suppression systems
- Avoid hot work and other spark-producing operations within the shutdown area
- Verify, by testing, that the fire-protection systems are operational
- Shut down or isolate any hazardous production operation in the area where the fire-protection system is shutdown
- "Lock out" or "tag out" impaired fire-protection systems
- Notify the public fire department, central station, or alarm company of the fire system shutdown and the extent to which the system is out of service
- Complete work in a timely manner to limit the duration of the shutdown
- Restore any fire-protection equipment, alarms, or detection devices that have been disconnected
- Verify, by testing, that the fire-protection systems are operational, that portable extinguishers are in place and fully charged, and that hose lines have been returned
- Notify plant personnel and the public fire department, central station, or alarm company that fire-protection systems have been restored

FIRE INSPECTIONS

Just as important as the maintenance of fire-protection systems is the implementation of an inspection program for the fire safety of plant operations. These fire inspections can be part of a larger safety inspection or specific to fire hazards or fire-protection systems. Once an adequate program has been established and implemented, inspections must be conducted by individuals knowledgeable in the operation and testing of the equipment and trained in completing the inspections. The inspections should be completed, at a minimum, on a monthly basis.

To simplify facility safety inspections, written forms specific to the occupancy and equipment are recommended. These forms should be comprehensive enough that no element of prevention or protection is overlooked. It is critical that the inspections identify all deficiencies, provide appropriate recommendations, and assign responsibilities for correction and follow-up activities. Possible areas to address in a fire-safety inspection include the following (Ladwig 1991, 338–39):

- Potential fuel sources, such as those associated with poor housekeeping, improper storage of ordinary combustibles, and improper use and storage of flammable or combustible liquids
- Potential ignition sources, such as those associated with smoking, electrical deficiencies, static charges, and heating appliances
- Life-safety issues, such as blocked exits, aisle ways, exit signs, and fire doors
- Compliance with procedures, such as hot work procedures, shutdown of fire systems, maintenance of fire systems, and emergency evacuation
- Fire-protection systems, such as alarm and detection systems, sprinkler systems, and portable fire extinguishers

Examples of fire-inspection forms are available from a variety of sources, such as OSHA, FEMA, NFPA, the local fire department, and the company's property-insurance carrier. The OSHA fire-inspection audit form is available on OSHA's website, where it is referred to as the Fire Safety Advisor. This Web-based fire-safety program can be downloaded and used by the public to complete a fire-safety inspection. NFPA publishes the *NFPA Inspection Manual*, which concentrates on the identification of unsafe conditions or deficiencies in buildings related to current fire codes and standards. This manual also provides occupancy-specific guidelines for fire inspections. Figure 10.2 provides an example from this manual of a fire-inspection form for an industrial occupancy (NFPA 1994b, 345):

Once the inspections are completed, the written forms or reports should be forwarded to facility management for review and action. For

Figure 10.2   Industrial-occupancy fire-inspection form

Property Name: _____   Owner: _____

Address: _____   Phone Number: _____

OCCUPANCY
Change from Last Inspection: Yes ☐   No ☐
Occupant Load:
Egress Capacity: Any Renovations: Yes ☐   No ☐
General Industrial ☐   Special-Purpose Industrial ☐   High Hazard ☐
High Rise: Yes ☐   No ☐   Windowless: Yes ☐   No ☐   Underground: Yes ☐   No ☐

BUILDING SERVICES
Electricity ☐   Gas ☐   Water ☐   Other ☐
Are Utilities in Good Working Order: Yes ☐   No ☐
Elevators: Yes ☐   No ☐
Fire-Service Control: Yes ☐   No ☐
Elevator Recall: Yes ☐   No ☐
Heat Type: Gas ☐   Oil ☐   Electric ☐   Coal ☐   Other ☐
In Good Working Order: Yes ☐   No ☐
Emergency Generator: Yes ☐   No ☐
Size:
Last Date Tested:
Date of Last Full-Load Test:
In Automatic Position: Yes ☐   No ☐
Fire Pump: Yes ☐   No ☐   GPM:
Suction Pressure: System Pressure:
Date Last Tested:
Date of Last Flow Test:
In Automatic Position: Yes ☐   No ☐
Jockey Pump: Yes ☐   No ☐

EMERGENCY LIGHTS
Operable: Yes ☐   No ☐
Tested Monthly: Yes ☐   No ☐
Properly Illuminate Egress Paths: Yes ☐   No ☐
In Good Condition: Yes ☐   No ☐

EXIT SIGNS
Illuminated: Internally ☐   Externally ☐
Emergency Power: Yes ☐   No ☐
Readily Visible: Yes ☐   No ☐

FIRE ALARM
Yes ☐   No ☐   Location of Panel:
Coverage: Building ☐   Partial ☐

Monitored: Yes ☐ No ☐
Method:
Type of Initiation Devices: Smoke ☐ Heat ☐ Manual ☐ Water Flow ☐
Special Systems ☐
Date of Last Test:
Date of Last Inspection:
Notification Signal Adequate: Yes ☐ No ☐
Fire Department Notification: Yes ☐ No ☐

FIRE EXTINGUISHERS

Proper Type for Hazard Protecting: Yes ☐ No ☐
Mounted Properly: Yes ☐ No ☐
Date of Last Inspection:
Adequate Number: Yes ☐ No ☐

FIRE-PROTECTION SYSTEMS

Type: Sprinkler ☐ Halon ☐ CO_2 ☐ Standpipe ☐ Water Spray ☐ Foam ☐
Dry Chemical ☐ Wet Chemical ☐ Other ☐
Coverage: Building ☐ Partial ☐
Date of Last Inspection:
Cylinder or Gauge Pressure(s): 1 psi., 2 psi., 3 psi., 4 psi., 5 psi.
Valves Supervised: Electrical ☐ Lock ☐ Seal ☐ Other ☐
Are Valves Accessible: Yes ☐ No ☐
System Operational: Yes ☐ No ☐
Sprinkler Heads 18″ from Storage: Yes ☐ No ☐

FIRE RESISTIVE (FR) CONSTRUCTION

Stairway FR: Yes ☐ No ☐ Hourly Rating:
Corridors FR: Yes ☐ No ☐ Hourly Rating:
Elevator Shaft FR: Yes ☐ No ☐ Hourly Rating:
Major Structural Members FR: Yes ☐ No ☐ Hourly Rating:
Floor-Ceiling Assemblies FR: Yes ☐ No ☐ Hourly Rating:
All Openings Protected in FR Walls and Floor-Ceiling Assemblies: Yes ☐ No ☐

HAZARDOUS AREAS

Protected by: Fire-Rated Separation ☐ Extinguishing System ☐ Both ☐
Door Self-Closures: Yes ☐ No ☐
Hazardous Materials: Yes ☐ No ☐
Properly Stored and Handled: Yes ☐ No ☐
Properly Protected: Yes ☐ No ☐
Are Lift Trucks Properly Stored: Yes ☐ No ☐
Is the Fuel Properly Stored: Yes ☐ No ☐
Is Fueling Done Properly: Yes ☐ No ☐
Are Extinguishers Provided: Yes ☐ No ☐
Hazardous Processes: Yes ☐ No ☐
Properly Protected: Yes ☐ No ☐

(continues)

Figure 10.2   Continued

HOUSEKEEPING

Areas Free of Excessive Combustibles: Yes ☐   No ☐

Smoking Regulated: Yes ☐   No ☐

Is Stock Stored Properly: Yes ☐   No ☐

Are Incompatible Materials Separated: Yes ☐   No ☐

Is Trash Removed on Regular Basis: Yes ☐   No ☐

INTERIOR FINISH

Walls and Ceilings Proper Rating: Yes ☐   No ☐

Floor Finish Proper Rating: Yes ☐   No ☐

MEANS OF EGRESS

Readily Visible: Yes ☐   No ☐

Clear and Unobstructed: Yes ☐   No ☐

Two Remote Exits Available: Yes ☐   No ☐

Travel Distance within Limits: Yes ☐   No ☐

Common Path of Travel within Limits: Yes ☐   No ☐

Dead-Ends within Limits: Yes ☐   No ☐

50% Maximum through Level of Exit Discharge: Yes ☐   No ☐

Adequate Illumination: Yes ☐   No ☐

Proper Rating on All Components: Yes ☐   No ☐

All Exit Enclosures Free of Storage: Yes ☐   No ☐

Door Swing in the Direction of Egress Travel (when required): Yes ☐   No ☐

Panic/Fire Exit Hardware Operable: Yes ☐   No ☐

Doors Open Easily: Yes ☐   No ☐

Self-Closures Operable: Yes ☐   No ☐

Doors Closed or Held Open with Automatic Closures: Yes ☐   No ☐

Corridors and Aisles of Sufficient Size: Yes ☐   No ☐

Stairwell Reentry: Yes ☐   No ☐

Mezzanines: Yes ☐   No ☐

Proper Exits: Yes ☐   No ☐

VERTICAL OPENINGS

Properly Protected: Yes ☐   No ☐

Atrium: Yes ☐   No ☐

Properly Protected: Yes ☐   No ☐

Are Fire Doors in Good Working Order: Yes ☐   No ☐

OPERATING FEATURES

Fire Drills Held: Yes ☐   No ☐

Employees Trained in Emergency Procedures: Yes ☐   No ☐

those deficiencies that are severe and present an imminent danger, facility management should be notified immediately so that corrective action can be initiated. Fire-safety inspections play a critical role in the overall safety program by providing a before-the-fact, proactive measure to identify and correct fire hazards before they result in loss incidents.

HOT-WORK-PERMIT PROGRAMS

A potential source of fire in most industrial operations involves the completion of hot work. Fire hazards may occur in the use of both gas and electric welding and in flame cutting because of the production of sparks. Sparks from cutting tend to be more hazardous because they are more numerous and are carried greater distances. Sparks, in the presence of flammable vapors, may start fires immediately. Smoldering fires, not apparent when the work is completed, may later burst into flame when no one is present. Work done by an outside contractor that requires cutting or welding should also be closely supervised. Approximately one of every three cutting and welding fires reported occurs while outside contractors are engaged in cutting and welding operations.

For this reason, OSHA developed standards (29 C.F.R. § 1910.252) requiring that a fire-prevention-and-protection plan be developed when welding, cutting, or other hot work is completed outside of a designated hot-work area. One specific requirement is that a fire-watch person be present whenever hot work is performed in a location outside the designated hot-work area where other than a minor fire might develop or any of the following conditions exist:

- Appreciable combustible material closer than 35 ft. to the hot work or more than 35 ft. away when the materials can easily be ignited by sparks
- Wall or floor openings within a 35-ft. radius
- Exposed combustible materials in adjacent spaces, including combustible materials in concealed spaces, such as between walls and below floors
- Combustible materials adjacent to the opposite side of metal partitions, walls, ceilings, or roofs, where hot work is performed, which are likely to be ignited by conduction or radiation

A hot-work-permit program requires that a permit be issued for all hot work (including permanent locations) conducted on or near a covered process. The permit should include the following information:

1. Date
2. Work to be performed
3. Location of job
4. Type of immediate firefighting equipment available, to include non-combustible covers
5. Fire watch assigned
6. Inspection of area before commencing work
7. Authorized signature of individual in charge of the permit system
8. Signature of the individual who authorized the job to indicate the area was inspected upon completion of work

The designated fire watch mentioned above must have fire-extinguishing equipment available and be trained in its use. He or she must also be familiar with the operation of the alarm in the event of a fire and shall watch for fires in all exposed areas. If a fire should occur, the fire watch should attempt to extinguish it only within the capacity of the available equipment or otherwise sound the alarm. The fire watch should be maintained for at least a half hour after completion of hot-work operations to detect and extinguish possible smoldering fires. Other precautions to consider prior to commencing hot work include the following:

- Sparks or molten metal should not be permitted to pass through doorways or through cracks or holes in walls and floors.
- All exposed combustibles should be moved a minimum of 50 ft. (15.3m) from cutting and welding operations. Noncombustible curtains must be used between the operation and combustible materials when adequate separation cannot be maintained.
- Floors should be swept clean, and wood floors should be wetted down or covered with a noncombustible fire blanket.

This chapter has discussed the role of the safety professional in fire-program management. It is critical to end this chapter with the understanding that once these fire programs are developed, it is line management's responsibility to implement these programs. The safety professional is frequently in a staff position that provides technical support to line management. Line management is responsible for the people and property within his or her area of supervision; common responsibilities including the following:

- To work closely with the safety professional and staff to ensure that fire-safety preplanning is completed prior to occupancy changes or the installation of new equipment or processes
- To enforce fire-safety procedures, such as maintaining exits free of all obstructions, not permitting smoking in fire-hazard areas, and following hot-work-permit procedures
- To work with the safety professional in selecting employees for program assignments and to ensure that these employees have been properly trained
- To ensure that emergency drills are held regularly and to work with the safety professional to evaluate the effectiveness of the emergency programs
- To work with the safety professional to establish priorities for inspection, testing, and maintenance of fire-protection systems

The programs discussed in this chapter play a critical role in the overall management of fire risks in an organization. However, a written program is only as good as its implementation, and management plays a critical role in both program implementation and evaluation.

CHAPTER QUESTIONS

1. What are the four primary steps in the fire-risk-management process?
2. What is one of the safety professional's primary roles in the risk-assessment step of hazard identification?
3. A basic risk assessment of a hazard involves identifying what?
4. When addressing the severity of a fire risk, it is important to consider both direct and indirect loss potentials. What are some examples of indirect losses?
5. What are some general options available for handling fire-risk exposures?
6. A properly conducted risk assessment can give management an idea of a facility's relative vulnerability to risk as well as what else?
7. Twenty years ago, emergency-response plans focused on fire and natural emergencies; however, such a narrow scope is no longer accept-

able with today's emergency risks having evolved substantially to include what other risks?

8. On a federal level, what are the three primary governmental agencies with regulatory responsibilities related to emergency response?

9. Identify three areas that must be addressed in a written emergency-action plan according to OSHA standards?

10. What is the primary purpose of the OSHA Chemical Process Safety Management standard?

11. What are three examples of duties that a fire brigade may perform during a fire emergency?

12. One of the purposes of the EPA Emergency Planning and Community Right-to-Know Act is to establish requirements for federal, state, and local governmental agencies, as well as many business facilities, regarding emergency response to environmental emergencies. Another major purpose of this act is to do what?

13. What is one of the purposes of the ICP published by the NRT?

14. Another important decision in planning a response strategy is determining the extent to which the organization is willing to commit time and money to developing and implementing an emergency-response plan. What are some examples of costs associated with the development and implementation of an emergency-response team?

15. Using the NRT ICP, the core plan is intended to do what?

16. One of OSHA's requirements for first aid is that, in the absence of an infirmary, clinic, or hospital in near proximity to the workplace that can be used for the treatment of all injured employees, a person or persons shall be adequately trained to render first aid. According to OSHA interpretations, what criteria are used to evaluate "near proximity"?

17. Identify two of the suggested measures for addressing the media as part of the overall emergency-response plan?

18. What is the primary reason for investigating loss incidents involving fires?

REFERENCES

Brannigan, Francis L. (1999). *Building Construction for the Fire Service.* Quincy, MA: NFPA.

Cote, Arthur, and Bugbee, Percy. (2001). *Principles of Fire Protection.* Quincy, MA: NFPA.

Cote, Arthur E., and Jim L. Linville. (1990). *Industrial Fire Hazards Handbook.* Quincy, MA: NFPA.

Crowl, Daniel A. (2003). *Understanding Explosions.* New York: Center for Chemical Process Safety.

Diamantes, David. (1998). *Fire Prevention, Inspection and Code Enforcement.* Albany, NY: Delmar Publishers.

Drysdale, Dougal. (1985). *An Introduction to Fire Dynamics.* New York: John Wiley and Sons.

Environmental Protection Agency (EPA). (2004a). *40 CFR 264: Standards for Owners and Operators of Hazardous Waste Treatment, Storage, and Disposal Facilities.* EPA.

EPA. (2004b). *Chemical Emergency Preparedness and Prevention*, at www.yosemite.epa.gov/oswer/ceppoweb.nsf/contents/epcraoverview.htm (accessed June 23, 2005).

EPA. (2004c). *Emergency Response Program—Community Relations*, at www.epa.gov/superfund/programs/er/hazsubs/commrel.htm (accessed June 23, 2005).

EPA. (2004d). *National Response Team*, at www.epa.gov/superfund/programs/er/nrs/nrsnrt.htm.

Friedman, Raymond. (1998). *Principles of Fire Protection Chemistry and Physics.* Quincy, MA: NFPA.

Government Information Technology Agency. (2004). *Arizona Statewide Standard Business Continuity/Disaster Recovery Plan*, at www.gita .state.az.us/policies-standards/html/p800_s865_bcdr.htm (accessed June 24, 2005).

Klinoff, Robert. (2003). *Introduction to Fire Protection*, 2nd ed. Clifton Park, NY: Delmar Learning.

Ladwig, Thomas H. (1991). *Industrial Fire Prevention and Protection.* New York: Van Nostrand Reinhold.

Moore, Wayne D., and L. Richardson. (2002). *National Fire Alarm Code Handbook.* Quincy, MA: NFPA.

National Fire Protection Association (NFPA). (1994). *Fire Protection Systems—Inspection, Test and Maintenance Manual*, 2nd ed. Quincy, MA: NFPA.

NFPA. (1994b). *NFPA Inspection Manual*, 7th ed. Quincy, MA: NFPA.

NFPA. (1997a). *Fire Protection Guide to Hazardous Materials,* 12th ed. Quincy, MA: NFPA.

NFPA. (1997b). *Flammable and Combustible Liquids Code Handbook.* Quincy, MA: NFPA.

NFPA. (2000a). *Fire Protection Handbook,* 19th ed. Quincy, MA: NFPA.

NFPA. (2000b). *NFPA 101: Life-Safety Code.* Quincy, MA: NFPA.

NFPA. (2002a). *Automatic Sprinkler System Handbook,* 2002 ed. Quincy, MA: NFPA.

NFPA. (2002b). *NFPA 1600: Recommended Practice for Emergency Management.* Quincy, MA: NFPA. .

Quintiere, James G. (1998). *Principles of Fire Behavior.* Albany, NY: Delmar Publishers.

Schneid, Thomas D., and Larry Collins. (2001). *Disaster Management and Preparedness.* Boca Raton, FL: Lewis Publishers.

Schram, Peter J., and Mark W. Earley. (1997). *Electrical Installations in Hazardous Locations.* Quincy, MA: NFPA.

Schroll, Craig R. (1992). *Industrial Fire Protection Handbook.* Lancaster, PA: Technomic Publishing Co.

Stringfield, William H. (2000). *Emergency Planning and Management.* Rockville, MD: Government Institutes.

U.S. Department of Labor (USDOL). (1976, January 27). OSHA, Standard Interpretations—Clarification of 1910.151 First Aid Training.

USDOL. (2002, April 18). OSHA, Standard Interpretations—Clarification of 1910.151 Medical Services and First Aid.

USDOL. (2004a). *Occupational Safety and Health Standards for General Industry, 29 C.F.R. §1910.38: Emergency Action Plans.* Washington, DC: U.S. Government Printing Office.

USDOL. (2004b). *Occupational Safety and Health Standards for General Industry, 29 C.F.R. §1910.39: Fire Prevention Plans.* Washington, DC: U.S. Government Printing Office.

USDOL. (2004c). *Occupational Safety and Health Standards for General Industry, 29 C.F.R. §1910.119: Process Safety of Highly Hazardous Chemicals.* Washington, DC: U.S. Government Printing Office.

USDOL. (2004d). *Occupational Safety and Health Standards for General Industry, 29 C.F.R. §1910.120: Hazardous Waste Operations and Emergency Response.* Washington, DC: U.S. Government Printing Office.

USDOL. (2004e). *Occupational Safety and Health Standards for General*

Industry, 29 C.F.R. §1910.156: Fire Brigades. Washington, DC: U.S. Government Printing Office.

U.S. National Response Team. (2005). *Working Together to Protect against Threats to Our Land, Air, and Water,* at www.nrt.org/production/nrt/nrtweb.nsf/homepage?openform (accessed June 23, 2005).

Vulpitta, Richard. (2002). *On-Site Emergency Response Planning Guide.* Itasca, IL: National Safety Council.

Appendix A: U.S. Environmental Protection Agency's Integrated Contingency Plan

A copy of this integrated contingency plan (ICP) can be obtained by calling the Resource Conservation and Recovery Act (RCRA) Superfund Hotline at (800) 424-9346 or by visiting the U.S. Environmental Protection Agency (EPA) website at www.epa.gov/oswer/ceppoweb.nsf/contents/staloc.htm. The following is the recommended ICP outline of an emergency-response plan, which includes a list of elements and a brief explanation (EPA 2004):

SECTION I—INTRODUCTION ELEMENTS

1. Purpose and Scope of Plan Coverage

This section should provide a brief overview of facility operations and describe in general the physical area and nature of hazards or events to which the plan is applicable. This brief description will help plan users quickly assess the relevancy of the plan to a particular type of emergency in a given location. This section should also include a list of which regulation(s) are being addressed in the ICP.

2. Table of Contents

This section should clearly identify the structure of the plan and include a list of annexes to facilitate the rapid use of the plan during an emergency.

3. Current Revision Date

This section should indicate the date the plan was last revised to provide plan users with information on the currency of the plan. More detailed information on plan update history may be maintained in Annex 6, "Response Critique and Plan Review and Modification Process."

4. General Facility-Identification Information

This section should contain a brief profile of the facility and its key personnel to facilitate rapid identification of key administrative information.

a. Facility name
b. Owner/operator/agent (include physical and mailing address and phone number)
c. Physical address of the facility (include county/borough, latitude/longitude, and directions)
d. Mailing address of the facility (correspondence contact)
e. Other identifying information (e.g., ID numbers, SIC code, oil-storage startup date)
f. Key contact(s) for plan development and maintenance
g. Phone number(s) for key contact(s)
h. Facility phone number
i. Facility fax number

SECTION II—CORE PLAN ELEMENTS

1. Discovery

This section should address the initial action the person(s) discovering an incident will take to assess the problem at hand and access the response system. Recognition, basic assessment, source control, and initial notification of proper personnel should be addressed in a manner that can be easily understood by everybody in the facility. The use of checklists or flowcharts is highly recommended.

2. Initial Response

a. Procedures for internal and external notifications, such as contact, organization name, and phone number of facility emergency-response coordinator, facility response-team personnel, and federal, state, and local officials.

b. Response-management system to instruct personnel in the implementation of a response-management system for coordinating the response effort. (More detailed information on specific components and functions of the response-management system may be provided in annexes to the ICP.)

c. Procedures for preliminary assessment of the situation, including an identification of incident type, hazards involved, magnitude of the problem, and resources threatened.

d. Procedures for establishing objectives and priorities for response to the specific incident, including the following:

  - Immediate goals and tactical planning (e.g., protection of workers and public as priorities)
  - Mitigating actions (e.g., discharge or release control, containment, and recovery, as appropriate)
  - Identification of resources required for response

e. Procedures for implementation of tactical plan

f. Procedures for mobilization of resources

The initial-response section should provide for activation of the response system following discovery of the incident. It should include an established twenty-four-hour contact point person and alternate, and instructions about whom to call and what critical information to provide. Plan drafters should also consider the need for bilingual notification. It is important to note that different incident types require that different parties be notified. Therefore, appropriate federal, state, and local notification requirements should be included in this section.

Procedures for preliminary assessment should provide information on problem assessment, establishment of objectives and priorities, implementation of a tactical plan, and mobilization of resources. In establishing objectives and priorities for response, facilities should perform a hazard assessment, using resources such as material safety datasheets or the *Chemical Hazard Response Information System Manual.* If a facility elects to provide detailed hazard-analysis information in a response annex, then a reference to that annex should be provided in this part of the core plan.

Mitigating actions must be tailored to the type of hazard present. For example, containment might be applicable to an oil spill but would not be relevant to a gas release. The plan holder is encouraged to develop checklists, flowcharts, and brief descriptions of actions to be taken to control different types of incidents. Relevant questions to ask in developing such materials include the following:

- What type of emergency is occurring?
- What areas or resources have been or will be affected?
- Do we need an exclusion zone?
- Is the source under control?
- What types of response resources are needed?

3. Sustained Actions

This section should address the transition of a response from the initial emergency stage to the sustained-action stage, where more prolonged mitigation and recovery actions progress under a response-management structure. This section of the core plan should be brief and rely heavily on references to specific annexes to the ICP.

4. Termination and Follow-up Actions

This section should briefly address the development of a mechanism to ensure that the person in charge of mitigating the incident can, in coordination with the federal or state on-scene coordinator, as necessary, terminate the response. In the case of spills, certain regulations may become effective once the emergency is declared over. The section should describe how the orderly demobilization of response resources will occur. In addition, follow-up actions associated with the termination of a response, such as accident investigation, response critique, plan review, and written follow-up reports, should also be outlined in this section. Plan drafters may reference appropriate annexes to the ICP in this section of the core plan.

SECTION III—ANNEX ELEMENTS

Annex 1. Facility and Locality Information

a. Facility maps
b. Facility drawings
c. Facility description or layout, including identification of facility hazards and vulnerable resources and populations, on and off the facility, that may be impacted by an incident

This annex should provide detailed information to responders on the layout of the facility and the surrounding environment. The use of maps and drawings to allow for quick reference is preferable to detailed written descriptions. These should contain information critical to the response, such as the location of discharge sources, emergency shut-off valves, and response equipment, and identify nearby environmentally and economically sensitive resources and human populations, such as nursing homes, hospitals, and schools. EPA regional offices, Coast Guard marine safety offices, and local emergency-planning committees (LEPC) can provide information on the status of efforts to identify such resources. Plan holders may need to provide additional detail on sensitive areas near the facility. In addition, this annex should contain other facility information critical to response and should complement but not duplicate information contained in the plan introduction section containing administrative information on the facility.

Annex 2. Notification
a. Internal notifications
b. Community notifications
c. Federal- and state-agency notifications

This annex should detail the process of making people aware of an incident, such as whom to call, when the call must be made, and what information or data to provide about the incident. The incident commander is responsible for ensuring that notifications are carried out in a timely manner but is not necessarily responsible for making the notifications. Regional contingency plans and LEPC plans should be consulted and referenced as a source of information on the roles and responsibilities of external parties that are to be contacted. This information is important to help company responders understand how external response officials fit into the picture. Call-down lists must be readily accessible to ensure rapid response. Notification lists provided in the core plan need not be duplicated here but should be referenced.

Annex 3. Response-Management System
This annex should contain a general description of the facility's response-management system, as well as specific information necessary to

guide or support the actions of each response-management function during a response.

A. GENERAL

If facility owners or operators choose to follow the fundamental principles of the National Interagency Incident Management System (NIIMS) Incident Command System (ICS), then they may adopt NIIMS ICS by reference rather than having to describe the response-management system in detail in the plan. In this section of Annex 3, planners should briefly address either of the following:

- Basic areas where their response-management system is at variance with NIIMS ICS
- How the facility's organization fits into the NIIMS ICS structure

This may be accomplished through a simple organizational diagram. If facility owners or operators choose not to adopt the fundamental principles of NIIMS ICS, this section should describe in detail the structure of the facility's response-management system. Regardless of the response-management system used, this section of the annex should include the following information:

- Organizational chart
- Specific job description for each position
- A detailed description of information flow
- Description of the formation of a unified command within the response-management system

B. COMMAND

1. *Commanders.* List facility incident commander and qualified individual, if applicable, by name and/or title and provide information on their authorities and duties. This section should describe the command aspects of the response-management system that will be used. The location(s) of predesignated command posts should also be identified.
2. *Information—internal and external communications.* This section should address how the facility will disseminate information internally and externally. Items to consider in developing this section include press-release statement forms, plans for coordination with the news

media, community-relations plans, the needs of special populations, and plans for families of employees.

3. *Safety.* This section should include a process for ensuring the safety of responders. Facilities should reference the responsibilities of the safety officer, federal or state requirements, and the safety provisions of the ICP. Procedures for protecting facility personnel should be addressed.

4. *Liaison—staff mobilization.* This section should address the process by which the internal and external emergency-response teams will interact. Given that parallel mobilization may be occurring by various response groups, the process of integration should be addressed. This includes a process for communicating with local emergency management, especially where the safety of the general public is concerned.

C. OPERATIONS
1. Operational response objectives
2. Discharge or release control
3. Assessment or monitoring
4. Containment
5. Recovery
6. Decontamination
7. Nonresponder medical needs, including information on ambulances and hospitals
8. Salvage plans

Response operations are driven by the type of incident; therefore, this section should contain a discussion of specific operational procedures to respond to an incident. Plan drafters should tailor response procedures to the particular hazards in place at the facility. A facility with numerous hazards is likely to have designed a series of procedures to address the nuances associated with each type of incident.

D. PLANNING
1. Hazard assessment, including facility hazard identification, vulnerability analysis, and prioritization of potential risks
   - This section should present a detailed assessment of all potential hazards present at the facility, an analysis of vulnerable receptors such as humans, the environment, and other facility-specific concerns, and a

discussion of which risks deserve primary consideration during an incident. By covering actions necessary to respond to a range of incident types, plan holders can be prepared for small, operational discharges and large catastrophic releases.

An important part of this planning process is reviewing facility changes that may affect the initial hazard assessment. Failure to conduct a formal review and authorization of such facility changes can lead to a variety of emergency incidents. A formal review program that establishes written procedures to manage any changes to facilities or to process chemicals, technologies, or equipment, including fire-protection equipment, can go a long way toward reducing the chances of unwanted hazards being introduced by facility changes.

2. Protection
   - This section should present a discussion of strategies for protecting the vulnerable receptors identified through the hazard analysis. Primary consideration should be given to minimizing those risks identified as high priority. Activities to be considered in developing this section include population protection, protective booming, dispersant use, in situ burning, bioremediation, water-intake protection, wildlife recovery and rehabilitation, natural remediation, vapor suppression, and monitoring, sampling, and modeling.

3. Coordination with natural resource trustees
   - This section should address coordination with government natural resource trustees. In their role as managers of and experts in natural resources, trustees assist the federal on-scene coordinator in developing or selecting removal actions to protect these resources. In this role, they serve as part of the response organization working for the federal on-scene coordinator. A key area to address is interaction with facility response personnel in the protection of natural resources.

   Natural resource trustees are also responsible to act on behalf of the public to present a claim for and recover damages to natural resources injured by an oil spill or hazardous-substance release. The process followed by the natural resource trustees, natural resource damage assessment (NRDA), generally involves some data collection during emergency response. NRDA regulations provide that the process may be carried out in cooperation with the responsible party.

Thus, the facility may wish to plan for how that cooperation will occur, including designation of personnel to work with trustees in NRDA.

4. Waste management
   - This section should address procedures for the disposal of contaminated materials in accordance with federal, state, and local requirements.

E. LOGISTICS

1. Medical needs of responders
2. Site security
3. Communications (internal and external resources)
4. Transportation (air, land, water)
5. Personnel support (e.g., meals, housing, equipment)
6. Equipment maintenance and support

This section should address how the facility will provide for the operational needs of response operations in each of the areas listed above. For example, the discussion of personnel support should address issues such as volunteer training, management, overnight accommodations, meals, operational/administrative spaces, and emergency procedures. The National Response Team recognizes that certain logistical considerations may not be applicable to small facilities with limited hazards.

F. FINANCE PROCUREMENT AND ADMINISTRATION

1. Resource list
2. Personnel management
3. Response equipment
4. Support equipment
5. Contracting
6. Claims procedures
7. Cost documentation

This section should address the acquisition of response resources and the monitoring of incident-related costs. Lists of available equipment in the local and regional area and the means of procuring such equipment as necessary should be included. Information on previously established agreements with organizations supplying personnel and equipment also should be included. This section should also address methods to account for resources expended and to process claims resulting from the incident.

Annex 4. Incident Documentation

a. Postaccident investigation
b. Incident history

- This annex should describe the company's procedures for conducting a follow-up investigation of the cause of the accident, including coordination with federal, state, and local officials. This annex should also contain an accounting of incidents that have occurred at the facility, including information on cause, amount released, resources impacted, injuries, response actions, and so forth. This annex should also include information that may be required to prove that the facility met its legal notification requirements with respect to a given incident, such as a signed record of initial notifications and certified copies of written follow-up reports submitted after a response.

Annex 5. Training and Exercises or Drills

This annex should contain a description of the training and exercise program conducted at the facility, as well as evidence that required training and exercises have been conducted on a regular basis. Facilities may follow appropriate training or exercise guidelines, such as the National Preparedness for Response Exercise Program Guidelines, as allowed under the various regulatory requirements.

Annex 6. Response Critique and Plan-Review-and-Modification Process

This annex should describe procedures for modifying the plan based on periodic plan review or on lessons learned through an exercise or a response to an actual incident. Procedures to critique an actual or simulated response should be a part of this discussion. A list of plan amendments and updates should also be contained in this annex. Plan modification should be viewed as a part of a facility's continuous improvement process.

A periodic review of the emergency-response plan by outside emergency-response agencies can provide valuable insight into the actions to be coordinated by both facility personnel and the outside agencies. Many of these outside response agencies may keep certain parts of the emergency-response plan for reference via hard copy or through the use of computers.

Annex 7. Prevention

Some federal regulations that primarily address prevention of accidents include elements that relate to contingency planning. This annex is designed to allow facilities to include prevention-based requirements, such as maintenance, testing, in-house inspections, release detection, site security, containment, and fail-safe engineering, that are required in contingency-planning regulations or that have the potential to impact response activities covered in a contingency plan.

Annex 8. Regulatory Compliance and Cross-Reference Matrices

This annex should include information necessary for plan reviewers to determine compliance with specific regulatory requirements. To the extent that plan drafters did not include regulatory-required elements in the balance of the ICP, they should be addressed in this annex. This annex should also include signatory pages to convey management approval and certifications required by the regulations, such as certification of adequate response resources or statements of regulatory applicability. Finally, this annex should contain cross-references that indicate where specific regulatory requirements are addressed in the ICP for each regulation covered under the plan.

REFERENCES

U.S. Environmental Protection Agency. (2004). *National Response Team— Integrated Contingency Plan*, at www.yosemite.epa.gov/oswer/ceppoweb.nsf/ vwresourcesByFilename/pr-2340.html.

.

Solutions to Chapter Questions

CHAPTER 1

1. Compare the fire-death rates in the United States to the fire-death rates in other industrialized countries.

   U.S. fire deaths, based on one million per population, are almost twice the average fire-death rates of other industrialized countries.

2. Effective fire prevention requires what three components?

   Effective fire prevention requires vigilance, action, and cooperation.

3. Describe the opportunities one has to intervene in a fire.

   - *Prevent the fire entirely.*
   - *Slow the initial growth of the fire.*
   - *Detect fire early, permitting effective intervention before the fire becomes too severe.*
   - *Suppress the fire automatically or manually.*
   - *Confine the fire in a space.*
   - *Move the occupants to a safe location.*

4. Differentiate between fire protection and fire prevention.

   Fire prevention is the elimination of the possibility of a fire's being started, while fire-protection strategies are designed to minimize the extent of a fire.

5. Describe some of the job activities a fire-protection engineer may engage in.

   Examples of fire-safety-engineering job aspects include evaluating buildings to determine fire risks, designing fire-detection-and-suppression systems, and researching materials and consumer products.

6. Describe the trends in fire-death experience in the United States since World War I.

   Overall, fire deaths in the United States have fallen nearly two-thirds since their peak levels around World War I.

7. What impact do fires have upon occupational fatalities and injuries in the United States?

   Data involving fires and explosions from 1992 to 2000 indicate that fires and explosions account for approximately 3 percent of all nonfatal occupational injuries and illnesses involving days away from work. Between 1992 and 2000, fires and explosions accounted for approximately 1,760 deaths in the workplace.

8. What are some major sources of ignition in the workplace based upon reported fires?

   The most common sources of ignition resulting in fires in the workplace are equipment, electrical sources, and open flames.

9. Describe some aspects of fire safety that OSHA has regulated in the workplace.

   OSHA regulates a variety of fire-prevention activities in the workplace, including fire extinguishers, life safety, fire-prevention plans, the control of ignition sources, and the proper handling of hazardous materials.

10. Describe OSHA's three key elements of fire safety.

    OSHA's three key elements of fire safety in the workplace are fire prevention, safe evacuation of the workplace in the event of fire, and protection of workers who fight fires or who work around fire-suppression equipment.

CHAPTER 2

1. T/F Deflagration is the burning of a gas or aerosol that is characterized by a shock wave.

   F

2. T/F Radioactive materials are those materials that spontaneously emit ionizing radiation.

   T

3. T/F Radiant heat transfer occurs through electromagnetic waves that are in the ultraviolet region and travel at the speed of sound.

   F

4. T/F The four major components of combustion are heat, radiation, smoke, and fire.

   F

5. T/F Sensible heat change is a change in the heat content of a material due to a temperature change only.

   T

6. T/F BLEVE stands for:
   a. Boiling-liquid expanding-vapor event
   b. Boiling-liquid expanding violent explosion
   c. Boiling-liquid enlarging-vessel explosion
   d. Boiling-liquid expanding-vapor explosion

   d

7. Specific heat is the amount of heat required to raise _____ of a substance by _____.
   a. 1 lb.; 1°C
   b. 1 lb.; 1°F
   c. 1 lb.; 1°K

   b

8. Thermal conductivity of metals
   a. Decreases as the temperature increases
   b. Increases as the temperature increases
   c. Decreases as the temperature decreases
   d. Increases as the temperature decreases

   a

9. In the NFPA labeling system:
   a. Blue indicates health hazards; red indicates fire hazards; yellow indicates chemical reactivity.
   b. Blue indicates fire hazards; red indicates chemical reactivity; yellow indicates health hazards
   c. Blue indicates chemical reactivity; red indicates fire hazards; yellow indicates health hazards
   d. Blue indicates fire hazards; red indicates health hazards; yellow indicates chemical reactivity

   a

10. When assessing the effect of heat on the body, two main factors determine the severity:
    a. Amount of body exposed and length of exposure

    b. Length of exposure and temperature
    c. Temperature and amount of body exposed
    d. None of the above
    b

11. List and then briefly describe the four elements of the fire tetrahedron.
*They are fuel, oxygen, heat/energy source, uninhibited free radical for-
mation.*

12. What are the five factors that influence heat transfer by convection?
*They are the density of fluid, the viscosity of the fluid, the coefficient of
thermal expansion, the specific heat of the material, and temperature
differences.*

13. What is the significance of the *North American Emergency Response
Guidebook*?
*Developed in cooperation with Canada and Mexico, its primary purpose
is to assist first aid responders in identifying the specific or generic classification of hazardous materials, allowing them to protect themselves and
the public during the response phase of a hazardous-materials incident.*

14. Smoke is the major killer in fires. Explain why.
*Smoke reduces visibility, irritates eyes and lungs, and contains lethal
gases.*

15. What is a hazardous material as defined by USDOT?
*It is any substance or material in a quantity or form that is capable of
imposing an unreasonable risk to the safety and health of an employee,
community, or populace.*

16. Explain the law of thermal dynamics.
*Heat energy always flows from hot to cold or from a higher energy state
to a lower energy state.*

CHAPTER 3

1. Describe some of the common electrical hazards that can result in fire
ignition sources.
- *Misuse of electric cords. This includes running the cords under rugs,
over nails, or through high-traffic areas and the use of extension cords
as permanent wiring.*
- *Poor maintenance. This entails a lack of a preventive maintenance
program designed to identify and correct potential problems before
they occur.*

- *Failure of ground. Failure to maintain a continuous path to ground can expose entire electrical systems to damage and can expose the workers using unprotected equipment to electrical hazards.*
- *Damaged insulation. Insulation protecting current carrying wires can become damaged over time, resulting in exposed wires. If the exposed hot and neutral wires touch, they can create a short circuit and an ignition source for fires.*
- *Sparking. Friction sparking is a form of mechanic heat created when two hard surfaces, at least one of which is metal, impact.*
- *Overloaded circuit. A circuit becomes overloaded when there are more appliances on the circuit than it can safely handle. When a circuit is overloaded, the wiring overheats, and the fuse blows or the circuit breaker trips.*
- *Short circuit. A short circuit occurs when a bare hot wire touches a bare neutral wire or a bare grounded wire (or some other ground). The flow of extra current blows a fuse or trips a circuit breaker.*

2. Differentiate between the various classes of flammable and combustible liquids.

   Flammable liquids are any liquids having a flash point below 100°F, except any mixture having components with flash points of 100°F or higher, the total of which makes up 99 percent or more of the total volume of the mixture.

   Combustible liquids typically require some external heating to produce a sufficient concentration of vapors. They include any liquid having a flash point at or above 100°F and are divided into two classes, Class II and III.

3. What import do the various classes and groups of flammable and combustible liquids have for the safety manager?

   The various classes of flammable and combustible liquids are used as factors for determining the amounts of liquids that can be stored in safety containers and flammable-liquid storage cabinets. The classes of liquids are also used to determine safe transferring methods.

4. Differentiate between the various hazardous-environment classes.

   Class I locations deal with the presence of flammable vapors, Class II locations deal with the presence of combustible dusts, and Class III locations deal with ignitable fibers and flyings.

5. What process should be followed when transferring a flammable liquid from a 55-gal. drum to a 5-gal. safety container?

   The flammable liquid should be transferred into the container by means of a device drawing through the top, or from a container or portable tanks by gravity through an approved self-closing valve. Adequate precautions shall be taken to prevent the ignition of flammable vapors. Class I liquids should not be dispensed into containers unless the nozzle and container are electrically interconnected through the use of a bonding wire. An alternative to using a bonding wire is the use of a metallic floor plate on which the container stands while filling is electrically connected to the fill stem. Transferring Class I liquids should not be done inside buildings unless adequate ventilation is provided.

6. What type of fire hazard does oxygen present in the workplace?

   Oxygen is an oxidizer, serving as an oxygen source for other materials that can be consumed as a fuel in a fire. Introducing pure oxygen to greases and oils can result in spontaneous combustion.

7. What fire-prevention and spill-control features would one expect to find on an aboveground storage tank that holds flammable liquids?

   Methods for controlling and preventing fires involving outside, aboveground tanks include the separation of storage tanks, diking and drainage, and venting.

8. Describe the safety features found in a flammable-liquid storage room.

   Safety features found in a flammable-liquid storage room include spill containment through the use of diking or drains, adequate ventilation, and appropriate electrical installations for hazardous environments. Fire-protection features include fire extinguishers and/or sprinkler system, rated fire doors, and walls constructed of fire-rated materials.

9. Describe the safety features of an approved safety container.

   Approved safety cans have a maximum capacity of 5 gal. with a spring-closing lid and spout cover. Safety cans are designed so that when they are subjected to heating, the can will relieve the internal pressure.

CHAPTER 4

1. Describe the mechanics of a BLEVE.

   The phenomenon known as a boiling-liquid expanding-vapor explosion (BLEVE) is the result of a liquid within a container reaching a tempera-

ture well above its boiling point at atmospheric temperature, causing the vessel to rupture into two or more pieces.

2. What is an oxidizer?

   In general, an oxidizing agent is a chemical substance in which one of the elements has a tendency to gain electrons.

3. What are four ways one can prevent boiler explosions?

   - *Proper maintenance*
   - *Inspections*
   - *Proper installation*
   - *Repairs made in accordance with codes*

4. What is an explosion?

   The term explosion is defined as a rapid release of high-pressure gas into the environment.

5. Describe some of the safety precautions one must take when transporting explosives.

   - *A competent driver should be with the vehicle at all times.*
   - *The driver or other attendant is not to leave the vehicle unattended for any reason.*
   - *Properly maintained vehicles shall be used.*

6. Define the various classes of oxidizers.

   - *Class 1 Oxidizers:*
     - Slightly increase the burning rate of combustible materials
       Do not cause spontaneous ignition when they come in contact with them
   - *Class 2 Oxidizers:*
     - Increase the burning rate of combustible materials with which they come into contact moderately
       May cause spontaneous ignition when in contact with a combustible material
   - *Class 3 Oxidizers:*
     - Severely increase the burning rate of combustible materials with which they come into contact
       Will cause sustained and vigorous decomposition if contaminated with a combustible material or if exposed to sufficient heat
   - *Class 4 Oxidizers:*
     - Can explode when in contact with certain contaminants
       Can explode if exposed to slight heat, shock, or friction

Will increase the burning rate of combustibles

Can cause combustibles to ignite spontaneously

7. Describe some of the safety precautions one must take when handling ammonium nitrate.

- *Store it in segregated areas.*
- *Store it in acceptable bins, storage containers, and the like.*
- *Do not mix it with other materials, such as flammable liquids like gasoline, kerosene, solvents, or light fuel oils, sulfur, and finely divided metals and explosives and blasting agents*

8. Describe some of the more common safety devices found on boilers.

- *Rupture disk device: a nonreclosing pressure-relief device actuated by inlet static pressure and designed to function by the bursting of a pressure-containing disk*
- *Safety relief valve: an automatic pressure-relieving device actuated by a static pressure upstream of the valve, which opens further with the increase in pressure over the opening pressure*
- *Temperature limit control: a control that ensures the boiler is operating within acceptable temperature ranges*
- *Low water cutoffs: an indicator of when water levels in the boiler have gotten to a low level that shuts down the heat source to the boiler*
- *Flame supervisory unit (igniter): a control that checks to ensure the gas is burning and prevents accumulation of gas in the room*
- *High and low gas-pressure switches: switches that monitor gas pressure going into the boiler*
- *Trial for ignition limiting timer (fifteen seconds): a timer that checks to ensure that the gas has been ignited and prevents the accumulation of gas in a room*

9. Describe some of the safety precautions one must take when using explosives.

- *Blasting should be performed only by qualified individuals.*
- *Procedures for loading explosives into blast holes, initiating the explosive charges, and dealing with misfires should adhere to applicable safety standards.*
- *Sources of ignition, such as matches, open light, or other fire or flame, should be prohibited at the blasting site to control the potential hazards associated with explosives.*
- *Because accidental discharge of electric blasting caps can occur from*

current induced by radar, radio transmitters, lightning, adjacent power lines, dust storms, or other sources of extraneous electricity, all blasting operations should be suspended and all persons removed from the blasting area during the approach and progress of an electrical storm.

CHAPTER 5

1. What is fire resistance?

    Fire resistance refers to the ability of a material or assembly to resist the effects of heat and flame from a fire. Therefore, fire-resistant construction would include the ease of ignition and flame spread of a building structure.

2. What are the three separate elements involved in a building fire?

    1. *The structural elements of the building. A structural element is a member that, if removed, will affect the structural stability of the building.*

    2. *The contents of the building.*

    3. *The nonstructural building elements. These include surface finishes, windows, interior vertical openings, decorative surfaces, air-conditioning systems, and the like.*

3. What does a Type 222 subclassification for a building signify?

    In a Type 222 subclassification, the exterior bearing walls, interior bearing walls, columns, and beams have a two-hour fire resistance.

4. What are three characteristics of steel that can reduce its performance in withstanding a fire?

    1. *Steel conducts heat, thereby aiding heat transfer.*

    2. *Steel has a high coefficient of expansion at elevated temperatures, which affects the steel structure because the ends of the structural member axially restrained and the attempted expansion due to the heat causes thermal stresses to be induced to the member. This stress, combined with those of normal loading, can cause a more rapid collapse.*

    3. *Steel will lose its strength when subjected to high temperatures.*

5. Why does gypsum have excellent fire-resistance characteristics?

    Gypsum products have a high portion of chemically combined water, and the evaporation of this water requires a great deal of heat energy.

6. How does ventilation play a role in the burning rates of materials?

    The burning rates of materials depend upon the available fuel surface area or the air available for combustion. When ample air is available, the burning rate of a fire depends upon the exposed surface area and the properties of the combustible material itself.

7. Why do high-rise buildings pose a unique fire risk?
   - *High-rise buildings affect fire department accessibility to the fire. Fire apparatuses have limitations in reaching the upper floors of the exterior of the building.*
   - *The height of the fire affects the number of fire service personnel required to deliver adequate types and amounts of equipment to the fire. More time and energy is required to deploy forces and equipment to the fire; as a result, these resources could be exhausted before firefighting forces can mount an attack.*
   - *Delays in deploying equipment and firefighters can indirectly affect fire growth, resulting in a fire of greater magnitude.*

8. What is fire loading, and what is it used for?
   The fire load is used to predict the severity of a fire to be anticipated in various occupancies. It is used to determine the resistance required of fire barriers and structural components.

9. What are some examples of ordinary-hazard occupancies?
   Examples of Ordinary-Hazard Group 1 Occupancies include bakeries and restaurant service areas. Examples of Ordinary-Hazard Group 2 Occupancies include libraries, dry cleaners, and woodworking facilities.

10. What are some perceived benefits of having a uniform national building code?
    - *It would provide one single set of building code requirements for code-enforcement officials, architects, engineers, designers, and contractors and manufacturers of homes.*
    - *It would provide uniform education and certification for building-code-enforcement officials.*

CHAPTER 6

1. Describe three types of human behaviors in fires.
   - *Convergence clusters occur when the occupants in a building that is on fire converge into specific rooms that they perceive as areas of refuge.*
   - *Panic behavior occurs when the occupants experience a sudden and excessive feeling of alarm or fear leading them to undertake extravagant efforts to secure safety.*

- *In reentry behavior, occupants who have successfully exited the building reenter for various reasons.*

2. What is an occupancy under the life-safety codes?
   An occupancy is the principal use of a structure.

3. What three things make up a means of egress?
   The means of egress has three parts: the exit access, the exit, and the exit discharge.

4. What are the illumination requirements for emergency lighting?
   Emergency lighting should be of sufficient illumination levels and maintained for at least 1.5 hours in the event of the failure of normal lighting. Emergency lighting illumination levels should be not less than an average of 1 foot-candle and, at any point, not less than 0.1 foot-candle, measured along the path of egress at floor level.

5. When does OSHA require a fire-prevention plan?
   A fire-prevention plan is required when there is a potential for fire hazards in the workplace.

6. What are the illumination requirements for exit signs?
   The exit signs must be illuminated to a surface value of at least five foot-candles and be distinctive in color. Self-luminous or electroluminescent signs that have a minimum luminance surface value of at least 0.06 foot-lamberts are permitted.

7. According to OSHA, does an emergency-action plan always have to be in writing?
   An employer with ten or fewer employees may communicate the plan orally to employees.

8. What occurred at the Imperial Food Products plant?
   The rupture of a hydraulic line and subsequent ignition of the oil resulted in twenty-five deaths and fifty-four injuries to workers.

Chapter 7

1. How does electrostatic spray painting work?
   In electrostatic spray painting, the spray material, such as paint, is negatively charged (while atomized or after having been atomized by the air or airless methods) through a connection of the spraying gun to a generator. The material being painted is positively charged; as a result, the difference in charge draws the particles toward the material to be coated.

2. What are acceptable methods of overflow protection on dip tanks?

To prevent the overflow of burning liquid from the dipping or coating tank if a fire in the tank actuates automatic sprinklers, one or more of the following shall be done:

1. *Drain boards shall be arranged so that sprinkler discharge will not flow into the tank.*
2. *Tanks shall be equipped with automatically closing covers.*
3. *Tanks shall be equipped with overflow pipes.*

3. Why is liquid-level control important in dip-tank operations?

Accidental overfilling of the tank or release of the liquid from the tank could result in a rapidly spreading fire.

4. How does an aerated-powder coating operation work?

An aerated powder is any powdered material used as a coating material that shall be fluidized within a container by passing air uniformly from below.

5. What is the maximum quantity of flammable or combustible liquids that can be stored in a coating-operation area?

The maximum quantity of liquid located in the vicinity of the dipping or coating process area shall not exceed a supply for one day or 25 gal. of Class IA liquids in containers, plus 120 gal. of Class IB or IC, Class II, or Class III liquids in containers, plus two portable tanks each not exceeding 2500 660 gal. of Class IB or IC, Class II, or Class IIIA liquids, plus twenty portable tanks each not exceeding 660 gal. of Class IIIB liquids.

6. When are dipping- and coating-operation areas considered hazardous environments?

Dipping and coating process areas where Class I liquids are used, or where Class II or Class III liquids are used at temperatures at or above their flash points, are considered hazardous locations; as a result, electrical equipment used in these areas must meet applicable codes. The hazardous-environment classifications can include the dip-tank area, drain area, and drying areas.

7. Describe the type of training workers in dipping and coating operations should receive.

Personnel involved in dipping or coating processes should receive documented training on the safety and health hazards associated with dip tanks, the operational, maintenance, and emergency procedures required, and the importance of constant operator awareness.

CHAPTER 8

1. T/F Fire alarm systems need to have at least three independent and reliable power supplies that are of adequate capacity for their application.

   F

2. T/F Radiant-energy-sensing fire detectors respond to an increase in the ambient temperature in their immediate vicinity.

   F

3. T/F Visible signaling is required when the average ambient-sound-pressure level exceeds 105 dBA.

   T

4. T/F In a proprietary supervising station, three operators are required to be on duty at all times so that there are always two people at the station when one is sent as a runner to an alarm location.

   F

5. T/F The primary purpose of a fire alarm reporting system is to send a signal or communication to an inside agency regarding a fire emergency.

   F

6. The trouble signal within a fire alarm system indicates:

   a. The operational status of the fire-protection systems being monitored

   b. The presence of a fire

   c. A problem or fault with a component or circuit of the alarm system

   d. None of the above

   c

7. Secondary power supplies serve as backup to the primary supply. This power supply must have enough capacity to allow the alarm system to operate for how many hours?

   a. 12

   b. 24

   c. 36

   d. 48

   b

8. For most fires, _____ detectors respond much faster than automatic sprinklers or _____ detectors.

a. smoke; heat

b. heat; radiant energy

c. spark; smoke

d. flame; smoke

a

9. The fire rating for rooms containing remote-supervising-station equipment should be:

a. 1 hour

b. 2 hours

c. 3 hours

d. 4 hours

a

10. Engine-driven generators and the batteries used in central-station facilities need to be tested how often?

a. Annually

b. Semiannually

c. Quarterly

d. Monthly

d

11. List and describe the three functions of an alarm system.

 1. To provide an indication and warning of abnormal fire conditions

 2. To alert building occupants and summon appropriate assistance in adequate time to allow for the occupants to travel to a safe place and for rescue operations to occur

 3. To be an integral part of an overall life-safety plan that also includes a combination of prevention, protection, egress, and other features unique to that occupancy

12. Explain what factors need to be considered when selecting an alarm system.

 The two most important factors are the speed and accuracy of the response to a fire with minimal chances of false alarms.

13. What is the primary purpose of signal annunciation.

 It is intended to enable responding personnel to identify the location of a fire quickly and accurately and to indicate the status of emergency equipment or fire safety functions that might affect the safety of occupants in a fire situation.

14. Maintenance, inspection, and testing records must be retained until

the next test and for one year thereafter. What information must be provided in these records.

The following must be provided: date, test frequency, name and address of property, name of person performing inspection, name/address/representative of approving agencies, designation of the detectors tested, functional test detectors, functional test of required sequence of operations.

15. What is a zone, and what are its criteria?

A zone is a defined area within a protected premises. A zone can define an area from which a signal can be received, an area to which a signal can be sent, or an area in which a form of control can be executed. Each floor of a building must be considered a separate zone. If a floor area exceeds 20,000 sq. ft., additional zoning should be provided. Zone length should not exceed 300 ft. in any direction. If the system serves more that one building, each building shall be indicated separately.

CHAPTER 9

1. What does the main-drain test indicate in a wet-pipe system?

The 2-in. main-drain test will alert the inspector of potential water-supply problems, such as inadequate water pressure and the presence of debris or obstructions in the water-supply line.

2. What does an inspector's test test for in a wet-pipe system?

The inspector's test replicates the opening of the remotest sprinkler head in the system.

3. What is a Class B fire, and what type of extinguishing medium is appropriate?

Class B fires involve flammable and combustible liquids, oils, and greases. Appropriate extinguishing mediums include carbon dioxide, aqueous film-forming foam, multipurpose dry-chemical (ammonium-phosphate), and halogenated agents.

4. How does a bulb-style sprinkler head work?

Bulb sprinklers have a glass bulb with liquid and an air bubble inside. As the liquid heats up, it expands, the air bubble disappears, and the glass bulb shatters, releasing a fitting that was holding back the water in the branch line.

5. It what types of situations are dry-pipe sprinkler systems most suitable?

Dry-pipe systems are used in facilities where the sprinkler system could be subject to freezing temperatures. In a dry system, air is under pressure in the system above the water-flow-alarm clapper valve.

6. Describe the three different classes of standpipe hose systems.

   Class I systems have 2.5-in. hose connections at designated locations in buildings for full-scale firefighting, intended for use by fire department personnel. Class II systems have 1.5-in. hose connections. They are intended for use as first aid measures by occupants and fire brigades to battle a fire before the fire department gets to the scene. With Class II systems, a hose, nozzle, and rack are typically installed on each hose connection. Class III systems are provided for both first aid response and full-scale firefighting.

7. What is the purpose of a fire department connection?

   The purpose for this type of connection is to allow the fire department to add additional water sources to the sprinkler system, thus increasing the water flow, or providing water flow that may be missing, to the sprinkler system.

8. What are the two major types of fire hydrants used in the United States?

   There are two major types of fire hydrants used in the United States: the dry barrel and the wet barrel.

9. What is the purpose of the water-flow check valve in a sprinkler system?

   The water-flow check valve serves two purposes. First, if there is water-pressure loss below the check valve, the clapper will remain seated and keep the water in the sprinkler system piping above the clapper valve in a wet-pipe system. The second purpose of the check valve is to activate a water-flow alarm in some systems.

CHAPTER 10

1. What are the four primary steps in the fire-risk-management process?
   - *Identification of fire and emergency hazards or events that could lead to significant loss*
   - *Quantification of risk, or the probability of a fire or emergency event will occur and incur loss consequences*
   - *Development and evaluation of alternative prevention and protection strategies to reduce the fire and emergency risk*
   - *Measurement to determine the effectiveness of strategies in reducing*

the fire and emergency risk associated with the implemented alternatives

2. What is one of the safety professional's primary roles in the risk-assessment step of hazard identification?

   The safety professional is responsible for providing the technical knowledge related to the fire codes and standards that may be used to identify the actual or potential fire hazards.

3. A basic risk assessment of a hazard involves identifying what?

   It involves identifying the probability and severity of potential fire losses.

4. When addressing the severity of a fire risk, it is important to consider both direct and indirect loss potentials. What are some examples of indirect losses?

   Indirect losses include business interruption, liability for injury or death, environmental contamination, and damage to company image.

5. What are some general options available for handling fire-risk exposures?

   - *Avoiding the risk by not completing the activity*
   - *Transferring the risk by purchasing insurance to cover potential losses or making alternate risk transfer arrangements, such as self-insurance*
   - *Providing loss-control improvements*
   - *Developing a risk-management program that includes a combination of the above*

6. A properly conducted risk assessment can give management an idea of a facility's relative vulnerability to risk as well as what else?

   It can indicate the facility's level of preparedness to handle a fire or other emergency and its ability to survive the emergency situation and remain in business.

7. Twenty years ago, emergency-response plans focused on fire and natural emergencies; however, such a narrow scope is no longer acceptable with today's emergency risks having evolved substantially to include what other risks?

   Emergencies now must encompass areas such as cyberterrorism, product tampering, biological threats, and ecological terrorism.

8. On a federal level what are the three primary governmental agencies with regulatory responsibilities related to emergency response?

   For the public sector, the primary governmental agency is the Federal Emergency Management Agency; in the private sector, the two primary agencies are the Occupational Safety and Health Administration and the Environmental Protection Agency.

9. Identify three areas that must be addressed in a written emergency-action plan according to OSHA standards?

   - *Procedures for reporting fires and other emergencies*
   - *Emergency escape procedures and emergency escape-route assignments*
   - *Procedures to be followed by employees who remain to operate critical plant operations before they evacuate*
   - *Procedures to account for all employees after emergency evacuation has been completed*
   - *Procedures to be followed by employees performing rescue or medical duties*
   - *Identification of the names or regular job titles of persons and departments to contact for further information or explanation of duties under the plan*
   - *Procedures for maintaining an alarm system that has a distinctive signal for each purpose and that complies with 29 C.F.R. § 1910.165*
   - *Procedures for designating and training a sufficient number of persons to assist in the safe and orderly emergency evacuation of employees*
   - *Procedures for reviewing the emergency-action plan with each employee covered by the plan when the plan is developed or the employee is initially assigned to a job, when the employee's responsibilities under the plan change, or when the plan is changed*

10. What is the primary purpose of the OSHA Chemical Process Safety Management standard?

    The primary purpose of this standard is to eliminate or minimize the consequences of catastrophic releases of toxic, reactive, flammable, or explosive chemicals.

11. What are three examples of duties that a fire brigade may perform during a fire emergency?

    - *Sound the alarm and aid in employee evacuation*
    - *Shut off machinery and utilities and ensure that fire-suppression systems are working properly and that fire doors are closed*
    - *Move motor vehicles away from the plant*
    - *Direct firefighters to the scene of fire*
    - *Stand by at sprinkler valves*

- *Extinguish the fire and maintain a fire watch after the fire is extinguished*
- *Assist with salvage operations and put fire-protection equipment back into service*

12. One of the purposes of the EPA Emergency Planning and Community Right-to-Know Act is to establish requirements for federal, state, and local governmental agencies, as well as many business facilities, regarding emergency response to environmental emergencies. Another major purpose of this act is to do what?

    Increase public knowledge of and access to information about the presence of toxic chemicals in communities, releases of toxic chemicals into the environment, and waste-management activities involving toxic chemicals.

13. What is one of the purposes of the ICP published by the NRT?
    - *To provide a mechanism for consolidating multiple facility response plans into one plan that can be used during an emergency*
    - *To improve the coordination of planning and response activities within the facility and with public and commercial responders*
    - *To minimize duplication of effort and unnecessary paperwork burdens and to simplify plan development and maintenance*

14. Another important decision in planning a response strategy is determining the extent to which the organization is willing to commit time and money to developing and implementing an emergency-response plan. What are some examples of costs associated with the development and implementation of an emergency-response team?

    Examples of costs include personal protective equipment, fire and other emergency equipment and supplies, medical costs, and training costs.

15. Using the NRT ICP, the core plan is intended to do what?

    It is intended to identify the essential steps necessary to initiate, conduct, and terminate an emergency-response action. These are recognition, notification, and initial response, including assessment, mobilization, and implementation.

16. One of OSHA's requirements for first aid is that, in the absence of an infirmary, clinic, or hospital in near proximity to the workplace that can be used for the treatment of all injured employees, a person or persons shall be adequately trained to render first aid. According to

OSHA interpretations, what criteria are used to evaluate "near prox-imity"?

In areas where accidents resulting in suffocation, severe bleeding, or other life-threatening or permanently disabling injuries or illnesses can be expected, a three- to four-minute response time, from time of injury to time of administering first aid, is required. In other circumstances (i.e., where a life-threatening or permanently disabling injury is unlikely), a longer response time such as fifteen minutes is acceptable.

17. Identify two of the suggested measures for addressing the media as part of the overall emergency-response plan?
    - *Designate a safe area that is away from the flow of emergency traffic for all media vehicles and for all media communications.*
    - *Maintain security in the designated media area and prohibit media representatives from access to the emergency area.*
    - *Identify a specific member of management to be the spokesperson for the company, and allow no other employees to talk with the media. The person selected should have experience in public relations and dealing with the media.*
    - *Send the media to appropriate areas to acquire video footage when necessary.*
    - *Provide informational packets with company information to the media.*
    - *Have legal counsel review all information prior to its presentation to the media, and keep questions from the media to a minimum.*

18. What is the primary reason for investigating loss incidents involving fires?

    The primary reason is to determine causes so that preventive measures can be taken to prevent future occurrences.

Glossary: Fire Safety Terminology

Acknowledge. To confirm that a message or signal has been received, such as by the pressing of a button or the selection of a software command.

Aerated powder. Any powdered material used as a coating material, which shall be fluidized within a container by passing air uniformly from below. It is common practice to fluidize such materials to form a fluidized powder bed and then dip the part to be coated into the bed in a manner similar to that used in liquid dipping.

Aerosol. A material that is dispensed from its container as a mist, spray, or foam by a propellant under pressure.

Alarm. A warning of fire danger.

Alarm-verification feature. A feature of automatic fire detection and alarm systems to reduce unwanted alarms wherein smoke detectors report alarm conditions for a minimum period of time or confirm alarm conditions within a given time period after being reset, in order to be accepted as a valid alarm-initiation signal.

Aliphatic. Refers especially to open-chain (noncyclic) hydrocarbons. Aliphatic hydrocarbons are major components of everyday materials such as turpentine, gasoline, and oil-based paints. Aliphatic hydrocarbons and their chemical derivatives are often quite flammable.

Approved. Approved for a purpose means that the equipment is suitable for a particular application, which is determined by a recognized testing laboratory, inspection agency, or other organization concerned with product evaluation as part of its labeling or listing program.

Autoignition temperature. The temperature at or above which a material will spontaneously ignite (catch fire) without an external spark or flame.

Blasting agent. The Occupational Safety and Health Administration defines a blasting agent as any material or mixture consisting of a fuel and oxidizer intended for blasting, not otherwise classified as an explosive and in which none of the ingredients is classified as an explosive, provided that the finished product, as mixed and packaged for use or shipment, cannot be detonated by means of a No. 8 test blasting cap when unconfined.

Boiling liquid expanding vapor explosion (BLEVE). The result of a liquid within a container reaching a temperature well above its boiling point at atmospheric temperature, causing the vessel to rupture into two or more pieces

Central-station fire alarm system. System that receives fire alarm signals and supervisory and trouble signals from a protected premise. These stations are controlled and operated by a person, firm, or corporation whose business is the furnishing of such systems.

Class I commodities. Noncombustible products that meet one of the following criteria: the noncombustible products are placed directly on wooden pallets, placed in single-layer corrugated cartons, or shrink-wrapped or paper-wrapped as a unit load with or without pallets.

Class II commodities. Noncombustible products that are placed in slatted wood crates, solid wood boxes, multiple-layer corrugated cartons, or equivalent combustible packaging material.

Class III commodities. Products made of wood, paper, natural fibers or Group C plastics with or without cartons, boxes, or crates and with or without pallets.

Class IV commodities. A product with or without pallets that meets any of the following criteria: it is constructed partially or totally of Group B plastics, consists of free-flowing Group A plastic materials, or contains within itself or its packaging an appreciable amount (5%–15%) of Group A plastics.

Class I hazardous locations. Locations in which flammable gases or vapors are or may be present in the air in quantities sufficient to produce explosive or ignitable mixtures.

Class II hazardous locations. Locations that are hazardous because of the presence of combustible dust.

Class III hazardous locations. Locations that are hazardous because of the presence of easily ignitable fibers or flyings, but in which such fibers or flyings are not likely to be in suspension in the air in quantities sufficient to produce ignitable mixtures

Class A fires. Fires that involve carbon-based products such as wood and paper.

Class B fires. Fires involving flammable gases and liquids.

Class C fires. Fires involving any combustible materials where electricity may be present.

Class D fires. Fires involving combustible metals, such as aluminum, magnesium, titanium, and zirconium

Combination detector. A device that either responds to more than one of the fire phenomenon or employs more than one operating principle to sense one of these phenomena. Typical examples are a combination of a heat detector or a combination rate-of-rise and fixed-temperature heat detector.

Combustible liquids. Typically, liquids that require some external heating to produce a sufficient concentration of vapors. Combustible liquids are any liquid having a flash point at or above 100°F and are divided into two classes, Class II and Class III.

Combustible material. A combustible material can be a solid or liquid. The U.S. Occupational Health and Safety Administration defines a combustible liquid as "any liquid having a flash point at or above 100°F (37.8°C), but below 200°F (93.3°C)."

Combustion. Can be defined as an exothermic chemical reaction between some substance and oxygen. Combustion consists of chain reactions involving free hydrogen atoms, H_2, hydroxyl free radicals, OH, and free oxygen molecules.

Dangerous when wet materials. Those materials that react with water to become spontaneously flammable or to give off flammable gas or toxic gas at a rate greater than one liter per kilogram of the material per hour.

Dead load. The weight of the building itself and any equipment permanently attached to or built on the building.

Deflagration. The burning of a gas or aerosol that is characterized by a combustion wave. The combustion wave moves through the gas and oxygen burning until all the fuel is used.

Density. The amount of something per unit volume. Most typically, one expresses the mass per unit volume for a solid or liquid, for example, 5.2 g/cm³. For gases or dusts, we might express this as grams per meter cubed.

Detector. A device suitable for connection to a circuit with a sensor that responds to a physical stimulus such as heat or smoke.

Detonation. The burning of a gas or aerosol characterized by a shock wave. With detonation, the shock wave travels at a speed greater than the speed of sound, and the wave is characterized by very high pressure that is initiated by a very rapid release of energy.

Dip tank. Examples of operations that can pose fire hazards include dip-tank operations in which objects are painted, dipped, electroplated, pick-led, quenched, tanned, degreased, stripped, roll-coated, flow-coated, and curtain-coated.

Dust. Fine, small particles of dry matter. Dust can be generated by handling, crushing, grinding, rapid impact, detonation, and breakdown of certain organic or inorganic materials, such as rocks, ore, metal, coal, wood, and grains.

Electric boilers. A power boiler, heating boiler, or high- or low-temperature water boiler in which the source of heat is electricity.

Electrostatic fluidized bed. A container that holds powder-coating material aerated from below so as to form an air-supported, expanded cloud of such material that is electrically charged with a charge opposite to the charge of the object to be coated; the object is transported through the container immediately above the charged and aerated materials in order to be coated.

Electrostatic spray painting. The spray material such as paint is negatively charged (while atomized or after having been atomized by the air or airless methods) through a connection of the spraying-gun to a generator. The material being painted is positively charged, and as a result, the difference in charge leads the particles toward the material to obtain the coating.

Endothermic process. One in which heat has to be supplied to the system from the surroundings.

Evacuation signal. A distinctive signal intended to be recognized by the occupants as requiring evacuation of the building.

Evaporation rate. The rate at which a material will vaporize (evaporate, or change from liquid to vapor) compared to the rate of vaporization of a specific known material. This quantity is a ratio; therefore, it is unitless.

Exit access. The route one must take to portions of the building that are protected from fire through their design, such as is the case in a hallway that has a two-hour fire rating.

Exit discharge. The portion of the exit that separates the exit from the public area.

Exothermic process. One that gives off heat. This heat is transferred to the surroundings.

Explosive. Defined by U.S. Department of Transportation as any substance or article, including a device, designed to function by explosion (i.e., an extremely rapid release of gas and heat) or that, by chemical reaction within itself, is able to function in a similar manner even if not designed to function by explosion.

Extra hazard occupancies. Those with the potential for the most severe fire conditions and therefore that present the most severe challenges to fire protection systems.

Fire alarm control panel. A system component that receives inputs from the automatic and manual fire alarm devices and might supply power to detection devices and a transponder(s) or off-premises transmitter(s). The control unit might also provide transfer of power to the notification appliances and transfer of condition to relays or devices connected to the control unit. The fire alarm control unit can be a local fore-alarm control unit or a master control unit.

Fire alarm signal. A signal initiated by a fire alarm-initiating device such as a manual fire alarm box, automatic fire detector, water-flow switch, or other device in which activation is indicative of the presence of a fire or fire signature.

Fire alarm system. A system or portion of a combination system that consists of components and circuits arranged to monitor and annunciate the status of fire alarm or supervisory signal-initiating devices and to initiate the appropriate response to those signals.

Fire brigade. An organized group of employees who are knowledgeable, trained, and skilled in at least basic firefighting operations. Even employees engaged only in incipient-stage firefighting will be considered a fire brigade if they are organized in that manner.

Fire load. The amount of heat released from a fire over a specific time period (rate) is based on the material's heat of combustion.

Fire point. The temperature at which a flame becomes self-sustaining so as to continue burning a liquid (at the flash point, the flame does not need to be sustained). The fire point is usually a few degrees above the flash point.

Fire prevention. The elimination of the possibility of a fire being started.

Fire protection. Basic tools of engineering and science to help protect people, property, and operations from fire and explosions (ASSE & BCSP, 2000, 23).

Fire resistance. The ability of a material or assembly to resist the effects of heat and flame from the fire.

Fire tetrahedron. Minimum components needed to have a fire. The components are the fuel, oxygen, heat, or some other type of energy source, and a chemical chain reaction.

Fixed-temperature detector. A device that responds when its operating element becomes heated to a predetermined level.

Flame detector. Flame detectors are categorized as ultraviolet, single wavelength infrared, ultraviolet infrared, or multiple wavelength infrared.

Flame spread. The rate at which a fire will spread from the point of origin to involve an ever-increasing area of combustible material.

Flammable. The U.S. Occupational Health and Safety Administration defines a flammable liquid under the General Industry Standards as any liquid having a flash point below 100°F, except any mixture having components with flash points of 100°F or higher, the total of which make up 99% or more of the total volume of the mixture. Under the Construction Industry Standards, a flammable liquid is defined as any liquid having a flash point below 140°F and a vapor pressure not exceeding 40 pounds per square inch (absolute) at 100°F.

Flammable aerosol. Defined by the U.S. Occupational Health and Safety Administration as "an aerosol which is required to be labeled flammable under the Federal Hazardous Substances Labeling Act (15 U.S.C. 1261). For the purposes of paragraph (d) of this section, such aerosols are considered Class IA liquids."

Flammable limits. Flammable limits apply generally to vapors and are defined as the concentration range in which a flammable substance can produce a fire or explosion when an ignition source (such as a spark or open flame) is present. The concentration is generally expressed as percent fuel by volume. Above the upper flammable limit (UFL), the mixture of substance and air is too rich in fuel (deficient in oxygen) to burn. This is sometimes called the upper explosive limit (UEL).

Flammable liquid. Any liquid having a flash point below 100°F, except any mixture having components with flash points of 100°F or higher, the total of which make up 99 percent or more of the total volume of the mixture.

Flammable solid. A flammable solid is defined by the U.S. Department of Transportation quite extensively (see 49 C.F.R. § 173.124). Three broad classes are desensitized explosives, such as those wetted with sufficient water, alcohol, or plasticizer to suppress explosive properties.

Flashover. A fire in an enclosed area that fosters the buildup of heat, and when the temperature reaches the ignition temperature of the majority of combustibles in the area, there is spontaneous combustion of the combustibles in the area.

Flash point. The lowest temperature at which a liquid can form an ignitable mixture in air near the surface of the liquid. The lower the flash point, the easier it is to ignite the material.

Fume. A cloud of fine particles suspended in a gas.

High-temperature water boiler. A water boiler intended for operation at pressures in excess of 160 psig or temperatures in excess of 250°F.

Hot-water heating boiler. A boiler in which no steam is generated, from which hot water is circulated for heating purposes and then returned to the boiler, and which operates at a pressure not exceeding 160 psig or a temperature of 250°F at the boiler outlet.

Initiating device. All types of sensors, ranging from manually operated fire alarm boxes to switches, that detect the operation of a fire-suppression system.

Interior finish. Class A materials have a flame-spread rating from 0 to 25. They are the best in terms of flame spread; in other words, the flame does not propagate as far with these materials as it would with the other classes of materials. Class B materials have a flame spread index from 26 to 75, and Class C materials have a rating from 76 to 200 (Cote & Bugbee 1991, 152).

Intrinsically safe. Equipment designed specifically for a hazardous environment. Intrinsic safety is a protection concept employed in potentially explosive atmospheres.

Ionization smoke detection. The principle of using a small amount of radioactive material to ionize the air between two differently charged electrodes to sense the presence of smoke particles. Smoke particles entering the ionization volume decrease the conductance of the air by reducing ion mobility. The reduced-conductance signal is processed and used to convey an alarm condition when it meets present criteria.

Latent-heat change. The change in the heat content of a substance when it undergoes a phase change only, no temperature change. Latent heat where liquid is converted to a gas is the heat of vaporization, while latent heat where a solid is converted to a liquid is the heat of fusion.

Light hazard occupancies. Occupancies or portions of other occupancies where the quantity and/or combustibility of contents is low, and fires with relatively low rates of heat release would be anticipated.

Listed. Equipment, materials, or services included in a list published by an organization that are acceptable to the authority having jurisdiction and concerned with the evaluation of products or services, that maintains periodic inspection of the production of listed equipment or materials or periodic evaluation of services, and whose listing states that the equipment, material, or service meets appropriate designated standards or has been tested and found suitable for a specified purpose.

Lower explosive limit (LEL). See lower flammable limit.

Lower flammable limit (LFL). If the vapor concentration in air is too low, there will not be enough vapors to ignite (also referred to as the lower explosive limit [LEL]). People commonly refer to the vapors as being too lean.

Magazine. Used for the storage of explosives and classified as either Class I or Class II magazines.

Manual fire alarm box. A manually operated device used to initiate an alarm signal.

Means of egress. Consists of three parts: the exit access, the exit, and the exit discharge.

National Fire Protection Association (NFPA). The NFPA is a private, non-profit organization and is the leading authoritative source of technical background, data, and consumer advice on fire protection, problems, and prevention.

Noncombustible material. A material that, in its intended form and used under the conditions anticipated, will not ignite, burn, support combustion, or release flammable vapors when subjected to fire or heat.

Occupant firefighting behavior. Behavior of individuals who have economic or emotional ties to a building.

Ordinary hazard occupancies. Subdivided into two groups. Group 1 includes occupancies where combustibility is low, quantity of combustibles is moderate, stockpiles of combustibles do not exceed eight feet, and fires with a moderate rate of heat release would be expected. Examples of Ordinary Hazard Occupancies Group 1 would include bakeries and restaurant service areas. Group 2 includes occupancies where the quantity and combustibility of contents is moderate to high, stockpiles do not exceed twelve feet, and fires with moderate to high rates of heat release would be anticipated.

Outside stem-and-yoke (OS&Y) valve. Valves that allow the building owner to shut off the water to the sprinkler system inside the property.

Oxidizing agent. A general definition of an oxidizing agent is a chemical substance in which one of the elements has a tendency to gain electrons.

Panic behavior. Behavior of persons in a fire who experience a sudden and excessive feeling of alarm or fear, leading to extravagant efforts to secure safety.

Photoelectric light-scattering smoke detection. Photoelectric light-scattering smoke detection is more responsive to visible particles (larger than 1 micron in size) produced by most smoldering fires. It is somewhat less responsive to black smoke than to lighter-colored smoke. Smoke detectors that use the light-scattering principle are usually of the spot type.

Process steam generator. A vessel or system of vessels comprising one or more drums and one or more heat-exchange surfaces as used in waste-heat or heat-recovery-type steam boilers.

Proprietary supervising station. A location to which alarm or supervisory signaling devices on propriety-firm alarm systems are connected and where personnel are in attendance at all times to supervise operation and investigate signals.

Pyrolysis. Simultaneous phase and chemical change caused by heat.

Pyrophoric. Materials that can ignite with no external ignition source within five minutes after coming in contact with air.

Reentry Behavior. Behavior of occupants who have successfully exited the building but, for various reasons, reenter. Typically, persons who reenter the building do so looking for loved ones, to assist others in exiting, and to assist with firefighting.

Remote-supervising-station fire alarm system. A system installed in accordance with this code to transmit alarm, supervisory, and trouble signals from one or more protected premises to a remote location where appropriate action is taken.

Safety factor. The ratio of the strength of a material prior to failure to the safe working stress. For example, a safety factor of ten would occur if the design load is only one-tenth of the tested strength.

Sensible heat change. The change in the heat content of a material due to a temperature change only, not phase change.

Smoke. Generally, a visible mixture of products given off by the incomplete combustion of an organic substance such as wood, coal, or fuel oil. This airborne mixture general contains small particles (dusts) of carbon, hydrocarbons, ash, and the like, as well as vapors such as carbon monoxide, carbon dioxide, and water vapor. Liquid droplets may also be present in the mixture.

Smoke detector. A device that detects visible or invisible particles of combustion.

Specific gravity. The ratio of the mass of a material to the mass of an equal volume of water at 4°C (39°F). Because specific gravity is a ratio, it is a unitless quantity. For example, the specific gravity of water at 4°C is 1.0, while its density is 1.0 g/cm^3.

Spontaneous combustion. Self-heating materials that exhibit spontaneous ignition or heat themselves to a temperature of 200°C (392°F) during a twenty-four-hour test period.

Spray booth. A power-ventilated structure provided to enclose or accommodate a spraying operation.

Type I construction. Buildings, commonly called "fire resistive," that have structural members, such as the frame, walls, floors, and roof, which are all noncombustible with a minimum specified fire-resistive rating.

Type II construction. A construction type in which the structural elements are entirely of noncombustible or limited-combustible materials; hence, the common name "noncombustible."

Type III construction. Commonly called "ordinary construction," a construction type where the exterior walls are noncombustible with a minimum two-hour fire-resistance, but the interior is constructed of combustible materials.

Type IV construction. Structural members are basically of unprotected wood with large cross-sectional areas; hence, the common name "plank," "timber," or "mill construction." Bearing walls, bearing portions of walls, and exterior walls must be noncombustible and have at least a two-hour rating.

Type V construction. A construction type where exterior walls and structural members are primarily made of wood or other combustible materials.

Unfired steam boiler. A vessel or system of vessels intended for operation at a pressure in excess of 15 psig for the purpose of producing and controlling an output of thermal energy.

Upper explosive limit (UEL). See upper flammable limit.

Upper flammable limit (UFL). If the vapor concentrations in air are above the UFL (also referred to as the upper explosive limit [UEL]), the vapors will not ignite. This is commonly referred to as the vapors being too rich.

Vapor. A gas-phase material that normally exists as a liquid or solid under a given set of conditions. As long as the temperature is below a certain point (the critical temperature, which varies for each substance), the vapor can be condensed into a liquid or solid with the application of pressure.

Vapor pressure. The vapor pressure of a liquid is the pressure exerted by its vapor when the liquid and vapor are in dynamic equilibrium. If we were to place a substance in an evacuated, closed container, some of it would vaporize. The pressure in the space above the liquid would increase from zero and eventually stabilize at a constant value, the vapor pressure.

Water-heater supply boiler. A closed vessel in which water is heated by the combustion of fuels, electricity, or any other source and withdrawn for use outside the system at a pressure not exceeding 160 psig and which should include all controls and devices necessary to prevent water temperatures from exceeding 210°F.

Zone. A defined area within a protected premises. A zone can define an area from which a signal can be received, an area to which a signal can be sent, or an area in which a form of control can be executed.

Index

7